THE
MISMANAGEMENT
OF TALENT

Employability and Jobs in the Knowledge Economy

Phillip Brown and Anthony Hesketh
with Sara Williams

D0912623

OXFORD
UNIVERSITY PRESS

OXFORD
UNIVERSITY PRESS

Great Clarendon Street, Oxford OX2 6DP

Oxford University Press is a department of the University of Oxford.
It furthers the University's objective of excellence in research, scholarship,
and education by publishing worldwide in

Oxford New York

Auckland Cape Town Dar es Salaam Hong Kong Karachi
Kuala Lumpur Madrid Melbourne Mexico City Nairobi
New Delhi Taipei Toronto Shanghai

With offices in

Argentina Austria Brazil Chile Czech Republic France Greece
Guatemala Hungary Italy Japan South Korea Poland Portugal
Singapore Switzerland Thailand Turkey Ukraine Vietnam

Published in the United States
by Oxford University Press Inc., New York

© Oxford University Press 2004

The moral rights of the author have been asserted

Database right Oxford University Press (maker)

First published 2004

British Library Cataloguing in Publication Data
Data available

Library of Congress Cataloging in Publication Data
Data available

ISBN 0–19–926954–8 (Pbk)
0–19–926953–X (Hbk)

2 4 6 8 7 5 3

Typeset by Newgen Imaging Systems (P) Ltd., Chennai, India
Printed in Great Britain
on acid-free paper by
Biddles Ltd., King's Lynn, Norfolk

Acknowledgements

We should like to thank the Economic and Social Research Council (ESRC) of Great Britain for funding the project on which this book is based. We also want to acknowledge the contribution of Dr Sara Williams who was employed as a research associate and undertook virtually all the graduate interviews and attended most of the assessment centres with us. She was also involved in some of the early discussions that helped to shape this book that was subsequently written by the principal authors. A number of people also helped us in various ways including Liz Brown, Cary Cooper, David Collinson, Ryan Conlon, Ralph Fevre, Steve Fleetwood, Carl Gilleard of the AGR, Dan Hecker of the US Bureau of Labor Statistics, Peter Hesketh, Martin Hird, Bob Jessop, Ian Jones, Hugh Lauder, Claire Smetherham, Michael Tomlinson, David Williams. Although crucial to the development of what follows, all of these people are absolved of any blame!

Without the cooperation of those we interviewed and the leading edge organizations that gave us a unique insight into the recruitment process this book would never have been written. For reasons of confidentiality the names of those involved in this study have been changed but they will know who they are so a big 'thank you' for your participation.

Colleagues at the School of Social Sciences in Cardiff, and at Lancaster University Management School and the Lancaster Institute of Advanced Studies in Management and Social Sciences have consistently supported and encouraged us to write this book. That support is greatly appreciated. We also thank the management and staff of The Abbey Hotel in Malvern for allowing two men to spend the best part of eight hours each day heatedly debating most of the content that follows. We also appreciate the role of Apple Education for providing us with the best kit money can buy.

Finally, to our children, all under the age of eleven, who found the most ingenious and welcome ways of stopping us from getting on with the writing of this book, and to Liz and Helen our respective partners who know more about management than we could even dream of!

Contents

Contents

List of Figures

List of Tables

1

The Promise

People are born with talent and everywhere it is in chains. Fail to develop the talents of any one person, we fail Britain. Talent is 21st century wealth.

Tony Blair[1]

The knowledge economy conjures a world of smart people, in smart jobs, doing smart things, in smart ways, for smart money, increasingly open to all rather than a few. Glossy corporate brochures present a future in challenging, exciting, and financially rewarding jobs for the winners in the competition for fast track management appointments, offering training, self-development, and rapid career progression. They also convey an image of enlightened employers actively seeking to diversify their talent pool, reflected in their approach to identifying, hiring, and retaining outstanding talent.

The challenge confronting governments around the world is to enhance the employability of the workforce. Every effort must be made to expand access to higher education, dismantle barriers to talent regardless of social circumstances, gender, or skin colour, and to harness human creativity and enterprise to meet the demands of employability in the new economy.

It represents a historic solution to the struggle for wealth creation based on the brains rather than the brawn of the workforce. It signifies a turning point in the evolutionary transformation from industrial to information rich, knowledge-based economies (KBEs).[2] It also offers a solution to the distributional question of 'who does what' within the allocation of work, especially as this is never far removed from the issue of 'who gets what' in terms of income, status, and life chances.[3] Indeed, we are told that the major problem is no longer the struggle for a limited supply of managerial and professional jobs, but the challenge of making sure that the workforce has the employability skills that enable them to take advantage of the high skilled, high waged jobs generated within the global economy.

Many people are investing their time, effort, and money in this promise. The socially disadvantaged are encouraged to 'aim higher' in preparation for high skilled employment, enticed with claims of a substantial knowledge dividend in terms of lifetime earnings for those with university credentials. But this promise does not come with a guarantee. A university degree is not enough to make one employable as credentials do no more than permit entry into the competition for tough-entry jobs rather than entry into the winner's enclosure.

Some Promising Questions

This book will examine this *promise*. First, it will examine the assumptions about education, work, and the labour market in a 'knowledge' economy. Does a KBE lead to a significant increase in the demand for highly educated 'knowledge' workers?[4] Is the problem of employability one of developing the appropriate attitudes and skills or does it reflect a mismatch between the aspirations of university graduates and labour market realities? Can the expansion of higher education and polices aimed at increasing social diversity overcome enduring inequalities in the allocation of jobs and life chances? To what extent can the political commitment to employability fulfil its policy objectives? Do the human capital assumptions on which these policies are premised offer an adequate framework for public policy or the management of human resources within organizations?

Second, how are companies redefining the employability skills of the future knowledge worker? Do employers believe that there is an expanding talent pool or a more intense 'war for talent'?[5] What makes a successful manager or future leader and how do companies seek to attract and select them?

Advances in the science of recruitment promise to remove the social bias that privileged those with the right school tie, accent, or family contacts, as candidates are scrutinized in the crucible of the assessment centre, where it is asserted that social pretence melts to reveal the core of individual employability. Assessment centres are the final recruitment events, that usually last between one and two days, where candidates are assessed across a range of competences involving a battery of assessment exercises such as group activities, individual interviews, administrative exercises, and psychometric tests.[6]

But how do employers differentiate between the employability of job applicants, and to what extent is social background, gender, ethnicity, or education a key factor? To what extent do the assessment centres used by most large companies allow them to identify 'objectively' the leaders of the future as they assert? Do new recruitment techniques reflect a significant change in managerial and leadership roles or can they be explained by other considerations that may have little to do with technical efficiency?[7]

Third, how do individuals understand, manage, and experience the competition for a livelihood? What strategies do they adopt to win an advantage in the competition for tough entry jobs? It is assumed that they will respond to the appropriate market signals in deciding whether to enter university or what jobs to go for. The fact that people rarely think or behave in these terms is well established as work is closely related to issues of self-identity.[8] Future knowledge workers not only judge job opportunities in terms of material rewards or status, but also intrinsic interest and self-development. As Giddens has observed 'class divisions and other fundamental lines of inequality, such as those connected with gender or ethnicity, can be partly *defined* in terms of differential access to forms of self-actualisation and empowerment'.[9]

Therefore, how do those seeking managerial and professional employment with leading blue-chip companies construct and manage their employability as they enter the labour market? How do they make sense of the competition for jobs and what measures, if any, do they take to improve their chances of finding suitable employment? How do they experience recruitment events such as assessment centres? How do they prepare for such events and what do they think employers are looking for? Do they try to present a true picture of 'themselves' or what they think employers want to see and hear? Moreover, are there any discernible differences in the way they understand and manage their employability in terms of social background, gender, and educational biography? Finally, how do those from similar—middle class—backgrounds seek to win a positional advantage in the competition for tough-entry jobs?

These questions point to the continuing importance of employment in shaping life-chances, lifestyles, and rewards. Indeed, a paradox of the KBE is that wage inequalities have increased at the same time that more people are gaining access to higher education. This not only reflects widening divisions between the work rich and work poor, but also growing divisions within middle-class occupations.[10] Who wins and loses in the competition for jobs therefore takes on new meaning in a context of a KBE, especially given the greater importance attached to issues of opportunity, justice, and cultural diversity.

It offers invaluable insights into the production, reproduction, and reshaping of social advantage and disadvantage: social inclusion and exclusion are two sides of the same coin. It also offers insights into how those at the upper echelons of companies are reorganizing and redefining job titles, work activities, and career opportunities in ways that concentrate rewards at the top of the hierarchy, despite the spread of highly qualified workers at virtually all levels of the organization. Therefore, the focus of this book is not only restricted to the issue of who wins in the competition for tough-entry jobs, but also considers why the job market is structured in the way that it is.

The Study

This book has things to say about employability from the top to the bottom of the jobs pyramid, but our fieldwork has focused on how university graduates managed their employability in the competition for 'fast track' managerial positions, namely, key positions within large multinational companies or leading public sector organizations, offering extensive training with the expectation of accelerated promotion into middle or senior managerial positions.

Much of the existing research has focused on large-scale surveys of education and social mobility, where labour market processes, including graduate recruitment, have remained under-researched.[11] Although large-scale surveys are indispensable, they fail to grasp the personal and social drama involved in the competition for a livelihood, lost in statistical details that chart class, gender, and racial inequalities in life chances. The purpose of this study is to capture the lived experiences of both the 'contestants' and 'judges' involved in the recruitment process.[12] It offers a unique insight into the realities of why some candidates win and others lose in the competition for tough-entry jobs.

Over a two-year period, fifteen leading edge private and public sector organizations were interviewed, along with ten interviews with policy stakeholders. All of the private sector companies were well-known multinationals that offered the prospect of international assignments and training opportunities for their fast-track appointments. Organizations were also selected to give a comprehensive picture across a range of business sectors including retail, financial services, telecommunications, manufacturing, and pharmaceuticals. These organizations were interviewed about their competitive strategies, human resources, and recruitment practices. This included a detailed examination of selection onto the managerial fast track, together with issues of diversity, employability, and managerial careers.

Six of these organizations were chosen as case studies, including two from the public sector. They gave us unique access to their assessment centres. The authors observed all aspects of the assessment process including the 'wash up' sessions at the end of these events where the fates of individual candidates were decided. This exposed the socially constructed realities of employability in the hiring process, where the personalities of potential candidates are dissected for organization fit and future leadership potential.

Sixty graduates were also interviewed. Of these, approximately half were re-interviewed over a period of eighteen months. They were drawn from applicants to the six case study organizations. This approach had the advantage of giving us a healthy sample of those who attended an assessment centre run by our case study organizations. Approximately 80 per cent of the graduates in this sample got through to the final round of the recruitment process. This is a much higher proportion than would be found if one adopted a random sample of applications. But given the lack of detailed knowledge about what happens at assessment centres and how they are experienced by both contestants and judges, this is a worthwhile price to pay.

It does, however, come with the caveat that it is not necessarily representative of all graduates entering the labour market. It only includes those who have applied for a fast-track training programme and it does not include large numbers of graduates who do not apply for fast-track positions because they do not want a career in management or feel that they have little chance of getting appointed. Yet, we will argue that our findings have far-reaching implications for an overall understanding of graduate employability in Britain, and in other developed economies, today.

Finally, evidence presented in this book also draws on employment data that has tracked recent changes in occupational structure and skill requirements in both the United States and Britain. This data offers an invaluable contribution to our understanding of employability in the KBE. It offers a 'reality check' that casts considerable doubt on the dominant discourse of knowledge capitalism. In a buoyant labour market with a demonstrable demand for knowledge workers it may be legitimate to focus on the 'private troubles' of individuals for a solution, but if there is a major over-supply of qualified candidates this is a 'public issue' and questions need to be raised about the current focus of government policy and the way organizations have so far responded to mass higher education.[13]

Lifting the Veneer of Employability

This book lifts the veneer of employability to expose serious problems in the way future knowledge workers are trying to manage their employability in the competition for tough-entry jobs; in how companies understand their human resource strategies and endeavour to recruit the managers and leaders of the future; and in the government failure to come to terms with the realities of the KBE.

The demand for high skilled, high waged jobs has been exaggerated. But it is something that governments want to believe because it distracts attention from thorny political issues around equality, opportunity, and redistribution. If it is assumed that there are plenty of good jobs for people with the appropriate credentials then the issue of who gets the best jobs loses its political sting. But if good jobs are in limited supply, how the competition for a livelihood is organized assumes paramount importance. This issue is not lost on the middle classes, given that they depend on academic achievement to maintain, if not advance, the occupational and social status of family members.

The reality is that increasing congestion in the market for knowledge workers has led to growing middle-class anxieties about how their offspring are going to meet the rising threshold of employability that now has to be achieved to stand any realistic chance of finding interesting and rewarding employment. The result is a bare-knuckle struggle for access to elite schools, colleges, universities, and jobs.[14] Therefore, a key argument in this book is that employability policies are flawed because they ignore the realities of 'positional' conflict[15] in the competition for a livelihood, especially as the rise of mass higher education has arguably done little to increase the employability of students for tough-entry jobs.

But a major problem confronting researchers interested in issues of employability is the lack of theoretically informed studies. The policy discourse is dominated by employer concerns about the supply of graduates, which has received little conceptual or empirical analysis. At best, it is informed by human capital assumptions that focus on the problem of how to develop the appropriate employability skills of the workforce. Issues concerning the demand for knowledge workers or the way organizations utilize the capabilities of those entering the workforce are largely ignored.[16]

In the following chapter we present a conceptual framework based on what will be called the duality of employability. This shows that access to tough-entry jobs not only depends on one's qualifications, knowledge, and social skills, but also on how one stands compared to other job seekers. It involves a positional competition where not everyone can win even if all the contestants are equally well qualified because there are invariably far more applicants than job opportunities. This leads us to present an alternative definition of employability to that which informs the current dominant discourse.

A contrast is then drawn between competing theories of education, jobs, and rewards in the KBE. *Positional consensus theory* is consistent with the dominant discourse of employability, that holds out the promises of knowledge-driven innovation leading to a high skilled, high waged economy. Hence, we will challenge the tenets of this approach and outline our approach based on *positional conflict theory*.[17] It will also introduce the key concept of 'personal capital' and explain why it has become increasingly important at the beginning of the twenty-first century.

In Chapter Three we examine the view that the KBE has led to a substantial increase in the demand for knowledge workers. This discussion will focus on data from the United States as well as Britain, given that the American economy is believed to be at the forefront of the knowledge revolution. Based on a re-analysis of Reich's acclaimed account of 'symbolic analysts',[18] we find little evidence to support the view that the demand for knowledge workers is growing rapidly. It is argued that the major problem is not the employability skills of individuals, although there is clearly room for improvement, but a failure to generate enough good jobs.

We also find increasing differentiation in the fortunes of recently qualified knowledge workers. While winners in the competition for jobs do not 'take all'[19] they do take the lion's share of the spoils. This is because the stakes have risen as access to the fast track has become even more important as companies downsize and delayer, reducing the opportunity for career advancement within organizations to a select few, worthy of career sponsorship. At the same time, the promotional literature of leading organizations entices more and more graduates towards a world of excitement, adventure, challenge, and personal development, which has led to increasing congestion in the market for managerial and professional jobs in most sectors of the economy. While there is some evidence of labour shortages the general picture is one of 'over-supply'. There are too many graduates chasing too few jobs.

Chapter Four moves from a macro analysis of the KBE to an examination of how organizations understand managerial talent and leadership potential. Much of the management literature has focused on the 'war for talent', 'winning the talent war', 'the talent edge', and the 'management of talent'. This chapter will examine the assumptions that underpin the 'talent wars' as it informs the recruitment of managers and future leaders.

Despite the rhetoric of organizational change and recruitment for diversity, companies have maintained an elitist view of managerial employability. The move to a mass system of higher education has not been mirrored within major organizations, where most have maintained a system of elite, fast-track recruitment. This is because they do not see a wealth of talent that could lead them to rethink the way they organize their businesses, think about leadership, or manage their human resources. Rather, many are locked into a Darwinian 'war for talent' that may bear little relationship to organizational efficiency. It would appear that no amount of higher education would significantly increase the supply of employable people!

Chapter Five draws on our interviews with graduates to explore the way young knowledge workers socially construct and manage their employability. The starting point for this analysis is the relationship between employability and self-identity. This recognizes that investments in 'personal' capital involve making investments in the self, rather than a simple pecuniary calculation made by rational self-seeking economic agents. How people manage their employability is much more than a technical matter of how well they adjust their competences to appropriate segments of the labour market, or how well they are able to manage careers information, or answer difficult interview questions. How they approach the labour market is saturated in social meaning. It is an expression of social being that reflects personal, cultural, and social resources that vary in terms of social background, gender, ethnicity, race, age, and educational biography. Moreover, even among those who shared similar cultural resources, they were packaged in different ways that had important implications for labour market outcomes.

Therefore, while there were common assumptions about their expectations of finding well-paid and rewarding jobs, to capture the differences in the way they understood and managed their employability, we identify two 'ideal types'—*Players* and *Purists*. The Players understood employability as a positional game. There was a recognition of other well-qualified competitors looking for the same jobs, this led them to market themselves in ways that conformed to the requirements of employers in order to win a competitive advantage. They used careers information and social contacts to 'decode' the winning formula, attended workshops that simulated group exercises at assessment centres, read books on how to answer difficult interview questions, and 'practiced' psychometric tests. They understood the task as learning to be competent at being competent.

Alternatively, the Purists viewed employability as winning a competitive advantage in a meritocratic race, where differences in individual achievement reflected innate capabilities, effort, and ambition. Work was viewed as an expression of the self. Securing the 'right' job involved developing good self-presentation skills so that employers could see the 'genuine article'. Hence, individual employability amounted to a 'technical puzzle' of finding employment that offered the right 'fit' with their knowledge, skills, and aspirations. These approaches to individual employability will be outlined in this chapter drawing on quotations from those we interviewed.

The rhetoric of the knowledge economy also speaks of a world of human creativity, initiative, and energy. It suggests that as companies come to rely on managerial and professional talent they have developed 'competency' based recruitment techniques that enable them to identify objectively the best person for the job irrespective of social background, gender, or personal contacts. This is also reflected in their commitment to diversity policies as competitive pressures impose stringent demands for talent based on performance rather than social convention. In Chapter Six we examine the textbooks and manuals used by human resource professionals that exude a confident air of 'objectivity' and 'precision' in current recruitment practices. Yet, the changing and difficult-to-define skill requirements of organizations raise serious doubts about the objectivity of hiring decisions despite genuine efforts on the part of recruiters to focus on a candidate's 'competence' to do the job in question.

The argument developed here challenges claims to scientific 'objectivity' espoused by the recruitment industry. Far from becoming more scientific, as the policy-makers and HR manuals would have us believe, the importance attached to the personal qualities of the candidate, such as drive, initiative, interpersonal sensitivity, and leadership skills, make it inevitable that recruitment decisions will continue to boil down to the science of 'gut feelings'. Moreover, although competency-based approaches are intended to benchmark the requirements of the job they are invariably used to assess the relative performance of different candidates.

Chapter Seven draws on our research evidence to expose the realities of how assessors try to identify the 'star performers' of the future. Leading private and public sector employers receive thousands of applications for fast-track management appointments. This has led to the widespread use of online applications to reduce costs. Typically, these applications are screened, for example, on university performance. Those that meet their basic requirements are offered an initial interview, often with a recent graduate. A formal aptitude, literacy, or numeracy test may also be used at this stage. Successful candidates are then invited to an assessment centre where most organizations assess four or five candidates per vacancy.

This chapter focuses on how organizations use these assessment centres to make their final decisions about who is to be selected. We examine who wins and why. How are the most employable candidates revealed to assessors in the recruitment process? It also shows how contestants prepare for assessment centres and what they make of the experience. Our analysis reveals a more complex picture than is commonly assumed, as there are genuine attempts by assessors to neutralize the impact of social class, gender, and ethnicity. But despite a high level of professional integrity, the organizational contexts in which recruitment decisions are made militate against cultural diversity. Consequently, even the best efforts of recruitment staff can do little to overcome the problem of cloning. That is, the tendency to recruit in their own image given the emphasis on 'social fit' and the need to recruit 'safe bets'. There is also increasing evidence that some candidates can successfully 'fake it' by learning the rules of the recruitment game.

A related problem is that it is difficult to predict the future performance of fast-track entrants. Indeed, their progress within the organization may reflect privileged access to training and career development unavailable to other employees within the organization. Therefore, the penultimate chapter will challenge the core assumptions about efficiency, justice, and diversity in the recruitment of elites. It will examine the human resourcing of the knowledge economy, the management of recruitment, and succession planning. It calls for a cultural revolution in the way these issues are understood. It argues that the war for talent mindset is based on vestigial thinking associated with outmoded ideas about the limited pool of ability, that contradicts much of the rhetoric about corporate innovation and cultural diversity. Many companies have yet to fully grasp the full implications of mass higher education, or in some cases, the requirements of knowledge-based productivity.

This directly challenges human capital assumptions about the nature of work efficiency in a knowledge economy. The social construction of managerial competence, talent, and leadership does not readily conform to the rhetoric of competitive advantage through people.[20] It is difficult to distinguish issues of managerial competence from broader issues of corporate branding and 'reputational' capital.[21] The 'best' companies want to recruit the 'best' people who are most likely to attend the 'best' universities, because they are the hardest to enter.

This may not simply reflect an unwillingness to change, but highlights unresolved positional issues within organizations in terms of who does and gets what. It raises issues concerning the very nature of knowledge work.[22] This is a new variant of an old problem of how companies try to convert the knowledge in a person's head into productive labour that contributes to corporate profits. There is therefore a need for a radical re-examination of the way existing business leaders understand talent, diversity, leadership, and organizational efficiency. Despite the rhetoric of the knowledge economy that purports to recognize the talents of all within the organization, companies have maintained fast-track recruitment that unduly privileges an elite.

In the final chapter we will return to the major themes of the book and examine the broader policy implications of employability. This will include the limitations of current government policies and the inherent contradictions associated with the duality of employability. It is argued that the policy focus on raising employability skills is flawed because it fails to understand the realities of the knowledge economy and the positional conflict that is engenders. This has profound implications for the way equality of opportunity has been reduced to little more than equality of access, which ignores the reproduction of unequal life chances and lifestyles.

It will also include an analysis of the social and economic waste associated with 'winner-takes-all markets', where the competition for the 'top' universities and jobs has attracted many more contestants but has not been accompanied by a commensurate expansion in the number of high-quality professional and managerial jobs. The 'real' vocational prizes are increasingly difficult to attain despite the acquisition of expert knowledge. It will also examine the contradiction in the way employability has been sold by companies that reflect the contradictions between competing pressures to maximize profits and minimizing risk on the one hand, and the need for innovation and forward planning, on the other.

Paradoxically, as companies have attempted to change the cultural assumptions about employment and career opportunities in an attempt to limit their responsibility for individual career development, they have created a rod for their own back. This has invited the next generation of knowledge workers to play the game, both in their strategies to win through in a competitive job market, but also by trading on one's curriculum vitae as a way of accelerating their promotion prospects along with their pay and fringe benefits. This is leading to major problems of productivity as well as retention that may lead some companies to reconsider the reasons why companies introduced organizational careers in the last century!

It will also reconsider the realities of employability from the vantage point of individuals. The rapid expansion of higher education is having a profound impact on the employability of highly qualified labour, but not in the way that people anticipate. Rather than being recruited into high skilled jobs, many potential knowledge workers are finding themselves in a competitive scramble for managerial and professional jobs that will leave many of them disappointed. This will not only lead to underemployment, where university graduates are in jobs that make little use of their formal training, but to unfulfilled personal and social expectations.

2

The New Competition

What each of us can achieve, all cannot.

Fred Hirsch[1]

The Win–Win Scenario

Today, debates about the assets, productivity, and competitiveness of companies focus on the quality of human resources, including managerial and leadership skills. Getting the right people, with the right knowledge, into the right jobs, is seen as essential for business success.[2] This debate reflects enduring issues about the demand for skills and how the best jobs are to be allocated. In the eighteenth century such questions were not at the forefront of Adam Smith's mind, given that the division of labour condemned most workers to jobs that made them 'as stupid and ignorant as it is possible for a human creature to become'.[3]

Yet, by the dawn of the twentieth century things were looking more optimistic as new technologies were believed to accelerate the demand for a skilled workforce.[4] This led to a major revision in the way the division of labour was understood.[5] In Emile Durkheim's classic study of the role of the division of labour in society, he saw it as a potential source of human fulfilment, social justice, and economic efficiency. But this could only be achieved if the competition for jobs was organized so that 'social inequalities exactly express natural inequalities'.[6] This gave the education system a central role in adjudicating the competition based on individual achievement. It also required an 'absolute equality' in the competition for a livelihood: inequalities in opportunities that did not reflect differences in the abilities and efforts of individuals were seen as inconsistent with the efficient and fair allocation of occupational roles.

Durkheim's view of a tightening bond between education, jobs, and rewards based on a 'meritocratic' competition[7] has dominated much of our thinking about education, employment, and social mobility throughout the last century. It also has much in common with human capital assumptions concerning the increasing value of people rather than machines. As Daniel Bell[8] observed, 'The post-industrial society, in its initial logic, is a meritocracy. Differential status and differential income are based on technical skills and higher education. Without those achievements one cannot fulfil the requirements of the new social division of labor ... there are few high places open without those skills.'[9]

Despite the increased proportion of managerial and professional jobs over the last century, this *consensus* view of meritocratic competition assumed that access to higher education would be limited to a few. This view has since been transformed. The competitive advantage of leading edge companies in the knowledge-based economy (KBE) no longer depends on the mass production of standardized goods and services that are made, monitored, distributed, and sold by vast armies of blue-collar and white-collar employees, but on technological innovation, applied knowledge and the intellectual capital of a highly skilled workforce.[10] There are new opportunities for people to use applied knowledge, initiative, and their creative energies in a wide range of occupations, including those working for small companies or in self-employment.

Goshal and Bartlett suggest that this requires a new approach to management, within a dynamic global environment in which competition is service-based and knowledge intensive. They argue that business leaders recognize, 'that human creativity and individual initiative were far more important as a source of competitive advantage than homogeneity and conformity ... Their challenge was not to force employees to fit the corporate model of the "Organization Man" but to build an organization flexible enough to exploit the idiosyncratic knowledge and unique skills of each individual employee'.[11]

Consequently, Ed Michaels and colleagues have argued that the question of how to identify, attract, recruit, and retain 'outstanding' talent is of paramount importance.[12] As a large slice of the workforce becomes 'knowledgeable', competitive advantage depends on recruiting the best talent. This 'war for talent' is seen to reflect the greater complexity of managerial roles due to globalization, deregulation, and rapid advances in technology, therefore,

> companies today need managers who can respond to these challenges. They need risk takers, global entrepreneurs, and techno-savvy managers. They need leaders who can re-conceive their business and inspire their people... over the coming two decades...companies will be competing intensely for the limited supply of very capable managers. Short-term fluctuations in economic activity will make the talent market a little looser or tighter from time to time, but the long-term trends are clear.[13]

From a consensus view, this competition for talent represents a further democratization of the workplace. Companies cannot rely on the leadership stereotypes of 'Oxbridge' or 'Ivy League' man. Going to a top university is no longer enough without the broad range of managerial competences that living within a cloistered elite is unlikely to develop. 'Diversity' has become an integral part of business success.[14] It presents the prospect of tough-entry jobs beyond those who previously saw them as a birthright.[15] Enlightened self-interest has led companies to develop policies aimed at widening their recruitment and the development of talent within the organization irrespective of gender, ethnicity, race, disabilities, or social background. To ensure that companies select the 'best' person for the job, many organizations in the private and public sector have adopted what they see as a more 'scientific' approach to recruitment. This is based on recruitment techniques that seek to match individual competence with the requirements of managerial and future leadership roles within the organization.[16]

Employability as Individual Empowerment

The consensus view also presents an optimistic interpretation of the new realities of global competition. These have forced companies to get smarter and to do 'more with less'.[17] Companies have become leaner, flatter, and more flexible, making them incompatible with the expectation of bureaucratic managerial careers.[18] Today, employees at all levels of the organization must remain employable even within the same job as work roles are subject to rapid change and consistently high levels of performance are demanded of everyone. Nobody can be cushioned from the realities of the 'bottom-line'. The contract of loyalty for job security, along with the prospect of career progression for white-collar workers has been abandoned.[19]

The shift in focus from employment to employability reflects the view that many companies are no longer able (or willing) to offer long-term career opportunities to their managers and professionals. Competitive pressures and the drive to increase shareholder value requires numerical flexibility that enables firms to restructure and eliminate 'surplus employees' whenever necessary.

This has led to the redefinition of the 'career', from a stepped progression within the same organization over an extended period, to that of the 'boundaryless' career.[20] The boundaryless career extends beyond the boundaries of specific organizations. It recognizes that all rather than a few privileged employees have a 'career' that may involve changing jobs on a regular basis. It highlights the need for marketable skills and external networks that offer invaluable contacts and job information. While the 'bounded' careers of the past subordinated individuals to the firm, and 'getting along meant doing what the firm wanted' and 'getting ahead meant being grateful for opportunities the firm brought your way',[21] the boundaryless career provides freedom and 'independence from...traditional organizational career arrangements'.[22]

The boundaryless career is closely related to the concept of employability. Traditional employment is viewed as a 'dependent state' whereas employability is concerned 'less with the availability of standard jobs than it is with the marketability of cumulative personal skills. Employment increasingly focuses less on filling predetermined work roles, and more on cultivating and using skills and capabilities. In the process, employment is coming to mean something at once more exciting and more temporary, driven by shifting personal competencies... by project activities...and by discovery'.[23]

However, the acid test of employability is employment. This is primarily a matter of whether people have gained the appropriate technical and social skills, networks, and business awareness, required to turn employability into a regular paycheck. Employability is understood as a 'supply side' problem as the demand for employment is taken for granted.[24] Therefore, in policy debates employability is typically defined as having 'the capability to gain initial employment, maintain employment and obtain new employment if required'.[25]

In these terms employability does not reflect the offloading of economic risk onto individuals, but a power shift at the heart of knowledge capitalism.[26] There is no longer any need for those with initiative, energy, or entrepreneurial flair to commit themselves to the same organization for decades in order to realise their career aspirations. If organizations depend on the knowledge and skills of the workforce, power rests with those that have the knowledge, skills, and insights that companies want. The shift away from long-term company careers have given knowledge workers greater freedom to job hop, adding value to their curriculum vitae with each appointment.

This has enabled highly qualified workers to short-circuit the organizational hierarchy to arrive in senior managerial positions often in their early thirties. Charles Leadbeater observes that:

> one of the most powerful social groups created by the knowledge economy are so-called 'knowledge workers': mobile, skilled, affluent, independent, hardworking, ambitious, environmentally conscious, people who can trade on their skill, expertise and intellectual capital. These knowledge workers will be highly mobile. For the elite there will be a transfer market, akin to the market for sports stars.[27]

Within much of the business literature, therefore, employability signifies a progressive movement that celebrates the liberation of the individual from reliance on the paternalism of the bureaucratic corporation. Employability not only reflects the new realities of business, but also changing lifestyles and cultural values. It is argued that younger workers want jobs that offer excitement and new challenges that are difficult for any single organization to provide. This has encouraged the creation of 'portfolio', 'boundaryless', or 'individual' careers that can include time-out from the labour market to pursue other interests. According to Bogdanowicz and Bailey, 'Generation X has joined the workforce of the new economy. Unlike the baby boomers who preceded them, generation Xers cannot and do not seek life-long employment, but they do crave life-long learning. They seek employability over employment: they value career self-reliance.'[28]

In sum, while it is rarely denied that big business has peddled employability rather than issues of job security and organizational careers, it is assumed to extend economic and personal freedom at least for those with marketable skills. As Peter Cappelli suggests

'While employers have quite clearly broken the old deal and its long-term commitments, they do not control the new deal [...] It is hard to see what could make employees give that control and responsibility back to the employer.'[29]

The High Skills, High Wage Economy

From a consensus view the enduring conflict between the aspirations of individuals for meaningful and interesting work and organizational efficiency has been resolved. Organizational success is seen to depend on the utility of talent rather than alienated labour. Self-development is the essence of work in a knowledge economy. Moreover, all can benefit from the transformation of work if people are willing to grasp the opportunities that are now available.[30] This reflects the social fluidity of post-industrial life. The decline of the linear life-course characterized by clearly demarcated roles for women and men along with significant socio-economic differences in educational and employment opportunities have given way to increasing individualization.[31] The primary ties of class, gender, and ethnicity are seen as less important in shaping social aspiration and life chances. Children no longer follow their parents into the same kinds of employment, more than ever before economic success is in the hands of the individual.[32] Consequently, the conflict that surrounded the competition for a few good jobs has been superseded by the problem of how to improve the employability of all.

The issue for governments is how to develop the employability skills of the population to meet the new challenges of business and to reap the benefits of high skilled, high waged work. Governments repeat employer accounts of the changing nature of employability in knowledge intensive organizations. Combined with the changing demands for technical and social skills, university graduates are expected to demonstrate a willingness to learn and reflect on learning, as well as develop self-promotional and career management skills.

Such ideas are given added salience by economic globalization. It is asserted that globalization has robbed governments of the power to protect domestic workers from foreign competition. There are no longer British, German, or American jobs, only British, German, or American workers.[33] There is nowhere to shelter from the forces that are shaping the global labour market. Individual and social welfare depends on the competitiveness of the knowledge, skills, and enterprise of the workforce.[34] These new realities are reflected in the changing distribution of economic rewards. The growth in income inequalities over the last twenty-five years is assumed to reflect the changing value of human capital. Those able to sell their knowledge, skills, and insights in the global economy have enjoyed a spectacular rise in economic fortune, whereas those with few marketable skills find their living standards under increasing pressure as they confront competition from other workers around the world willing to work for a lot less.[35]

This argument is used to explain the incomes of the top echelons of business enterprise. In 1970 the chief executives of *Fortune* 100 companies in the United States received 39 times more that the average worker, by the end of the 1990s this had increased to 1,000 times the pay of ordinary workers.[36] The policy implication is that these vast differences in income can be narrowed by increasing the value of human capital of all, rather than a few, so that many more people can benefit from the returns to individual and public investments in education. Such arguments have led to an expansion of higher education and lifelong learning. Moreover, because 'learning is earning' it is argued that those who stand to benefit through increased salaries should pay more towards the cost of their studies.[37]

At the same time, governments also acknowledge employer concerns that those leaving schools, colleges, and universities often lack the appropriate knowledge, commitment, and business awareness to take advantage of these new economic opportunities. Traditional concerns about the employability of the unemployed and unqualified have been extended to those entering the job market from university. Knowledge workers cannot assume that there are jobs 'out there' waiting for them. They must take responsibility for their own employability. After all, no democratic government can be responsible for making people learn or to be enterprising.

This has led governments, especially those of a neo-liberal persuasion in Britain and America, to limit their role to 'supply-side' issues, such as education, training, and the deregulation of labour markets, making it easier for companies to hire-and-fire. Little surprise then, when New Labour in Britain was to herald 'education as the best economic policy we have'.[38] The exponential growth in opportunities for higher education in Britain also reflects a political commitment to extend opportunity to all, removing the historical barriers to university that confronted those from lower socio-economic backgrounds.

Gone are the days when only the few are educated beyond their early teens. Higher education has become a mass pursuit and success in the job market is a matter of developing the knowledge and employability skills that employers now demand. The major policy challenge is how to encourage more students from non-traditional backgrounds to take advantage of the new opportunities that are open to them.

Hence, employability is presented as a 'win–win scenario'. It is a source of individual and national prosperity that rests on the talents and achievements of individuals. The old economy inevitably involved the rationing of good jobs. Within the new global economy the potential for knowledge work is greatly increased if nations can win a competitive advantage in the 'knowledge wars'. By raising the educational standards of all to international benchmarks of excellence, nations can become magnet economies attracting a disproportionate share of the global supply of high skilled, high waged jobs.[39] This, it is argued, has transformed the competition for a livelihood. While individual achievement must remain the basis for educational and job selection, equalizing the competition for a livelihood is no longer the essence of social justice because we have entered a global rather than a domestic competition for jobs.

Redefining Employability

The above account is at best complacent. There is a *new* competition for managerial and professional jobs, but it is far removed from the frictionless world described so far. A major weakness of the consensus view is that it ignores differences in the power of individuals and social groups to enhance their employability at the expense of others. The idea that the domestic competition for jobs has lost its intensity (and political significance) because there is knowledge work available for those with the appropriate employability skills is not supported by the evidence that will be explored in detail in the following chapter. Evidence drawn for the United States and Britain will show that the expansion of higher education cannot be explained by an exponential increase in the demand for knowledge workers.

This casts doubt on policy assumptions that define employability as a technical problem of ensuring that labour market entrants have the skill sets that match the requirements of employers. Rather than focus exclusively on employability skills, we need to focus on the occupational structure.[40] A growing supply of knowledgeable workers does not mean that they will find knowledge work. Managerial and professional jobs remain at a premium. The labour market is a mechanism for rationing as well as allocating job opportunities that may leave large numbers of employable candidates struggling to find suitable work. Therefore, we need to examine the changing nature of *positional conflict* that characterizes the struggle for credentials, employability, and jobs.

Equally, the view that the domestic competition has become less important because more knowledge workers now operate in a global labour market is a simplification of existing realities for most workers.[41] Some occupational elites operate in a global rather than a local context,[42] but they accumulated elite credentials and other cultural assets within national and local contexts. How domestic competitions are organized continue to be important to understanding the fates of the eventual winners and losers. Where we are born and grow up continues to structure our labour market opportunities whether local, national, or international.[43] Equally, it is capital that has greater mobility than workers. Workers from different countries come into competition when companies make decisions about where to invest in new plants, offices, or research capability. These decisions will include a number of considerations such as proximity to markets, political stability, transportation networks, social overheads, wage costs, incentives in the form of cheap rents, tax holidays, government grants, as well as skill levels and the quality of education and training.

Indeed, if the creation of a high skill, high wage economy depends on a general upgrading of the skills of the labour force, tackling the problem of domestic inequalities in income and opportunities becomes *more* rather than less important with economic globalization. Globalization does not resolve the problem of domestic positional competition. The rich and the poor are still related. Access to elite schools, colleges, and universities along with the credentials they bestow remains a key factor in determining future life-chances. The question of social justice will continue to depend on how individual nations states frame the competition for a livelihood.[44]

To understand the realities of the *new* competition we require a fresh analysis of employability in the knowledge economy. Here, the occupational structure and the demand for different kinds of workers is believed to shape the employability of individuals. If five well-trained brain surgeons applied for a suitable vacancy, it is inevitable that four surgeons will not get job offers. Likewise, at times of labour shortages the long-term unemployed become 'employable', whereas when jobs are in short supply they become 'unemployable' if there is a ready supply of qualified job seekers willing to take low skilled, low waged jobs.[45]

Employability cannot, therefore, be defined solely in terms of individual skills or characteristics. This is because it exists in two dimensions—the relative and the absolute.[46] Virtually all policy statements on employability fail to grasp this *duality of employability*. Policy debates have concentrated on the issue of whether those in the job market have the appropriate skills, knowledge, commitment, or business acumen to do the job in question. This *absolute* dimension of employability is not inconsequential. When most jobs are low skilled and workers interchangeable, the skills and personal qualities of employees are of little interest or relevance to employers.[47] But the increasing importance attached to human resources reflects their intrinsic value as a source of efficiency, innovation, and productivity. The personal is productive.

In subsequent chapters it is shown that this focus on the knowledge, skills, and personalities of individuals is also mirrored in the rhetoric of corporate recruitment. The emphasis on managerial competences gives the impression that what determines who is offered employment depends on whether candidates meet the appropriate benchmark standard. This creates the impression that all those capable of fast-track appointments are made offers and the rest are not up to the grade for whatever reason. This neglects the fact that some job applicants are employable but not offered posts because of a mismatch between supply and demand—there are simply not enough vacancies.

This is why employability also needs to be defined as a *relative* concept that depends on the laws of supply and demand within the market for jobs. If there were more jobs than applicants for professional and managerial workers, the expansion of higher education would pose less of a problem. We could assume that all candidates with the appropriate qualifications and skills would get appointed. But this is far removed from the realities of the labour market, even when the economy is buoyant. The aggregate demand for different categories of workers, whether skilled or unskilled and the supply of potential recruits, differentiated according to their credentials, skills, experience, sex, race, or age form the opportunity structure within which individual employability is cast.

Employability not only depends on whether one is able to fulfil the requirements of specific jobs, but also on how one stands relative to others within a hierarchy of job seekers. It cannot be understood outside of this duality. Therefore, in this book the employability of individuals will be defined as *the relative chances of getting and maintaining different kinds of employment.*

This definition focuses on the relative chances of individuals from different social classes, genders, or ethnic groups gaining access to various kinds of employment. This does not ignore the importance of technical skills or the knowledge requirements of specific appointments. Their absence is likely to rule out anybody who does not possess them. But it is possible to be employable and not in employment.

The reference to different kinds of employment is especially important when considering the highly educated. There is a huge range of jobs in complex societies. These involve vast differences in training, skills, knowledge, and income. But even those with few formal qualifications are capable of undertaking many kinds of employment in knowledge-driven economies. Whether they find employment will depend on whether there are other more qualified or experienced people looking for the same kinds of work. A key question is, therefore, employable for what? Going to university may make somebody less likely to be unemployed, but their studies may not lead to the jobs and careers associated with a university degree in the past.

There is also a 'subjective' dimension to understanding how people approach the competition for jobs and labour market outcomes, as issues of employability are intimately connected to the question of the self and social identity.[48] People tend to limit the range of jobs they apply for to those they feel (correctly or otherwise) they have a chance of getting, as well as to what they think is appropriate. An obvious example is the way gender socialization has shaped the labour market for men and women in ways that continue to have a significant impact on the gender composition of the occupational structure.[49] This subjective dimension has become more important because employability depends on the personality package that needs to be sold in the competition for tough-entry jobs (see below).[50]

The subjective dimension of employability is not restricted to the candidates for jobs. Employers also operate with explicit and implicit assumptions about the management and leadership qualities of different 'types' of people. The embodiment of 'talent' is a social construction that will reflect the cultural values of organizations and the wider society. Differences in the labour market outcome of black students, when compared with the performance of equally qualified white graduates, suggests that a complex set of factors come into play that compound the disadvantage of many ethnic minority groups.[51] As we will go on to argue these may not stem from racist attitudes but from 'indirect' discrimination, woven into the institutional fabric of the workplace and the wider society. These are issues to which we shall return. But to grasp the full implications of the new competition we need to explain the causes of increasing social congestion in the market for elite jobs, the changing significance of the credential, and changing conceptions of the 'model' manager.

Stakes and Ladders

Differences between winners and losers within employment have always existed. But the race to income inequality in the 1980s and 1990s in the United States and Britain has led to a dramatic increase in the stakes. The idea of a 'winner-takes-all' job market may exaggerate these trends, as Frank and Cook admit 'it would be more accurate to call them "those-near-the-top-get-a-disproportionate-share market". But this is a mouthful, and hence our simpler, if somewhat less descriptive, label'.[52] Nevertheless, income inequalities have not only widened between those with advanced credentials against high school graduates, but they have widened within occupational categories such as managers and professionals.[53]

These trends also cast considerable doubt on claims that there has been a power shift in the direction of knowledge workers. They do not simply reflect returns to human capital, but as we have noted, the structure of occupations. Equally, the winner-takes-all character of labour markets does not correspond to the distribution of raw talent, but cultural assumptions harboured by organizations, that have profound implications for productivity, diversity, and careers. This suggests that we need to look at the way jobs are socially defined, alongside any consideration of knowledge requirements of specific occupational roles, that is, how employees are 'positioned' in the hierarchy of authority, status, responsibility, knowledge, and rewards. Therefore, access to fast-track appointments becomes more important in flatter organizations where there are fewer opportunities of achieving senior positions or for those who are not on the fast track to prove their worth through internal career opportunities. Even pension provision is characterized by increasing inequalities between senior executives and other managers and professionals within the same firms.

Equally, the vast majority of knowledgeable workers can only capitalize on their knowledge within employment, and even in employment they remain vulnerable to redundancy as the cull of knowledge workers in Silicon Valley testified. Georg Simmel observed almost a century ago, that the freedom of employees is invariably matched by the freedom of employers. While employees are free to change employers, they are not free from the need to make a living.[54]

The insecurity that this imposes on the workforce greatly limits their sense of freedom, precisely because they are not free from everyday financial constraints. In a buoyant labour market the balance of power between employees and employers is disguised by a ready supply of job opportunities, but when the economy begins to slow and unemployment increase, the realities of *flexible* labour markets are thrown into sharp relief. The collapse of organizational careers and the downsizing of companies have led to a democratization of job insecurity. This is associated with an intensification of work leading to a culture of long hours, and a lack of clearly defined career opportunities. This requires employees to stay fit in their present job and to remain fit in the wider job market. For some this is a source of empowerment but it depends on working long hours, consistently meeting short deadlines, maintaining good mental and physical health, and significant investments of time, effort, and money in career maintenance.

The political obsession with waged work as the only meaningful way to improve one's life-chances or express one's social contribution has also raised the employment stakes. Rather than alleviate the problems associated with job insecurity and unemployment, governments in Britain and America have impoverished the welfare provision aimed at the losers in the competition for jobs. This has not only left middle-class families in 'fear of falling'[55] but also worried about the future prospects for their children, as there are few guarantees that children from the middle classes will maintain, let alone surpass, the social positions of their parents.[56]

This problem also reflects changes in the occupational structure, especially since the 1950s. As a larger proportion of families came to view themselves as middle class, it is more difficult for daughters and sons to achieve a higher social status than their parents. In other words, they have to run faster to stand still. As Boudon observed, the distribution of social status tends to change less rapidly in industrial societies than the distribution of levels of education',[57] and because 'individuals who have a better educational level are also more likely to have a better social background...it is also more difficult for them to reach a higher social status than their father, simply because the father's status is more likely to be high in the first place'.[58]

This kind of status congestion in the occupational structure helps to explain why positional considerations increase over time in affluent societies. It also highlights the limits to inheritance, as the middle classes are dependent on educational credentials and the job market to perpetuate family status.

In the United States there is evidence of the seriously rich attempting, and succeeding, to rig inheritance laws to make it easier for them to pass wealth onto their offspring. In a context of increasing positional competition they are seeking to reproduce their advantage through wealth and ownership rather than credential competition. This is not to say that they will not buy access to elite kindergartens, schools, colleges, and universities, as this is an important source of cultural and social capital, but having enough money to remove the need for waged work is an invaluable insurance policy.[59]

The extent to which this is happening and whether it represents a precedent that other developed economies will follow remains to be seen, but this is not an option for the middle classes that need to translate their cultural advantage into 'hard' (e.g. credentials) and 'soft' (e.g. personal qualities) currencies to be exchanged in the market for jobs.[60] Success in the paper chase and a 'winning' personality hold the key to inheritance for the middle classes. They may inherit some material wealth but usually this represents a fringe benefit. It pays for skiing holidays, a second home or private education, but it is inadequate to support a middle-class lifestyle. This depends on a reasonable degree of success in the job market. The middle classes have little option other than to capitalize on their cultural assets via education, given the need to acquire credentials from tough-entry schools, colleges, and universities.[61]

For the lower socio-economic classes the limitations of inheritance are different. The digital divide, lack of money for books, often cramped housing conditions, and poor local job prospects, place them at a distinct disadvantage. The de-industrialization of vast regions of Britain and America robbed working-class neighbourhoods of access to jobs that offered a decent income. A commitment to equal opportunities and positive discrimination offers virtually the only chance of breaking the cycle of disadvantage, through the formal economy.

Education and the Deregulation of Talent

For much of the twentieth-century access to university had been used to regulate the supply of well-qualified entrants into the market for managerial and professional jobs.[62] But Western governments, especially those adopting market policies, have found it difficult to resist calls for wider access to higher education. This has opened new opportunities to working class, older, and ethnic minority students to gain graduate qualifications and at the same time removing the problem of access to higher education from middle-class families.[63] Women are now encouraged to compete on equal terms with men.[64] Although inequalities in subject choices, pay, and promotion prospects remain, women, especially from middle-class backgrounds are serious contenders for credentials and managerial and professional employment.[65] Women now achieve more top-class degrees than men, but they do not have the same exchange value in the job market compared with males achieving the same grade.[66]

While the expansion of higher education appears to extend access to professional and managerial employment to more people, and raise expectations of middle-class lifestyles, 'more means different'. It has led to greater differentiation in the perceived 'quality' of both students and universities. This has served to intensify competition for the 'best' schools, colleges, and universities that are judged to give access to the most prestigious vocational prizes.

However, this is more than a competitive struggle for credentials, income, or power. It also reflects concerns about self-identity, self-development, and life-style that also contribute to market congestion in fashionable and glamorous areas of employment, such as the media, consultancy, and the fashion industry.[67] Many want jobs that give them scope for personal expression and development and to use their knowledge, skills, and creativity, in ways that make a difference to the world around them. This has produced more competitors in the competition for fast-track jobs, played for raised stakes that not only determine what they will earn, but also who they will become.

Credentials: A Weakening Currency

It is commonly assumed that the competition for jobs is a competition for credentials. But the relationship between credentials and occupational position is less clear as more people gain access to university credentials. The labour market prospects of university graduates are diverging in terms of income, status, and opportunities for self-development. This leads people to find new ways of gaining a positional advantage. But this also becomes more difficult to achieve as people adopt the same tactics, such as trying to secure access to elite universities or through gaining more advanced credentials such as a Masters in Business Administration (MBA). As Fred Hirsch suggests, 'If everyone stands on tiptoe, no one sees better'.[68] The result is credential inflation.

If more people gain the qualifications previously required for professional or managerial jobs, and if the numbers of these jobs does not expand to meet the supply of qualified people, the value of the credential will decline. The idea of credential inflation is akin to the idea of monetary inflation.

The more money there is in circulation, the less you can buy with the same amount of money, because increases in the money supply makes prices rise. A high school diploma was quite valuable in the 1920s, because only a small percentage of the population had it; one could 'purchase' a good managerial job with it at that time.[69]

But as more people acquire credentials their value in the jobs market declines. This leads to a demand for more advanced degrees, but as Randall Collins goes on to predict, 'If in the future everyone had a Ph.D., law degree, M.B.A., or the like, then these advanced degrees would be worth no more than a job in a fast food restaurant, and the competition would move on to still higher degrees.'[70]

Credential inflation also has implications for job competition because it will tend to favour those from wealthy backgrounds who are able to meet the costs associated with an extended competition for credentials as employers lift their entry requirements in an attempt to reduce the flood of applicants.[71] This becomes more significant as the financial burden of positional competition confronting individuals and families is rapidly mounting on both sides of the Atlantic. But rather than constantly lift entry requirements, employers may differentiate more in terms of the 'quality' of the credential, does it, for instance, carry the imprimatur of an 'elite' or a 'second chance' institution? This, of course, is nothing new. Companies have been targeting elite institutions in search of 'high flyers' for decades.

But inflationary pressures can lead to a different outcome that relates to both the problem of legitimating inequalities in the way organizations treat graduates with the same credentials and to changing models of managerial efficiency. For many jobs more advanced forms of education and training may be seen as counterproductive (i.e. too academic, specialized, or leading to 'unrealistic expectations'). Employers may place less emphasis on credentials by extending their recruitment criteria.[72] As one employer explained 'paper qualifications are the first tick in the box and then we move onto the real selection'. Thus, there is a change in the way employers appropriate credentials.

The Rise of Personal Capital

In bureaucratic organizations credentials were seen as a certificate of organizational suitability. The spread of bureaucracy and the use of education as a way of qualifying people for different kinds of employment went hand-in-hand. Within the bureaucratic paradigm managerial work was based upon depersonalized relationships, which involve clearly defined roles, rules, and procedures.[73] The assignment of these roles was based on technical expertise assessed through formal examination. Efficiency depended on the development of the 'bureaucratic' personality, characterized by a high degree of conformist and rule-following behaviour.[74]

There was also a clear separation between the private social world of the individual and the public 'visible' role of the corporate official, at least during the exercise of official duties. The preservation of personal space and intimate relationships divorced from the impersonal and public performance of bureaucratic routine is a dominant feature of the bureaucratic personality, as Robert Merton noted in his classic description, 'the structure is one which approaches the complete elimination of personalised relationships and non-rational considerations (hostility, anxiety, affectual involvement, etc.)'.[75]

The requirements of bureaucratic efficiency were mirrored within the education system. The ideology of meritocracy asserted that the competition for credentials must focus on individual achievement irrespective of social or personal considerations. The disciplined, rule-following behaviour required to obtain advanced level credentials offered employers valuable information, both about the individuals' levels of technical expertise and their suitability for managerial roles. The value of education as a screening device for employers was also enhanced because access to higher education was severely restricted.

Today, employers argue that the kinds of people they are looking for has changed and that the credential tells them less about what they need to know about a candidate when making their recruitment decisions. This reflects the changing demands organizations are placing on a new cadre of managers and professionals. Organizations have attempted to articulate a range of 'competences' required to fulfil managerial and professional roles, including those with leadership potential. Considerable importance is attached to personal and social skills alongside any consideration of the knowledge requirements of the job.[76] Knowledge that remains in people's heads is useless to employers. It is the way the knowledge in people's heads is communicated, applied, and extended with others that really counts. Unless people can work together in a constructive fashion, productivity and profits will suffer. As Harry Scarbrough has noted, 'Knowledge work is less a matter of the application of predefined expertise and more a joint product of human interactions with informational and intellectual assets', often delivered through information and communication technologies.[77]

In this changing context of work, managers are expected to be self-directed, work in project teams, network with customers and clients, initiate change, and work to tight deadlines. According to Peter Drucker this reflects a shift from 'managing the work of people' to 'managing for performance', where the starting point is 'the definition of results'.[78] Greater importance is, therefore, attached to recruiting people who can 'hit the ground running'. Whether in the private or public sector they are expected to be 'oven-ready' rather than being locked away in training schools in the hope that they will deliver results in the medium term.[79]

This has led employers to extend the range of managerial competence to include interpersonal sensitivity, good communication skills, persuasiveness, drive, resilience, adaptability, self-confidence, good judgement and problem-solving skills, together with creativity and business awareness. The model of managerial leadership has shifted from the *bureaucratic* to *charismatic* personality. Max Weber was the first to draw this distinction, but he restricted the definition of charismatic leadership to a small number of extraordinary individuals among the religious prophets, military heroes, political leaders, and social reformers. Weber noted that:

In contrast to any kind of bureaucratic organization of offices, the charismatic structure knows nothing of a form or of an ordered procedure of appointment or dismissal. It knows no regulated 'career', 'advancement', 'salary', or regulated and expert training of the holder of charisma or of his aids. It knows no agency of control or appeal, no local bailiwicks or exclusive functional jurisdictions; nor does it embrace permanent institutions like our bureaucratic 'departments', which are independent of persons and of purely personal charisma.[80]

This restricted use of charisma seems less appropriate as many features of the inexorable shift to the 'iron cage' of bureaucracy have been halted if not reversed. The charismatic personality has been 'normalized' at the beginning of the twenty-first century. Shils suggests that the normal form of charisma is more attenuated and dispersed.[81] Indeed, Weber anticipated 'the routinization of charisma' as it adjusts 'to the conditions of the economy, that is, to the continuously effective routines of workaday life'.[82]

The charismatic personality represents changing forms of symbolic control in knowledge intensive organizations.[83] It celebrates those managers who seek to undermine the structures of routine action and rule-following behaviour; where inner determination, drive and strength is given greater weight than conformity to external bureaucratic controls; where recognition, authority, legitimacy, and rewards are achieved through 'proving one's worth' rather than derived on the basis of one's position in the organizational hierarchy. In essence, the charismatic personality is the opposite of the bureaucratic, in that it assumes 'personalized' relationships with colleagues and the need for mutual compatibility, as much as the acquisition of expert knowledge.[84]

However, these charismatic qualities are not only important because they denote the ability to work with others or leadership potential, but also because they represent the essence of knowledge work itself. As Mats Alvesson has suggested:

the ambiguity of knowledge and the work of knowledge-intensive companies means that 'knowledge', 'expertise' and 'solving problems' to a large degree become matters of belief, impressions and negotiations of meaning. Institutionalized assumptions, expectations, reputations, images, etc. feature strongly in the perception of the products of knowledge-intensive organizations and workers.[85]

The value added associated with many knowledge intensive industries (i.e. consultancy; financial services), stems from convincing clients that large fees are a legitimate price for professional knowledge. Therefore the emphasis on managerial charisma is not important only because it is seen to facilitate the productivity of knowledge utilization. The 'personal' is also product in that the presentation of self is the embodiment of corporate value. Whoever is recruited has to be convincing not only to colleagues, but also to clients and customers. They must define and epitomize valued knowledge. This involves standards of appearance, speech, deportment, and social confidence that demonstrates that one is in tune with clients, customers, and partners, as firms are entrusting the individual with the knowledge claims of the organization. The extent to which this embodiment of the firm matters will obviously depend on the nature of the business, but the more businesses are encouraged to get closer to clients and customers, the more personalized 'micro-branding' becomes a defining feature of elite employability.

These changes in the job market and work context have contributed to the rise of personal capital. But we have no doubt that whatever changes have taken place in the workplace, the rise of personal capital was inevitable in a context of mass higher education. This reflects the problem of legitimating recruitment decisions when large numbers of people acquire the credentials that were previously restricted to a small minority. Rather than lacking the appropriate credentials, candidates are now excluded for lacking the personal qualities for managerial and leadership roles.

Defining Personal Capital

Personal capital does not refer to the size of one's bank balance, but to the extent the self can be packaged to capitalize on those personal

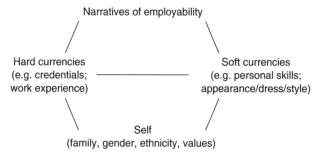

Fig. 2.1 The social construction of personal capital

qualities valued by employers. The self is a key economic resource, 'who you are' matters as much as 'what you know' in the market for managerial and professional work.[86] Therefore, personal capital depends on a combination of *hard currencies* including, credentials, work experience, sporting or music achievements, etc. and *soft currencies*, including interpersonal skills, charisma, appearance and accent (see Figure 2.1).

Employers have not abandoned their trade in *hard currencies*. The education system still grades each cohort of students with greater intensity. The average student in the United Kingdom confronts over a hundred formal examinations even before they enter college or university. Yet, problems associated with screening large numbers of applicants have led them to target particular colleges or universities, and to make greater use of summer placements and internships, along with encouraging existing employees to 'introduce' potential employees to the company. Therefore, the examination hall is the anteroom of the job centre not of the director's office.

Alongside these hard currencies we have argued that the *soft currencies* of employability have assumed greater importance as charismatic rather than bureaucratic qualities become part of the explicit criteria of managerial competence, including an emphasis on self-reliance, social confidence, and interpersonal sensitivity. As the definition of managerial qualities comes to focus on personal charisma, the 'rules of entry' and 'rules of the game' become increasingly personalised. It is more difficult to hide one's 'self' and cultural inheritance behind the veiled screen of technical expertise.[87] The 'whole' person is exposed in the assessment of managerial competence, which reflects the widespread use of student profiles, assessment centres, and staff appraisal schemes.[88]

And the greater the emphasis upon self-reliance and emotional involvement,[89] the greater the demand for recruits to exhibit a personal affiliation to colleagues and the organization.[90]

Hence, a greater part of everyday life is being subsumed within an economic calculus. This 'economy of experience' has become more important as the social background, gender, and ethnic identity of job applicants became increasingly 'visible' and significant for entry to managerial and professional jobs, irrespective of one's academic credentials.[91] The classroom ceases to be the dominant place of learning. This is not only because the period of learning has been extended into later life, but also that it has trespassed most of the institutional barriers between the home, education, work, and leisure. The boundaries between education and everyday life are collapsing. One of the principles of meritocratic competition was the creation of a competition played out in purpose-built arenas (schools, colleges, universities) where social differences were to be removed to reveal differences in innate character and ability.

The economy of experience highlights the importance of capitalizing on other 'extracurricular' activities that can be used to demonstrate the range of managerial competences that organizations have benchmarked as indicative of elite employability. This includes activities such as 'canoeing up the Amazon backwards' as one recruiter half-jokingly observed.[92] Such activities demonstrate drive, determination, and creative thinking. More mundane examples are voluntary work or extensive travel during a gap year after university.

But personal capital amounts to more than 'credentials + key skills'.[93] The value employers attach to both hard and soft currencies depend on how they are packaged as a *narrative* of employability. This involves being able to present one's experiences, character, and accomplishments in ways that conform to the competence profiles scrutinized by employers. Elite employability is no longer a by-product of elite class membership. The self has to be packaged as a life story full of productive promise. Of course, this is not only important in the competition for jobs, but is also an essential feature of career development, especially when employees are expected to take command of their own careers. Even university academics are now expected to create stories that embellish their curriculum vitae in ways that demonstrate their indispensable contribution and international reputations, whenever they seek a pay rise, senior promotion, or a new academic post.

This definition of personal capital is far removed from the technicist assumptions of human capital theory, where there is little sense of the integrity of the self or the social construction of identity, and little attention to issues of power, cultural capital, or positional conflict.[94] People do not enter the education system or labour market *tabula rasa*, like empty vessels instinctively guided by economic self-interest.[95] People are differently positioned in the competition for credentials or access to cultural practices that conform to the expectations of leading employers. The more attuned one's family and educational background to the rhythm and culture of the organization, the more one's everyday activities are likely to count as indicative of managerial potential.

Pierre Bourdieu has made a significant contribution in demonstrating how the middle classes have capitalized on their cultural assets via the education system as employers introduced bureaucratic entry and promotion procedures, based on the credential, throughout the twentieth century.[96] The idea of cultural capital (and that of *habitus*) has been helpful in explaining why those from more privileged backgrounds are able to 'capitalise' on their cultural assets within the competition for credentials and jobs, which are denied to those from disadvantaged backgrounds. Decades of research have shown that when one shares the same culture as teachers and the school, it does not guarantee academic success but it greatly increases the probability of achieving it.

Bourdieu consistently emphasized the importance of human agency as well as structural barriers to opportunity. Defining habitus as 'an acquired system of generative schemes objectively adjusted to the particular conditions in which it is constituted',[97] Bourdieu demonstrates how our experiences and actions reflect wider social and cultural inequalities that are difficult for those from disadvantage backgrounds to overcome.[98] These inequalities are not merely cognitive, they are embodied in us, and consequently experienced in part through what Bourdieu refers to as bodily *hexis*:

Bodily hexis is political mythology realised, *em-bodied*, turned into a permanent disposition, a durable manner of standing, speaking and thereby of feeling and thinking...The principles em-bodied in this way are placed beyond the grasp of consciousness, and hence cannot be touched by voluntary, deliberate transformation, cannot even be made explicit.[99]

The problem is that the concept of habitus, like that of cultural capital, is a rather blunt instrument when attempting to explain recruitment into tough-entry jobs. This is because most of those who make it to the final assessment centres, where employers decide on whom to appoint, often share similar cultural resources on which to capitalize in the job market. A key issue is, therefore, how those from similar backgrounds manage their employability in different ways. Our study is primarily an exploration of positional conflict within the middle classes.[100] What we are attempting to capture is the way that the knowledge workers of the future perceive, prepare, package, and present 'themselves' in the recruitment process. When the focus is on within group rather than between group differences, the concept of *personal capital* is required to understanding how some winners in the education system maintain a winning streak in the job market, while other credential holders lose out. In terms of the middle classes the management of individual employability is largely a question of how similar cultural resources are translated into personal capital in different ways. And this cannot be achieved without a nuanced understanding of self-identity.

Within the middle classes there are competing views of how the competition for a livelihood should be played, along with the nature of personal achievement. We found differences in ethical purpose and the value individuals attach to playing by the rules. Established assumptions about the rational self-optimizing individual within economic theory finds little support in most studies of real life experiences.[101] Issues of personal capital are intimately related to the innermost secrets of the self. While some people may be able to 'fake it' in adapting themselves to the perceived requirements for getting a job, others may be unwilling to play the game or lack the social confidence that is required to 'put across' a different persona.[102]

This relationship between what it takes to win a competitive advantage in the competition for tough-entry jobs and its personal and social costs, calls for a detailed investigation of differences in the values, strategies, and accounts of both contestants and judges. It also reminds us that the value of personal 'capital' (direct and indirect flows of income)[103] depends on the judgements of others. Individual claims to leadership potential are of little value unless they are authorized by employers. Moreover, the capital value attached to specific personal characteristics can go up or down independent of individual activities or performance. As we noted above, it will depend on the personal capital of others. If, for example, universities started to offer training courses in how to succeed in interviews, group exercises, and publish examples of successful narratives of employability, those that appear to be good at handling assessment centres today, may be judged as mediocre in the future as more people learn to play the recruitment game.

Prior to examining these issues we need to examine the rhetoric of the 'knowledge economy' in light of the available evidence, and to consider what this evidence tells us about the relationship between credentials, jobs, and rewards in the new economy.

3

What Knowledge Economy?

> There is a lot of fuzzy thinking about the knowledge economy and globalisation and international competition and all the rest of it, and that needs to be examined very carefully because we could be going for a large picture and miss out on the specifics that really count.
>
> *(Policy-Maker Interview)*

You may be reading this on your return home from work. You might be one of the 15.5 million managers working in the American business and financial sectors, or perhaps one of the 3.5 million managers at work in the United Kingdom.[1] But spare a thought for the 2.3 million janitors and cleaners who are only just now going to work in the United States to clean up the mess you have made today. Perhaps you stopped before getting on a train—the parts of which were built by some of the 13 million production workers in the United States—to pick up a burger cooked for you by one of the 522,000 fast food workers, and handed to you by one of the 2.2 million servers at the disposal of hungry Americans. You may be tucking into a sandwich sold to you by one of the 147,000 transportation attendants, and prepared earlier today by one of the 205,000 workers who prepare food for consumption away from the premises on which it was made. This book may well have been bought from a website that called upon one of the

86,000 credit authorizers to deem you eligible to carry out the financial transaction, and it will have then needed to be packaged by one of the 1.1 million packers, and finally delivered by a combination of the 688,000 postal workers who ensure Americans receive their mail each day. All of these services in the world's largest knowledge-based economy need to be managed. But for every individual with the title manager in the US economy, there are another four workers who are either making the product or serving you with it. We are emphatically not as the knowledge economy guru Charles Leadbeater has suggested, *Living on Thin Air*.[2]

In this chapter we first review the evidence for the claims made by policy-makers regarding the contemporary shift to a so-called knowledge-based economy (KBE). We then, second, move on to examine the evidence presented by policy-makers in the United States, the world's largest KBE, initially by using policy-makers' own interpretations of the available occupational data, and then via our own re-categorization of the same data. The so-called KBE thesis is exposed to a new evaluation in the light of our findings. The portents of our re-evaluation are not good for those who advocate the alleged shift to a KBE. The final section of the chapter then attempts to think through the ramifications of our scaling down of the size of the proportion of knowledge workers in contemporary economies and what this means for the dramatic increase in graduates on both sides of the Atlantic—the fruits of successive administrations' faith in the alleged increased demand by the KBE for high skilled, high value-added labour regarded by many to be best provided through a bachelor's degree.

A Knowledge Economy

In her introduction to the voluminous report recently compiled by the US Department of Labor on the American workforce, Secretary Chao describes training programmes as 'effective "venture capital" for the 21st century workforce'.[3] In doing so, the Secretary of Labor appears to have overlooked one of the harsh lessons confronting financial investors across the global economy: that the value of investments can go down as well as up. Like it or not, very few people can avoid the financial misery when the economy takes a nosedive. Falling stocks and shares in New York or Tokyo have implications for those who have shares invested in the London Stock Exchange. In a global economic world, what affects an American's mortgage or pension affects the value of the mortgage or pension of somebody living in rural northern England or in downtown Kowloon.

Unlike financial capital, human capital appears to be impervious to such fluctuations. Or at least this is what we have been led to believe by those advocating the relentless pursuit of increased knowledge and skills. Knowledge reaches the parts other forms of capital cannot reach. It can enhance the economic returns of individuals, regions, and nation states; it can grant a healthier life to those fortunate enough to acquire knowledge, and even, so we are told, promote greater spiritual fulfilment. Crucially, its elixir transcends the peaks and troughs of the performance of the global economy. Human capital is worth having in the bad times as well as during the good. Moreover, you can measure the difference, even if you cannot feel it. Policy-makers on both sides of the Atlantic never miss an opportunity to point to the 'knowledge-differential' and its impact on our rewards in the labour market (See Figure 3.1).

In just two decades, the earnings gap between a college and high school graduate in the United States has widened from 38 to 70 per cent.[4] The minister for higher education in the United Kingdom continually refers to the additional £400,000 a graduate will earn during his or her lifetime. This is why, the government informs us, a higher

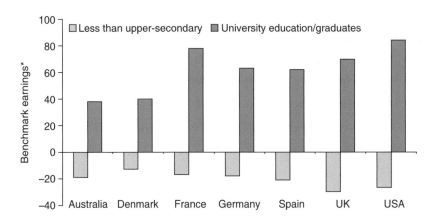

Fig. 3.1 Earnings according to education level: various countries

Source: OECD data in A. Wolf (2002), *Does Education Matter?* (London: Penguin).

education in the United Kingdom like that of the United States has to be paid for by its fortunate beneficiaries. This is the philosophy of the 'something for something society' trumpeted so fondly by the British Prime Minister, and one in which there are 'no rights without responsibilities'.[5]

It is not just about what we are paid. The way we do business has changed beyond all recognition. As we have seen in previous chapters, capitalism has redefined itself into a new and 'stable rhetorical form, in common usage in business and government, and seeping into popular culture'.[6] The language is now of 'high added value' and 'high performance work organizations' who 'attempt to provide workers with the information, skills, incentives, and responsibility to make decisions essential for innovation, quality improvement, and rapid response to change'.[7] In the new knowledge economy we have moved from high volume to high value work.[8] Work now requires knowledge workers who supply and manage their own knowledge to find out how existing knowledge can best be applied to produce results.[9]

Contrary to popular belief, knowledge workers are not a new phenomenon. While the talk of knowledge work today focuses on the whiz-kid 'creatives' and consultants of the new economy,[10] others point to the knowledge-based work conducted over generations by, among others, witch doctors, church priests, and the global entrepreneurs of the shipping industry. Its role in economic competition between nations also has a long pedigree as David Landes has observed, in the early eighteenth century France sent out 'explorers' to acquire the secrets of new British technologies, and in 1718 it 'launched a systematic pursuit of British technicians: clock- and watchmakers, woollen workers, metallurgists, glassmakers, shipbuilders'.[11] This led the British to pass laws prohibiting the emigration of certain skilled craftsmen. It is also difficult to assess the economic value of knowledge as it can take many diverse forms and not all forms are equally productive; 'knowledge is extremely heterogeneous in nature, and its value is not intrinsic but depends on its relationship to the user, so it cannot be quantified in the same terms as physical objects such as land or industrial capital'.[12]

This has not prevented some commentators from suggesting that knowledge work is ubiquitous. 'Quite simply', observes one of the KBE's chief proponents, James W. Cortada, 'everyone is a knowledge worker.'[13] He continues, 'it is the process of expansion and diversification that has created the need to understand better who is a knowledge worker'.[14] As we will see in the next chapter, the clamouring by organizations to recruit the brightest and the best has reached an unprecedented level of intensity. The British Prime Minister has also provided his full support to meeting the challenges of the new knowledge-driven economy. In his *Foreword* to a policy document of the same title, Tony Blair sets out the new imperative facing modern nation states:

The modern world is swept by change. New technologies emerge constantly, new markets are opening up. There are new competitors but also great new opportunities. Our success depends on how well we exploit our most valuable assets: our knowledge, skills, and creativity. These are the key to designing high value goods and services and advanced business practices. They are at the heart of a modern, knowledge driven economy. This new world challenges business to be innovative and creative, to improve performance continuously, to build new alliances and ventures. But it also challenges Government: to create and execute a new approach to industrial policy.[15]

The political economy of the KBE is one of unprecedented opportunity, under the constant threat of being left behind. The shift to high value-added skills is presented as inexorable. Indeed, some of the more wild estimates of the contemporary economic climate suggest that as much as 70 per cent of the US workforce can be categorized as a knowledge worker.[16] It is such estimates that have fuelled nation states across the globe to engage in a major expansion of their higher education systems. Again, as we have seen, the logic is remarkably straightforward. In a world where knowledge work is becoming ubiquitous it is of paramount importance to create a workforce of individuals with the skills and creativity to rise to the demands of the new economic climate. The greater the proportion of the workforce with the requisite skills, the increased likelihood of economic success for the nation state in question.[17] Only then, so goes the policy rhetoric, will we be able to move into a state of full employment.

The rhetoric from business unashamedly focuses on the process of doing knowledge work. 'These days', writes Charles Leadbeater 'most people in most advanced economies produce nothing that can be weighed: communications, software, advertising, financial services. They trade, write, design, talk, spin and create; rarely do they make anything. The assets they work with are just as ephemeral as their output'.[18] The challenge facing modern day business is to make that what is ephemeral and ideational manifest, explicit and codified and consequently exploitable. In business speak top managers need to view the firm as a portfolio of competencies, which in turn require constant definition and reinvestment.[19]

Competence requires skills, and skilled activity is 'about the creation of highly valued certainties from uncertainty, highly valued actions and outcomes, and a highly valued moral order'.[20] Specific vocational skills are increasingly being replaced by generic skills that are largely performative and aesthetic in nature, and crucially, the adequacy of which is largely contested. The generic has become the new vocational. There are no certainties in the new KBE, only constant recapitulations of dominant generic themes such as teamwork, creativity, leadership, and innovation to specific domains such as IT, finance, management, retail, or consultancy. A whole academic field has recently grown up alongside the rhetoric of competence and human resource management devoted specifically to the economic measurement of returns on investment to learning and development.[21] Recent contributions to this field remain largely quantitative, simplistic, and unconvincing, failing to capture the complexities of the process of measuring the impact upon organizational performance of knowledge work.

The capacity of the KBE to reconstitute our individual identity is still being contested. Al Gini's *My Job My Self* describes the process through which 'work becomes our mark of identity, our signature on the world: to work is *to be* and not to work is *not to be*'.[22] Who or what we want to be is limited only by our own aspirations. The self is critical in the rise of a new 'institutionalized individualism', the manifestation of which for Ulrich Beck is intertwined with our working selves:

Most of the rights and entitlements of the welfare state, for example, are designed for individuals rather than for families. In many cases they presuppose employment. Employment in turn implies education and both of these presupposes mobility. By all these requirements people are invited to constitute themselves as individuals: to plan, understand, design themselves as individuals.[23]

The availability of suitable work to enable new knowledge workers to 'constitute themselves' is viewed as axiomatic. Our analysis of the actual opportunities open to those who aspire to be new knowledge workers paints a different picture, however. It is to this analysis we now turn.

What Knowledge Economy?

The principal justification for the advent of the KBE lies in the shift from an unskilled or low skilled economy to one based on high skills and high wages. The following extract taken from a report combining the US Departments of Commerce and Labor is indicative of the genre:

As recently as the 1950s, 20 percent of the workforce was professional, 20 percent was *skilled*, and 60 percent was *unskilled*. In dramatic contrast, by 1997, professionals continue to be about 20 percent of the workforce, yet less than 20 percent are *unskilled* workers, and more than 60 percent are *skilled* workers. This great change in the composition of the labor market signals the dramatic shift of the U.S. economy and workforce has been undergoing—a shift that is likely to continue in the coming years.[24]

Such claims do not sit easily with available data on occupational change on both sides of the Atlantic. This is made all the more perplexing by the observation that occupational change projections emerge from the same government departments as policy documents advocating the shift from a low skills to a high value, high skills economy. Consider, for example, the following extract from President Bush's own *XXI Programme*, a policy initiative designed specifically to tackle the development of the US workforce:

Most new jobs will arise in occupations requiring only work-related training (on-the-job training or work experience), even though these occupations are projected to grow more slowly. *This reflects the fact that these occupations accounted for about 7 out of 10 jobs in 2000.*[25]

This is wholly at odds with the claims of those advocating the rise of the KBE. Far from dominating the workforce, the above observation from the US Bureau of Labor Statistics (BLS) concedes that no more than 30 per cent of all working Americans are in occupations requiring a bachelor's degree. For every job requiring a degree, there are more than two, which do not. This is not to suggest that occupations not requiring a degree do not add high value. What concerns us here is that the BLS's own observation that the majority of Americans do not requiring a degree for their work, contradicts the high skills, high value-added claims of the proponents of the KBE thesis. Clearly, a more detailed analysis of occupational activity is required.

The Data: USA

We begin our analysis with one of the major advocates of the KBE thesis—Robert Reich and his book *The Work of Nations*. Reich's central claim was that the future standard of living of Americans rested not on the amount of capital in the nation's core corporations and industries but the worldwide demand for American's specific skills and knowledge.[26] The shift from high volume to high value requires the development of products and services that meet exactly the requirements of customers for which they are prepared to pay a significant premium. Such high-value businesses according to Reich 'cannot easily be duplicated by high-volume competitors around the world'.[27] Consequently, future business strategies must centre upon specialized knowledge. It is this requirement that led Reich to form his now famous exposition of the skills of the 'symbolic analysts' (knowledge workers):

Look closely at these high-value businesses and you see three different but related skills that drive them forward. Here, precisely, is where the value resides. First are the problem-solving skills required to put things together in unique ways (be they alloys, molecules, semiconductor chips, software codes, movie scripts, pension portfolios, or information). [...] Next are the skills required to help customers understand their needs and how those needs can be met by customized products. [...] The key is to identify new problems and possibilities to which the customized product might be applicable. The art of persuasion is replaced by the identification of opportunity. Third are the skills needed to link problem-solvers and problem-identifiers. [...] Those occupying this position in the new economy were typically called 'executives' or 'entrepreneurs' in the old, but neither term fully connotes their role in high-value enterprise. Rather than controlling organizations, founding businesses, or inventing things, such people are continuously engaged in managing ideas. They play the role of strategic broker.[28]

In Reich's new economy, not everybody can be a symbolic analyst. On the contrary, alongside the *symbolic–analytical services*, which incorporate the problem-solving, problem-identifying, and strategic brokering activities of knowledge workers, are two additional categories of 'competitive positions in which Americans find themselves'.[29] In contradistinction to the strategic brokering of knowledge workers were *routine production services* entailing 'the kinds of repetitive tasks performed by the old foot soldiers of American capitalism in the high volume enterprise'.[30] Crucially, these repetitive and routine tasks are not solely the domain of the traditional blue-collar workers described in government documents and theories advocating the shift to the KBE. On the contrary, routine production service workers also include:

> routine supervisory jobs performed by low- and mid-level managers—foreman, line managers, clerical supervisors, and section chiefs. [...] Routine production services are found in many places within a modern economy apart from older, heavy industries [...]. They are found even amid the glitter and glitz of high technology. Few tasks are more tedious and repetitive, for example, than stuffing computer circuit boards or devising routine coding for computer software programs. [...] The foot soldiers of the information economy are hordes of data processors stationed in 'back offices' at computer terminals linked to world-wide information banks.[31]

A third category of workers identified by Reich, those conducting *in-person services*, are similar to routine production workers in that much of what they do also entails simple and repetitive tasks, with pay being a function of hours worked or work performed. Also like routine production, in-person services workers 'need not have acquired much education (at most, a high school diploma, or its equivalent, and some vocational training)'.[32] The primary difference to routine production workers is that the tasks performed by in-person services are person-to-person. Individuals need to have a pleasant demeanour, to smile, and have the personal and performative aesthetic skills often surrounding the discourse of employability in the KBE. Significantly, because person-to-person transactions are commodified and consumed immediately and in real time, they cannot be exported spatially on a global scale in the same way that routine production or symbolic–analytical services can be.[33]

Regardless of how your job is officially classified (manufacturing, services, managerial, technical, secretarial, and so on), or the industry in which you work (automotive, steel, computer, advertising, finance, food processing), your real competitive position in the world economy is coming to depend on the function you perform within it. Herein lies the basic reason, according to Reich, why incomes are diverging. 'The fortunes of routine producers are declining. In-person servers are also becoming poorer, although their fates are less clear-cut. But symbolic analysts—who solve, identify, and broker new problems—are, by and large, succeeding in the world economy.'[34]

Reich attempted to quantify the proportion of the US labour force represented by these three discrete categories. This was a task not without its problems, as he acknowledged.[35] As many as a quarter of the jobs in the US economy were unclassifiable largely because he did not categorize government employees such as teachers or civil servants, and because some traditional job categories overlap with more than one of the three categories he identified. Nevertheless, Reich's reworking of the government's data enabled him to calculate that in 1990 routine production workers accounted for 25 per cent of the American workforce and that their share was declining. In-person services equated to roughly a third of the workforce (30 per cent) and their numbers were growing rapidly. Crucially, both routine production and in-person workers each outnumbered symbolic analysts (20 per cent),[36] although the latter category, according to Reich, had significantly mushroomed in the previous four decades:

The proportion of Americans who fit [the symbolic analyst] category has increased substantially since the 1950s (by my calculation, no more than 8 percent of American workers could be classified as symbolic analysts at mid-century), but the pace slowed considerably in the 1980s—even though certain symbolic-analytical jobs, like law and investment banking, mushroomed.[37]

The question, now, more than a decade after Reich's initial analysis is the extent to which workers in the globe's largest knowledge-based economy are distributed across the three types identified by Reich? We have already seen how writers like Cortada[38] have suggested that as much as 70 per cent of the US labour force were knowledge workers in the 1990s, a figure roughly supported by Peter Drucker's *Post-Capitalist Society*.[39] Such discrepancies serve to highlight that trying to identify the extent of knowledge work in today's economy is a complex and treacherous task.[40]

The actual figures for the year 2000 along with projections for 2010 are presented in Table 3.1.[41] In presenting Table 3.1 we have incorporated those public sector workers—most notably the 8 million individuals working in education in the United States during 2000—left out by Reich, because they did not fit into his thesis of work being defined in relation to the global job market. Given our interest in the extent of knowledge work within the 'national' economy it was important to include public sector workers because it included important groups of knowledge workers such as teachers and senior public

Table 3.1 The US workforce based on a threefold classification of occupations

Work[a] classification	1983 (a)	1994 (a)	2000 (a)	2010 (p)
Knowledge worker (K-W)	22	24	29	31
In-person services (I-P)	44	45	45	44
Routine production (R-P)	34	31	26	25

[a] These figures include the 25% of the workforce, mainly public sector workers left out by Reich.

Notes: (a) = actual numbers; (p) = projected numbers.

administrators. For the purposes of this analysis we also use the term knowledge worker (KW) rather than symbolic analyst.

A number of observations with ramifications for the KBE thesis can be observed from the data presented in Table 3.1. First, our analysis appears to reject Cortada's calculations that knowledge workers were the largest category of economically active individuals during the previous two decades. By our calculations, the proportion of knowledge workers (22 per cent) was less than half that of Cortada's estimations for the 1980s (52 per cent), and significantly less during the 1990s (24 per cent and 70 per cent, respectively). During the 1980s and 1990s a greater proportion of Americans were working in routine production-related occupations than in what we now describe as KBE jobs. Second, proponents of the KBE thesis will draw some satisfaction from the observation that in 2000 the proportion of those that might be classified as knowledge workers (29 per cent) outnumbered those classified as doing routine production work (26 per cent). Furthermore, the *actual* proportion of those engaged in knowledge work in the United States in 2000 exceeded the *estimations* for those in the knowledge worker category for 2005 by the BLS in 1995.[42] For the first time in American history, at least on this interpretation of these data, the proportion of those thinking for a living outnumbered those who were undertaking routine production.[43] At 29 per cent of the workforce in 2000, only an additional 2 per cent rise, or 3 million workers, are required to hit the estimated total for 2010.[44]

Nevertheless, the bifurcation of the US economy by 2010 into, at best, a third of the workforce engaged in knowledge work on the one hand, and a quarter occupied in routine production services on the other reveals the major occupational role of the in-person services category. This reading of occupational data is one well supported by a number of commentators advocating the rise to prominence of a largely service sector-based economy in the United States during the 1980s and 1990s.[45] Twenty-first-century America will remain a service intensive economy, with people providing direct services to others whether they are beautifying, caring, feeding, or protecting them. The prospect of living on thin air looks increasingly like a thesis based on nothing more than hot air.

This view is supported by data that examines occupational categories with the *fastest* and *largest* jobs growth in the American economy. Table 3.2 shows those jobs with the fastest jobs growth. This offers a picture of the knowledge economy in line with the proponents of the KBE. It predicts that most of the fastest growing jobs require advanced levels of education and training. But when we compare the actual numbers of these jobs with those occupational categories with the largest jobs growth, that is, those jobs in which most people will find employment, we are presented with a very different picture of the US economy (see Table 3.3).[46]

The 80/20 Economy

Our unease about how these data have been compiled led us to a more detailed process of re-categorization and recoding of each individual occupational category used by the BLS, nearly 1,000 in all, to establish a more accurate reading of the distribution of knowledge work across the world's largest KBE. In undertaking this task we found that the distinction between in-service person occupations and routine production work was somewhat arbitrary. Many of the 23 million Americans involved in office and administrative support, for example, are engaged in the administration of 'standard procedures and codified rules' of Reich's routine production services.[47] But our primary focus was on the classification of knowledge workers. We did not simply code individual occupations as knowledge workers if the typical entry qualification required was that of a bachelor's degree. We were not trying to establish the credentials required to secure the job. We did not want to conflate the issue of employer entry requirement with the actual use of knowledge within specific occupational roles.[48] Instead, we coded each job on the basis of what the day-to-day work of the

Table 3.2 Top ten fastest growing occupations in the United States, 2000–2010

Occupation	Employment		Change		Quartile rank by 2000 median hourly earnings	Education and training category
	2000	2010	Number	Per cent		
Computer software engineers, applications	380	760	380	100	1	Bachelor's degree
Computer support specialists	506	996	490	97	2	Associate degree
Computer software engineers, systems software	317	601	284	90	1	Bachelor's degree
Network and computer systems administrators	229	416	187	82	1	Bachelor's degree
Network systems and data communications analysts	119	211	92	77	1	Bachelor's degree
Desktop publishers	38	63	25	67	2	Post-secondary vocational award
Database administrators	106	176	70	66	1	Bachelor's degree
Personal and home care aides	414	672	258	62	4	Short-term on-the-job training
Computer systems analysts	431	689	258	60	1	Bachelor's degree
Medical assistants	329	516	187	57	3	Moderate-term on-the-job training

Source: US Bureau of Labor Statistics.

occupation entailed against each of the three categories. For example, within the 703,000 media and communications occupations in 2000, we coded writers and editors as knowledge workers: the work they are engaged in repeatedly requires their 'manipulations of symbols—data, words, oral and visual representations'.[49]

Table 3.3 The occupations with the largest jobs growth in the United States, 2000–2010

Occupation	Employment		Change		Quartile rank by 2000 median hourly earnings	Education and training category
	2000	2010	Number	Per cent		
Combined food preparation and serving workers, including fast food	2,206	2,879	673	30	4	Short-term On-the-job training
Customer service representatives	1,946	2,577	631	32	3	Moderate-term on-the-job training
Registered nurses	2,194	2,755	561	26	1	Associate degree
Retail salespersons	4,109	4,619	510	12	4	Short-term on-the-job training
Computer support specialists	506	996	490	97	2	Associate degree
Cashiers, except gambling	3,325	3,799	474	14	4	Short-term on-the-job training
Office clerks, general	2,705	3,135	430	16	3	Short-term on-the-job training
Security guards	1,106	1,497	391	35	4	Short-term on-the-job training
Computer software engineers, applications	380	760	380	100	1	Bachelor's degree
Waiters and waitresses	1,983	2,347	364	18	4	Short-term on-the-job training

Source: US Bureau of Labor Statistics.

Another example might be that of the three quarters of a million data in-putters who are engaged in the routine work of keying in data at a computer station or the 38,000 IT specialists involved in desktop publishing. Both data in-putters and desktop publishers may have

Table 3.4 Revised classification of knowledge work in the American economy

Category	2000 (a)%	Number million	2010 (p)%	Number million
Knowledge worker (K-W)	20	29.1	22	36.9
In-person services (I-P)/ Routine production (R-P)	80	116.5	78	130.8
	100	145.6	100	167.7

Source: Authors' re-categorization of BLS data.

degree-level qualifications. But the nature of their work is different in relation to the knowledge intensive work of software developers or database administrators. The results of this re-categorization of occupations at the individual level are displayed in Table 3.4.[50]

The economy to which most commentators point as being the ideal typical KBE on our reading has no more than 20 per cent of its workforce—some 29 million out of a total of 145 million workers—primarily engaged in what might be described as knowledge work. For every knowledge worker actively at work in the US economy, another four workers are engaged in routine production or person-to-person service occupations. Far from being a KBE, US citizens participate in what might be described as the *80/20 workforce* in which most workers find themselves serving or making things rather that thinking for a living. It is difficult, on this reading, to support the up-skilling thesis or the shift to high value-added skills pointed to by policy-makers and the principal proponents of the KBE thesis. Workers are becoming more knowledgeable but the 'permission to think' for a living is far from commonplace. Knowledge is certainly being worked harder. But far from the much-trumpeted increased demand for knowledge workers, there is simply increased demand for additional workers whose labour activates this knowledge in the form of manufacturing or selling products in their various guises. Knowledge *worked*, then, does not necessarily require certificated knowledge *workers*.[51] Rather than 'average' skill levels increasing, there is a polarization in the opportunity for people to use their knowledge and skills in the workplace. As Harry Braverman claimed some thirty years ago:

Since, with the development of technology and its application to it of the fundamental sciences, the labor processes of society have come to embody a greater amount of scientific knowledge, clearly the 'average' scientific, technical, and in that sense 'skill' content of these labor processes is much greater now than in the past. But this is nothing but a tautology. The question is precisely whether the scientific and 'educated' content of labor tends toward *averaging*, or, on the contrary, toward *polarization*. If the latter is the case, to then say that the 'average' skill has been raised is to adopt the logic of the statistician who, with one foot in the fire and the other in ice water, will tell you that 'on the average,' he is perfectly comfortable.[52]

Of more concern, perhaps, is our observation that the United States has not thought itself out of the recession it found itself in at the beginning of the twenty-first century after ten years of unprecedented growth.[53] Our calculations suggest that the proportion of knowledge workers is set to increase only by two percentage points, or 3 million new jobs to 2010. This is not welcome news for the hundreds of thousands of college graduates hitting the US labour market each year, or, for that matter, the 30 million workers in the United States who already hold a bachelor's or postgraduate degree qualification.[54] Many highly qualified individuals who have recently entered the job market may be left with little prospect of finding an interesting and rewarding job that utilizes their expert knowledge.

The Data: UK

So what of the United Kingdom's KBE? *The Future of Higher Education*, published in 2003 by the British government, reaffirmed the Labour Government's stance that the best strategy is one of adopting a high skill KBE.[55] According to the minister for education and skills, 'our future success depends upon mobilizing even more effectively the imagination, creativity, skills and talents of all our people [which] depends on using that knowledge and understanding to build economic strength and social harmony'.[56] Exactly how much the United Kingdom relies on its faith in the KBE is revealed later in the same document where it is suggested that 80 per cent of the 1.7 million new jobs to be created by 2010 will be in occupations that normally recruit those with higher educational qualifications.[57]

Like the United States, however, the United Kingdom's economy is far from being that of a KBE. On the contrary, our reading of data from the same source utilized by the *The Future of Higher Education*, raises some interesting questions both about the harsh reality of the current situation and that of the UK economy of the future. Table 3.5 summarizes the pattern of employment in the United Kingdom based on the threefold classification used in Table 3.1.[58]

This shows that the United Kingdom has a higher proportion of workers engaged in knowledge work than those in the US economy.[59] Although these headline figures may look superficially impressive we are unable to re-analyse how the broad occupational categories (e.g. science and engineering professionals; associate health professions) have been compiled as for the US data. We are reliant on the aggregations of occupations used in the standard occupation classification codes (SOC) utilized by the Department for Education and Skills, and this should lead us to treat these figures with considerable caution.

On this evidence the proportion of the United Kingdom's workforce engaged in knowledge work has risen just five percentage points in two decades from 27 per cent in 1981 to nearly one in every three workers by 1999 (32 per cent). The in-person category appears to be proportionately smaller in the United Kingdom than in the United States, hovering around one in every five workers. Routine production jobs represent a greater share of the UK workforce than in the US economy, albeit dropping from 56 per cent in 1981 to just under half (47 per cent) of the workforce in 1999. The work conducted by those in the United Kingdom also appears to be polarizing into those fortunate enough to be engaged in knowledge work on the one hand, and those trapped in relatively low skilled and highly routinized work on the other. The reality of the UK occupational structure, then, like that of the United States, appears to fall a long way short of the rhetoric of the KBE thesis.

This is no better illustrated than in the future projections for the UK economy (Table 3.5). These are based on statistical work by Richard

Table 3.5 Percentage distribution of UK labour force, 1981–2010

Reich classification	1981 (a)	1999 (a)	2005 (p)	2010 (p)
Knowledge worker (K-W)	27	32	39	41
In-person services (I-P)	17	21	22	22
Routine production (R-P)	56	47	39	37

Notes: (a) = actual; (p) = projected.
Source: Extrapolated from data from the Department for Education & Skills (see footnote 58).

Wilson and colleagues who estimate that the proportion of the UK workforce engaged in knowledge work will rise from 32 per cent in 1999 to 39 per cent in 2005, and, crucially, outnumbering those involved in routine jobs, which is estimated to retract sharply by 2010 (falling from 47 per cent in 1999 to 37 per cent by 2010).[60] Exactly how these projections have been compiled remains something of a mystery. We are simply told that they are extrapolated from the UK Labour Force Survey 1994–1998 'using a detailed converter developed in collaboration with the Office for National Statistics'.[61]

Interestingly, this approach allegedly enables UK projections to 'avoid the more extreme results that can arise from simply extrapolating changes at the more detailed occupational level as is done by the Bureau of Labor Statistics in the US'.[62] This observation is all the more perplexing when we take into consideration that the BLS's data can be seen to indicate little change for the US economy, whereas the UK estimates for change appear to be far more extreme in relation to the accelerating growth in the proportion of knowledge workers. The shift towards a knowledge economy appears to be one based more on political hope than economic fact. It is to the meeting between aspiration and the reality of the occupational labour market we turn to next.

Nice Work, if You Can Get It

Sitting alongside the rhetoric of the KBE thesis is the claim of the unprecedented need for an increasing number of graduates to meet our alleged rising skill needs on the one hand, and to keep up with our economic competitors who invest more in their higher education on the other:

In a fast-changing and increasingly competitive world, the role of higher education in equipping the labour force with appropriate and relevant skills, in stimulating innovation and supporting productivity and in enriching the quality of life is central. The benefits of an excellent higher education system are far-reaching; the risk of decline is one that we cannot accept.[63]

The argument stands or falls on there being suitable opportunities for knowledge work for the increased numbers of graduates who are already participating in the mass system of higher education created during the previous fifteen years of unprecedented expansion in the United Kingdom, mirroring the post-war expansion of higher education in the United States. Here again, data is in short supply, but rhetoric abounds:

Graduates derive substantial benefits from having gained a degree, including wider career opportunities and the financial benefits that generally follow. On average, those with a higher education qualification earn around 50% more than non-graduates.[64]

In the provocatively titled *Who's Not Working and Why* Frederick Pryor and David Schaffer reject the central thrust of the KBE thesis that an increasing proportion of the workforce needs increased education, skills, and training to cope with the demands of knowledge work. They concede that there has been some increase in the demands for skills, education, and functional literacy during the last quarter of a century but they also note that the actual education levels of the workforce have increased faster than the demand for educated workers. Their analysis of the entire US labour force data between 1970 and 1995 led them to conclude that 'American workers have more education than is needed.'[65] Crucially, they shed light on something of an ominous development in the US labour force that has been suspected, and is now confirmed:

An increasing share of university-educated workers are taking jobs where the average educational level has been much lower. In some cases this may represent a technological upgrading of the occupation; *in most cases, however, it appears that other factors are at work in this process of downward occupational mobility.*[66]

The authors offer two other factors which may be responsible for the downward mobility of college graduates. First, and again in contradistinction to the KBE thesis, Pryor and Schaffer point to clear evidence that the number of jobs requiring relatively low levels of education has increased at a faster rate than the number of prime-age workers with a high school diploma or less. Far from the number of jobs requiring higher skills levels outpacing the rate at which the United States can educate suitable numbers, the reverse now seems to be true; there has been a more rapid increase in jobs requiring low education levels than the numbers leaving the US education system with low levels of qualifications to undertake such jobs. This, suggest Pryor and Schaffer, may well account for the displacement or 'bumping effect' of those with relatively higher levels of credentials having to take jobs where the level of education required to actually do the job is much lower. Here, once again, we detect the distinction between knowledge *worked* and knowledge *worker*.

A growing body of evidence is also pointing towards graduate underemployment in the United Kingdom,[67] sitting alongside other accounts about the skills needs of most UK businesses.[68] Some of this research suggests that up to 40 per cent of university graduates are in non-graduate jobs.[69] A recent large-scale investigation into credential inflation in the United Kingdom also concluded:

[I]t is clear that the increase in graduates has not filtered across the industrial and -occupational structure in the way that would be expected if the [knowledge-based economy] thesis were correct. There has been a trend for the average status of both first and second jobs to decline. [. . .] It therefore seems that while the life-course might have an effect, there remains a structural tendency towards overqualification which has a negative effect on employment.[70]

Tucked away in the statistical report referred to by *The Future of Higher Education* is a section with three different future assumptions about the direction of UK occupational growth.[71] These predictions are important because Table 3.5 is based on the most 'optimistic' reading of the data.[72] It is based on what is called the *trend* assumption, which simply suggests that demand for high skills jobs are extrapolated from past rates of change during the 1990s. It is hardly surprising, then, that estimates based on one of the largest economic growth periods in recent times should predict an explosion in the future demand for graduates. Given the recent downturn of both the US, and to a lesser degree the UK economies, geopolitical instability resulting from the 'War on Terrorism', and current trends in 'off-shoring' involving a growing proportion of high skilled jobs to low waged economies, the trend assumption appears overly optimistic. Based on the 80/20 economy in the United States, for the British economy to raise the proportion of knowledge workers to 40 per cent of the workforce would require it to double the proportion of people in knowledge work in the United States!

The business of estimating the demand for graduates is clearly far from an accurate science.[73] The *First Destination* data utilized by funding bodies for higher education and the UK government is also notoriously inaccurate, largely because of low response rates and its incapacity to even reveal what graduates are doing just six months after graduation— barely time to have returned from their well-earned vacations to initiate the search for a suitable post.

A better indicator is the Association of Graduate Recruiters' (AGR) *Salaries and Vacancies Survey* that has been conducted on an annual basis for the last thirty years. The AGR has long represented the views of the major graduate recruiters in the United Kingdom collecting data and commissioning various research projects into the graduate recruitment market place. Although indicative only of the demand of the so-called 'blue-chip' organizations for graduates, the membership of the AGR provides the most accurate picture of those organizations in the United Kingdom who represent a significant share of those who recruit and develop tomorrow's knowledge workers. The waxing and waning of demand from these organizations for the product of our universities probably provides a more accurate yardstick for organizational demand for graduates in the United Kingdom.[74] Our extrapolation of the actual numbers of UK graduate vacancies available in blue-chip companies based on the AGR's annual survey is presented in Figure 3.2.[75]

By our calculations, the 400 or so organizations which comprise the AGR's membership offered a total of 25,000 vacancies for graduates during the current Labour administration's first year in office. In the

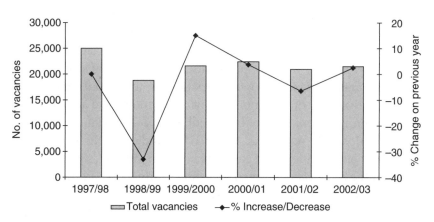

Fig. 3.2 Blue-chip graduate vacancies in the United Kingdom, 1997–2003
Source: Data extrapolated from AGR Graduate Recruitment Surveys 1997–2003.

same year a total of nearly 400,000 graduates completed their studies at a higher education institution;[76] a ratio of sixteen graduates applying for every graduate job offered in the United Kingdom by blue-chip organizations according to our reworking of AGR data.

Interestingly, a year later, blue-chip organizations slashed their recruitment by a third in the face of concerns about the Asian financial cirsis and global recession.

The following year, vacancies in the same companies moved in an upward direction but, crucially, not to a level achieved in 1997/1998 (21,620 compared to 25,000, respectively). Despite a rise on the previous year of 2.5 per cent, the number of graduate vacancies available in 2003 (21,500) has still not reached the actual level of vacancies available in 1997/1998 when the Labour Party came to power. This evidence raises serious doubts about the anticipated demand for knowledge workers in the UK economy, with the ratio of graduates to jobs available in blue-chip organizations rising to 20 : 1.[77] The very latest data paints an even drearier picture, suggesting that the actual number of applications for each graduate job is on average 35 : 1, although this latter data is distorted by a large number of graduates making multiple applications to a limited number of blue-chip organizations.[78]

The policy discourse that surrounds the returns to a graduate education is also overwhelmingly based on the data provided by the AGR survey. Consequently, this survey's reported starting salary of £20,000 available to those graduates who secure a post with one of the blue-chip organizations reported in the AGR survey represents the average starting salary of only the top 5 per cent of the graduate labour market. These are the posts dreamt about by young, aspiring university students as they weigh up the returns to what will now be a significant and personal investment in their personal capital. Nevertheless, a recent large-scale analysis points to wide variations in the labour market perceptions and activity of students in higher education[79] and actual experiences within what might now be described as a 'non-standard' labour market.[80] Moreover, additional research has indicated the existence of wide variations in differential earnings between graduates in relation to gender in the three years immediately after graduation and beyond (see Table 3.6).[81] Crucially, this same research derived from large-scale projects concluded that the findings 'reveal persistent inequalities among highly qualified employees which cannot be wholly explained by differences in qualifications, occupational variables or employment participation'.[82]

Table 3.6 Average annual earnings of graduates, 1999–2000

Age	Males (£)	Females (£)	% by which average male earnings exceeded those of females
20–24	16,738	14,592	14.7
25–29	23,302	20,154	15.6
30–34	30,448	24,939	22.1
35–39	36,948	27,774	33.2
40–44	36,949	26,691	38.4
45–49	36,696	26,113	40.5
50–54	38,153	26,549	43.7
All ages under 60	32,555	23,630	37.8

Source: Purcell, K. (2002), table 1, p. 6.

It is this varied picture of differential outcomes within the labour market that policy-makers choose to ignore when convincing students and their parents that higher education is a good investment.

Our analysis shows that there is no prospect of the graduate labour market expanding in line with the increased supply of graduates. According to the latest available projections for the United Kingdom over the next decade, something like 1.3 million people will leave their jobs each year either for new ones or to retire.[83] If, as we have estimated above, something like a third of these jobs are in what might be classed as knowledge work occupations, we can estimate that each year 400,000 new graduates are competing for approximately 416,000 knowledge worker posts with the 7.8 million graduates already at work in the UK economy. This might well account for why recent research suggests as many as 40 per cent of graduates are not actually using their university-acquired skills in their work.[84]

Some of the key issues raised by this chapter concern how to raise the demand for high skilled work within the economy, and how leading edge companies are responding to the growing supply of highly educated job applicants. The following chapter begins to expose how employers are responding to the rise of mass higher education.

4

The War for Talent

As in ancient times, talent has become the coin of the realm. Companies that multiply their human talents will prosper. Companies that don't will struggle.

Ed Michaels et al.[1]

People are being encouraged to invest in a university education in the promise of improving their chances of becoming a knowledge worker in the future. But while governments eulogize the new economy and the spread of high skilled, high waged work that they predict, much of the management literature has focused on the 'war for talent'.[2] Numerous books have appeared since the late 1990s with titles including, *The War for Talent*, *Winning the Talent Wars*, *The Talent Edge*, and *How to Compete in the War for Talent*. Some of this exuberance can be explained by the overheated American economy at century's end. But it also reflects current thinking about the knowledge economy, global economic competition and organizational change, and the view that these changes are putting more pressure on organizations to attract, develop, and retain 'truly' talented people. Therefore, even at times when labour markets slacken and companies look to reduce their labour costs, the assumptions that underscore the 'talent wars' remain.

This discourse around the war for talent (WfT) is important to consider because the competition for managerial jobs and careers is shaped by the way companies understand the nature and distribution of employable people. It also offers an insight into the mindsets of those responsible for the recruitment of managers and potential leaders in leading edge companies that will be the focus of subsequent chapters. This chapter will examine how organizations interpret and respond to the WfT discourse, making use of quotations from authors that espouse the WfT, company literature,[3] and employer interviews. A critical assessment of the WfT and its implications for wider issues of employability will be the subject of a later chapter, *The Wealth of Talent*.

Talent Management: A Strategic Business Challenge

Consultants at McKinsey and Company have perhaps done most to promulgate the 'war for talent' as what they regard as a strategic business challenge and driver of corporate performance.[4] In line with the dominant discourse of the knowledge-driven economy discussed in previous chapters, it is asserted that knowledge has become more important than money, land, or machines. The value of human capital has never been greater, given the increasing value of 'intangible assets such as proprietary networks, brands, intellectual capital, and talent'.[5] As one of our participating global consultancy companies told us:[6]

The company doesn't actually own anything, it doesn't actually own any buildings or cars or lap-tops or anything. The main asset is what's between people's ears and as a global organization we have the highest proportion of graduates than any other, its something like 90 per cent graduates...Our stock is intellectual ability. But not only technicians, meant in the broadest sense, but people that are able to handle clients well, conclude deals, and are generally very competent business people.

But as the knowledge economy is seen to widen the potential for more and more people to be involved in the accumulation, manipulation, and distribution of knowledge, which Michaels and his colleagues estimate to have increased from 17 to 60 per cent since 1900, competitive advantage is believed to depend on the outstanding performance of a few. What constitutes talent is being transformed as the acquisition of knowledge becomes widespread 'more knowledge workers means it's more important to get great talent, since the differential value created by the most talented knowledge workers is enormous'.[7] Likewise Cohen observes in *The Talent Edge*, that:

Traditional markets are being redefined, new economies are rapidly developing, and technology and new trade agreements are levelling the playing field globally. In this context, the need for skilled and competitive labor is ongoing. The talent of top performers has become the critical difference between those companies that grow and innovate, and those that falter or merely survive.[8]

Within this discourse, the value of outstanding talent will continue to mount as the knowledge economy continues to develop. Michaels and his colleagues are inspired to historical comparisons with Winston Churchill's famous epigraph, 'Never in the field of human conflict was so much owed, by so many, to so few.' But as they explain:

the war for talent, thankfully, lacks the fire and bloodshed of the Battle of Britain (sic). Nevertheless, just as the RAF was able to accomplish the impossible by segmenting its fighting force, companies can achieve higher performance by differentiating between their high, average, and low performers. If more companies had the discipline and courage to differentiate their talent this way, they, too, could accomplish the impossible.[9]

Such arguments present the fast track and other ways of differentiating high performing individuals or potential talent as a vital part of the armoury of any organization that seeks to prosper in the new economy. It has become imperative that companies try to identify the most talented individuals capable of becoming future senior managers and executives. In this study, virtually all of the companies interviewed for this book saw the fast track as a route to senior managerial if not executive leadership positions. Most viewed the fast track as an integral part of their succession planning, and an essential requirement if they were to attract the best candidates. They also recognized that although the fast track was aimed at university graduates, increasing numbers entering the job market inevitably meant that more of these graduates would be appointed to jobs that did not offer the same opportunities for rapid career progression. Talking about the fast track, a household named company in the financial sector told us:

When we recruit we are looking for the future leaders. We've already started to say that we will recruit less in the future... There are lots and lots of graduates out there if it's graduates that you need, who might aspire to be a sales person or a sales team leader but don't see themselves particularly going above that level, and you don't want a leadership programme there for them against their will... So we need to open up, it's probably an organizational fault that there hasn't been another route in.

For another leading telecommunications company the fast-track programme existed:

To grow our own talent for the future. At the moment we are developing technology that no one has, it is basically learn as you go... it's... a way of getting bright graduates in so that we can develop our own talent. So even within HR, where there isn't a labour shortage of HR officers, you're having someone coming in at ground level, doing placements within the business and having a really good understanding of the company... We did a whole massive piece of work... to question fundamentally do we need graduates, is it worth making a big investment? The answer was 'yes, of course... but what do you see the graduates doing?' Bums on seats will lead to the future, we want to recruit the senior managers, execs and directors of the future... so we're actually going to tell the graduates how we're going to do that.

However, it was generally believed that there would be greater differentiation between graduates in the future which would challenge the equation that 'graduate recruitment = fast track'. As an international software company told us after taking on around 400 university graduates:

I don't want 400 high flyers, because there are not 400 high flying jobs. We are not an internally aggressive, or internally competitive company... There is no, x is better than y, there isn't that feeling in here, there isn't that feeling that you have to really, you have to bust a gut, or you have to be seen to be working late. Those people who want to go and work that late, can work that late, but also there are jobs in IT that are not high flying consultancy jobs and so you don't want, you want a balance which is what we try to get.

Here, the existence of the fast track was seen to reflect the requirements of a differentiated workforce, but the selection of those who will go on to 'great things' is viewed as a personal choice about what is appropriate for the individual rather than a consequence of business imperatives and problems of career blockages in lean organizations.[10]

The Rising Demand for High-Calibre Managerial Talent

In the WfT the demand for high-calibre managers reflects a more challenging business context, doing more with less, more quickly and within a global environment. Companies today need managers who can respond to these challenges through enterprise, creativity, and leadership. This demand for managerial talent is evident in the requirements companies make of those looking for fast-track managerial appointments. Corporate brochures and websites proclaim that they are the best company to work for, but that only the best candidates are likely to have the personal capital that they are looking for:

What matters to us is the potential to reach a senior level fast. Everyone who joins us must be able to offer flexibility, enthusiasm, commercial acumen, independence, initiative, communication skills, an enquiring mind and the ability to plan, organise, analyse and evaluate. Teamworking—on a local and international level—is vital to the success of projects, so the way you relate to people is as important as the way you manage responsibility . . . we're looking for tomorrow's managers and technical specialists. Real decision-makers. So we need to employ innovative, self starting people who can think on their feet and handle responsibility. (Adtranz)

We believe that our ambitious plans can only be achieved by attracting and developing the very best talent, who bring enthusiasm and commitment to the service they provide to their clients, as well as to their own personal development . . . our competitive advantage comes from our people . . . Work at Ernst & Young is demanding, we aim not only to meet but to exceed our clients' expectations. The type of people who can achieve this will have . . . been involved in a variety of activities at university but have juggled their time well and consistently met deadlines. Not been satisfied with tried and tested methods but will have continuously tried to improve things and enjoyed being part of a changing environment . . . The most striking characteristic of people at Ernst & Young is their strong sense of individuality and the wide variety of skills, knowledge and experience they possess. (Ernst and Young)

Our success flows from the people making up the team, and our future depends on attracting and retaining those who share our eagerness to challenge the status quo. So we offer challenging responsibilities and ample development prospects... We know that maintaining our position of world leadership depends on having the best people working with us. (Vodafone)

Our people will always be Logica's biggest asset. In an environment that fizzes with a unique combination of technical innovation and creative flair, it's their talent, inspiration and sense of adventure that drive the business forward... That's why whenever it's time for a new member to join the team, we look for those who share our inquisitive and resourceful approach... However powerful the technology, what sets us apart from the competition is the talent and energy of our people. Our success is driven by dynamic, resourceful individuals who refuse to compromise and constantly strive for ever more innovative solutions... There are certain things we look for in our employees. We like them to think for themselves, so initiative is important. As is commitment. We expect 100% at all times. (Logica)

We're looking for talented, confident people who know where they're going. People who are not content to be a cog in a big machine, but want to be leading from the front in an organization that is changing lives. (National Health Service, NHS)

You will offer a strong and consistent record of high academic success. You will be able to demonstrate you have used your intelligence to solve problems, find creative solutions and use excellent judgement; think strategically and analytically, and be more confident and ambitious than the majority of your peers. We are keen to attract high-quality, highly literate and numerate applicants from a variety of degree subject backgrounds. (Robson Rhodes)

We have established a reputation for technical excellence through continuing innovation in pioneering technologies and have only achieved this by attracting, developing and retaining some of the best, most flexible talent available. We employ outstanding individuals with technical disciplines to work in meaningful roles with a bias in... technical and product development and manufacturing, with occasional opportunities in one of the support professions. (RayChem)

Meeting the Demand for Talent when the Career Bargain has been Broken

The discourse of the talent wars also highlights new rules of engagement as corporate-downsizing since the late 1980s 'broke the traditional covenant that traded job security for loyalty'.[11] Organizations no longer rely on nurturing talent based on long-term employment for the reasons noted in Chapter Two. But at the same time that companies were demanding greater flexibility over employment contracts, there has also been growing concerns about how organizations are going to retain their talented managers. According to Woodruffe, 'the independence of knowledge workers is...a consequence of the deliberate moves by firms to empower them and make them free'.[12] Breaking the psychological contract of security for loyalty removed many of the constraints and old taboos associated with frequent job-hopping, as Michaels and colleagues noted, 'it had become a badge of honour to have multiple companies on one's resume'.[13] The full implications of this shift to a market-driven employment relationship[14] is captured by Tulgan in his observation that:

if you create a free market for anything, including talent, the people with the most value to sell are going to leverage it for everything it's worth. And that's what's happening...Success now is defined by the open market, and that means the sky is the limit. No single organizational hierarchy puts a cap on your potential. Go wherever opportunities take you. That is the essence of the free-agent mind-set.[15]

This has much in common with those who characterize the US and UK labour markets in terms of winner-takes-all.[16] But the polarization of incomes that is associated with the growing disparities between 'winners' and 'losers' is not understood in negative terms, as such disparities are assumed to reflect the market value and contributions of individuals that had been artificially restricted by outdated agreements that limited the remuneration of individual employees for social or political reasons.[17] But it is not only income that is being leveraged, as Michaels and his colleagues also observe, 'more than ever, talented individuals have the negotiating leverage to ratchet up their expectations for their careers. The price of talent is rising'.[18]

All for the Best

In the WfT how companies attract, hire, and manage talent has therefore assumed paramount importance. Recruitment assumes considerable importance, ensuring that they recruit the right people. As Michaels and his colleagues once more inform us, 'excellent talent management has become a crucial source of competitive advantage. Companies that do a better job of attracting, developing, exciting, and retaining their talent will gain more than their share of this crucial and scarce resource and will boost their performance dramatically'.[19] They must do this according to the 'new realities' summarized by Michaels and his team in the following terms:[20]

The old reality	The new reality
People need companies	Companies need people
Machines, capital, and geography are the competitive advantage	Talented people are the competitive advantage
Better talent makes some difference	Better talent makes a huge difference
Jobs are scarce	Talented people are scarce
Employees are loyal and jobs are secure	People are mobile and their commitment is short term
People accept the standard package they are offered	People demand much more

A striking feature of this discourse is in the way in which work is packaged to appeal to potential fast-track employees. This is far removed from the '9–5, keep your nose clean and don't rock the boat' world of the corporate bureaucrat. Employers are attuned to what they perceive the best are looking for from prospective employers, sometimes informed by focus groups discussions or surveys of new hires. To enhance their appeal the very essence of a fast-track job is transformed within the virtual world of recruitment websites. You will find little about the constraints on individual interests and opportunities in the corporate pursuit for profit. For those that make it onto the fast track, work is consumption. The transition from university to work is reversed. Those with real talent can leave behind a life of endeavour for which there may have been little purpose beyond a good grade and enter a world where one is given real responsibility and where one's creative energies can be released within a fast-moving environment that offers almost limitless opportunities and scope for self-development. This includes challenging responsibilities, teamwork, and friendship, along with a competitive salary:

> As a company, we're aiming as high as we can get. We think and operate globally. We see no limits to what we can achieve. Are you equally ambitious? Can you handle the challenges you'll meet on the way? ... You'll be working with colleagues from every continent and culture. So what does that mean for you? A world of opportunity. Quite literally, limitless—you can go as high and as far as you want. (BAE Systems)

> Do you want to be responsible for your own business area, have interesting career prospects both at home and abroad? Do you want the chance to show initiative and creativity in a fast changing business environment? If so, then you are the person we want to join our team at Adtranz. (Adtranz)

> Today you'll start building your career. Tomorrow too. In fact, at Ernst & Young you'll never stop. Our global learning programme ensures you'll continue to develop your business thinking throughout your career. It's a commitment we make to you the day you join us. In return, we know you'll help us develop innovative solutions for the world's great companies. Through teaming, learning and leadership, at Ernst & Young you can achieve so much more. Why stop now? (Ernst & Young)

> Logica is not like most organizations. The buzz, the excitement, the sense of adventure combine to create a more stimulating environment ... Discover how you can contribute to the fizz and to the creative vision underlying our success ... Do you like the excitement of working at a start up, but don't want to take on the risks? Logica may be the right place for you. (Logica)

> Show us you can excel and we'll show you an open road upwards. (Hobsons Publishing)

The reward of a fast-track appointment is the preservation and development of one's individuality. They are more than a cog in the machine, but someone whose efforts, skills, and talents could make a difference to the company. Gone are the days of the off-the-shelf career package with neat diagrams of what can be expected of a fast-track trainee at various stages of their career. They are now greeted with an individual development plan that will include various training modules usually over a one or two-year period. Some of this training will be generic, focusing on such things as communication and presentation skills, project management, or working towards professional examinations. Other aspects of training will be specifically tailored to the individual's needs based on discussions with a mentor (who is usually a senior member of staff) or someone in the human resource management team. The message is clear: 'you are a valued individual, there are outstanding opportunities awaiting you, but you must take responsibility for managing your employability'.

This presents a conundrum for organizations against a backdrop of 'not for life' employment. In a UK survey of 362 adverts for graduate appointments in 2001 we found only one explicit promise of job security. But we found little of the celebratory rhetoric of the 'free agent' shifting jobs and adding value to their CVs, when we spoke to those doing the hiring at the grass roots. These companies were willing to invest a lot of resources in the training and development of their fast-trackers. At the same time it was acknowledged that few organizations could honestly say that they offered a career for life.

Indeed, this study highlights a major tension between the celebratory rhetoric of market individualism that drives the WfT, and the needs of businesses (rather than financial markets) to develop the productive capabilities of the workforce in a collective enterprise. Many companies have become increasingly aware of the downside of downsizing and the market-driven workforce. There is considerable scepticism about being able to buy in able managers and executives as and when they are required. Many commented on the importance of organizational culture and institutional memory. A lot of the rhetoric about corporate change has often portrayed institutional memory as trained incapacity. This fits well with ideas about the weightless economy and the explosion of business start-ups in Silicon Valley.[21] But most companies need people, especially at senior levels, to understand and share the values of the organization. They need people who have seen similar 'problems' before, people who know how to manage the process of problem solving, even if the specific problem requires a unique solution. These companies are concerned about succession planning and place considerable value on growing their own talent:[22]

We expect it to happen because history tells us that it will and that is certainly what I was … told to do, if you want to get on in your career you don't stay with a company any more than two years, but as a recruiting company we don't want that, and we certainly don't encourage people to only stay a couple of years. We provide a twelve month training programme so if we lose them twelve months after that it is an awful lot of money for next to no payback … We have suffered at about the three/four years level because they will do training for a year, do one, maybe two jobs, and then say, 'Now what?' But we certainly don't encourage people to go after a couple or three years, we want some people to stay so we have got the experience. (Manufacturing Sector)

We have gone from, 'You manage your own career', to, 'Well, actually, there's a risk in that, in that you lose some of your top people which you have invested heavily in, and it's a bit daft to lose them if they don't really choose to go and they could be a good asset for the future. (Financial Sector)

You know some people stay over five years and are really happy and we don't really want to lose them at all...I think it is a mixture of graduates. You do get some graduates who are jobs for life and I think where that has happened it is the ambitious ones because they can see how much scope there is within the organization. There are some graduates at the moment, who are really making things happen for themselves which is really wonderful to see. Some people will always see it as a stepping stone and that's fine, I guess different ambitious people have different ways of how they want their future to be. (Telecommunications Sector)

In one of the information technology companies it was believed to be virtually impossible to keep people because of the opportunities within the wider job market. However, retrenchments in the IT sector have reduced these opportunities and increased the risks associated with moving to another company. However, this organization has tried to make a virtue of the 'free agent' mindset:

I think a certain amount of churn is very healthy and we get other people in from organizations after a couple of years. Obviously we want to hold on to our high flyers but we can't. I think people especially in this industry will do their two/three years and move around and generally graduates look at portfolio careers now, the idea of a job for life just doesn't exist anymore and they don't want to do that...but it is not so much of an issue now as the economy is a bit tighter, not like two years ago when they were just recruiting like mad ...On a plus side, we tend to use it to sell careers in the company because you can have a portfolio career without leaving, which is quite handy to do. I don't necessarily think it is a bad thing at all as long as you have the right staff at the right time...the fact that they are going to go in three or four years time. As long as you can deliver and you are always going to want to hang onto your top people, that is my personal view and it is not a corporate view. (IT Consultants)

Some of the employers were also concerned about how to manage the expectations of graduates, who were typically seen to have inflated ideas about the speed of their ascent into leadership roles and their overall worth to the business world. The fact that this was, at least in part, a consequence of the way companies presented themselves as dream-makers for the chosen few, escaped most of them:

> We don't call it a fast track. But essentially who else makes someone head of graduate recruitment after 12 months? So it is quite a fast track. But we don't call it as such...if you call it fast track you are then managing expectations. Some 21 year olds thinking they can take on the world and think they can become a senior manager at the age of 22. So I think there is something in there about managing expectations and also not pissing off the staff that you have. We have an internal promotion policy and graduates...have a very high profile so therefore there is opportunity to move up faster. It's down to individuals. (Telecommunications Sector)

Talent: A Limited Commodity?

In the WfT discourse it is not only assumed that talent has become more important, but also that it remains in limited supply.[23] Yet, those who advance such views find it difficult to define highly talented managers. In general terms, talent is often seen as 'the sum of a person's abilities—his or her intrinsic gifts, skills, knowledge, experience, intelligence, judgement, attitude, character, and drive. It also includes his or her ability to learn and grow'.[24] It is then acknowledged that 'defining great managerial talent is a bit more difficult. A certain part of talent eludes description: You simply know it when you see it',[25] like when senior managers and executives look in the mirror!

It is then acknowledged that there is no universal definition of great managerial talent because it will vary depending on organizational context, including the nature of the business, organizational culture, and management style. Each company is, therefore, encouraged to:

> understand the specific talent profile that is right for it...We can say, however, that managerial talent is some combination of a sharp strategic mind, leadership ability, emotional maturity, communications skills, the ability to attract and inspire other talented people, entrepreneurial instincts, functional skills, and the ability to deliver results.[26]

Ultimately we are told that 'talent' is a 'code for the most effective leaders and managers at all levels who can help a company fulfil its aspirations and drive its performance'.[27] Although far from satisfactory at least Michaels and his colleagues have a shot at a definition. Others such as Tulgan see little point in trying to define 'talent' because:

You know very well that a single truly great person on your team is worth two, three, four, or five mediocre ones. The difference in value is hard to quantify, but the truth of the matter is clear: Nobody is more valuable than that person you can rely on without hesitation. That person almost always gets the job done right and ahead of schedule, takes exactly the right amount of initiative without over-stepping, makes the tough judgement calls as well as the easy ones, and makes it look routine.[28]

The nature of talent is central to the ideas in this book and it will be systematically explored in a later chapter. Here, we will limit ourselves to considering the nature of this discourse and how the companies that we interviewed responded to some of its key elements. Clearly, companies are being encouraged to develop and invest in something they have little idea how to identify and specific to each company. Moreover, while Michaels et al. define talent in terms of performance, fast-track recruitment is as much about identifying potential as current performance. Yet, most of the companies interviewed in this study were reasonably confident that the focus on behavioural competence enabled them to define and capture what they were looking for, as we will show in the following chapter.

Managerial Talent: Born or Made?

Despite these problems of definition it is also confidently asserted that there is a limited pool of talent capable of rising to senior managerial positions. Indeed this reflects a long-standing assumption in Western culture that there is a limited pool of ability from which any given generation can draw.[29] The fast track has traditionally been assumed to reflect innate differences in the capabilities of employees. Tight restrictions on the numbers of university students for much of the last century reinforced the assumption that there was a limited pool of talent capable of benefiting from a university education. 'Naturally' it was from this elite that people were chosen for accelerated career progression within the corporate hierarchies of the time. However, the expansion of higher education since the late 1980s has made it very difficult to sustain this view of a cognitive elite, as the limited pool of ability comes to resemble an ocean of untapped talent. We have already seen that employers now argue that the demonstration of cognitive ability is only one aspect of what it takes to become a senior manager in innovative, fast-moving businesses. As one employer told us, today 'you have to be across the board and not just clever'.

Assumptions about innate qualities are extended to include drive, resilience, confidence, and creativity in definitions of managerial talent. This 'spiritual dimension of power'[30] echoes the Darwinian search for the 'fittest' personalities with the appropriate personal, people, and task skills. The growing demand for managers of the future to exhibit charismatic qualities has done little to alter the Darwinian view of most recruiters. Whereas in bureaucratic organizations the recruitment process was explicitly targeted on the search for raw intellectual talent and technical expertise, it is now extended to include the 'gift' of charisma. This is clearly an example of social gifts being translated into natural gifts.[31] This does not mean that recruiters all think that leaders are born rather than made. Indeed, social Darwinism does not depend on innate differences in genetic capacities but the drive and moral courage of individuals to adapt to their environment to become business or political leaders. As Graham William Sumner noted in the late nineteenth century, 'class distinctions simply result from the different degrees of success with which men have availed themselves of the chances which were presented to them'.[32]

Many of the recruiters we spoke to shared the view that drive, persistence, and self-reliance are integral to managerial success as we will discuss in the chapter on 'picking winners'. Most also shared the view that the rise of mass higher education had not increased the pool of managerial and leadership talent. Some complained about the poor quality of some candidates:

We do seem to be getting more people coming through and you'll say, 'Well, who the hell was that that I just had to sit with for half an hour?' Because either they talked a complete load of rubbish or they spoke so quickly you couldn't understand a word of it, or they just couldn't get the sentences out and you think, 'These are graduates!' I think, 'Is this me? Am I expecting too much? Have I been in the job too long?' But I'm assured it is not me...the academic level has slipped and...that would be carried through the universities, because if they are starting lower they can't expect them to get up to where they were. On the other side of it, the social skills don't stack up to me, because...graduates now have done so much more than anybody that I went to school with...I don't know perhaps they decide they will travel for six months but they are not being quite as extensive or whatever it is but maybe the bigger group has only come about by the bottom-line dropping down a bit. (Manufacturing Sector)

Despite such views a major concern of other recruiters was the large numbers applying for fast-track appointments. In the financial sector we were told:

The quality is definitely still there. There is no less quality...On the basis of 4–5,000 applications, we very easily get what we're looking for, I'm not so sure there's a war...for talent...at this stage, it's more a war of turning them away.

There was also considerable ambiguity about whether managerial talent is born or made. Recourse to 'nature' is seductive because it removes social and ethical responsibilities from those who need to make difficult judgements about the future careers and life-chances of others. If differences between candidates reflect innate characteristics then the fast track represents a legitimate way of trying to capture the 'nature' of things. Whereas, if employers are making judgements about differences in social experiences, it raises awkward questions as management and leadership skills could be developed through training and other learning opportunities. This ambiguity was captured in the following discussion about whether leaders are born or made:

We hope to see someone that has the potential before we want to invest.

So they are born not made?

[laughter] Is that the time! I've no idea but I think our process works on the assumption that they are born. You spot that potential and then you develop it. I think that's the assumption we work on and whether it's right or not I don't know...they have been born but there are other things they have done as we've been saying about developing them. You would hope to see that 'something' and then develop it if they've been born with it...They've done other things that just build on that because there is something innate about them that, 'I want to go on, I want to be the leader of that senior management team, to go on their expedition to the Himalayas. I want to do this, and I want to do that, and I want to be part of this group.' There is just something, and I think drive kept coming through to me when you were talking, you know about the drive to go out there and find my placement rather than keep going to their mentor and keep asking 'where do you think I should go next?' The drive to want to do better, the drive and the aspiration of 'I want to be there, I want the challenge.' So I think everything in life then just builds...It's like rolling a snowball, you build it up...so perhaps we don't work on the ethos that they are born but we work on the ethos that by the time they come to us they should have developed something of themselves that we can spot... Does it have to be one of these, it could be both, some could be born, some could be made. (Financial Sector)

Diversity: Tapping the Pool for Talent?

Within the literature on the war for talent there is remarkably little mention of cultural diversity. Michaels and colleagues have only one reference to diversity and that is in a case-study description of a company that had tried to broaden its recruitment profile. However, an extensive literature on diversity issues aimed at HRM professionals has emerged in the last twenty years. There are numerous definitions of diversity but all are based on a respect for individual and cultural differences. Kandola and Fullerton suggest that 'the fundamental argument for managing diversity is the benefit derived from recruiting, retaining and promoting the best people regardless of their background, ethnicity, accent, sex, hair colour, or other individual characteristics'.[33]

The advocates of greater cultural diversity within organizations have not been slow in making the business case. Individual differences are championed as a source of competitive advantage because companies that diversify staffing are more likely to reflect the profile of their customers or clients. It is also seen to offer companies greater variation in the way they handle new and novel circumstances, or when they are competing in international markets. Greenslade suggests that 'cultural diversity creates an environment in which...the talent and attributes of people from different backgrounds and heritages are fully valued, utilised and developed. Such an environment, we believe, can achieve superior business results.'[34]

The question of cultural diversity challenges organizations to examine their assumption about 'the best' and what they look like. While Johnson and Redman's conclusion is somewhat premature, that 'organizations that operate globally have come to recognize that talent is by no means restricted to prime-age Caucasian males!',[35] virtually all the organizations that participated in our research have bought into the rhetoric, if not the realities, of managing diversity. Most companies have developed explicit policy statements on diversity that are featured prominently in their recruitment literature. Deliberate attempts are made by most organizations to ensure that their websites and brochures avoid the message, 'if you are not a white male or female with an Oxbridge degree don't bother applying for a job here because you don't stand a chance of getting in'. The widespread use of personal profiles of successful fast-trackers is used to convey the message that they recruit a diverse range of people. These profiles will often include an Asian woman, Afro-Caribbean man, and someone from a 'new' university.

In part this is a pragmatic response to the problem of competing for 'the best' that are assumed to be concentrated in a small number of elite universities. For organizations that are looking for large numbers of new hires or who feel that they are not at the top of the 'pecking order' of companies that offer starting salaries in excess of £30,000 a year, they have an incentive to broaden their net (and their organization's appeal).

The logic of this approach is neatly captured in the advice offered by Woodruffe. In the search for talent he suggests that 'a winning answer is to look in the less obvious places and overcome the obvious temptations to confine one's efforts to good departments of 'better' universities'.[36] He recommends that companies widen their net in the trawl for talent:

If the organization has concluded it needs to recruit greater diversity, it needs to make itself attractive to such people, quite apart from protecting them once they have joined. To make itself attractive, perhaps it needs to present itself as welcoming of differences and not rigidly defined in terms of its organizational personality. The more rigid the definition, the more it will restrict itself to people 'like us'. It therefore needs to present images in its recruitment literature of diverse people who have been successful employees.[37]

Some organizations have clearly taken this advice:

We've just got a diversity sponsor...because we're...quite young, it's a bit sophisticated for us! With graduate recruitment it's not something we discourage but not something we actively encourage. So it's difficult because with something like the brochure...I'm always conscious that it is slightly staged. I make sure we have a cross section of representatives so it can be anything from having a white engineer but doing yoga, which is challenging the stereotypes. Making sure we have a female Asian person in our adverts and a male Asian person in our adverts and in our brochure. (Telecommunications Sector)

This year we have gone quite in-depth on the website, having case studies that we are going to swap around throughout the year...someone says about their typical day and there is a picture on there so it is trying to make it a lot more familiar to people...because it is hard as an undergraduate to actually imagine yourself having finally got through this process and in a job. So to try and make it appeal a little bit more and [suggest] there are people here doing this, and this is the university they went to, and somebody might think 'oh I went to that university and they are obviously looking for people like me'. (Manufacturing Sector)

But what was firmly engrained in the minds of HR staff was that the selection of the best employees was paramount. Actively promoting diversity was encouraged to increase the range of applicants but there was a unanimous view that they would always take the 'best' candidate:

I did the personnel undergrad interview and sat there and talked to an Asian girl who had got through the first stage...she didn't get through at the next stage, but she didn't get through for the same reasons that other people didn't get through, it wasn't because her colour was the wrong one. I mean we are based in the Midlands where we are surrounded by all sorts of different-coloured people, and short and tall and fat and thin and all the rest of it, and to me...the colour of your skin is the same as whether you are fat, thin, tall or short. So we haven't got a published policy...but we do look at the numbers...to make sure that what we are doing is correct. But we won't go out and positively say this is who we are going to go for. (Manufacturing Sector)

The issues organizations are grappling with in respect to diversity, recruitment, and talent management are also captured in the following discussion with two female HR professionals. They begin by recognizing the problem of implementing diversity policies when executive board members reflect a legacy of Oxbridge Man:

Suddenly we've got a new Equality and Diversity Director who is very visible and we talk about E & D in everything we do...I suppose from a graduate recruitment perspective, if you're just looking at pure race and age, we have a fairly good record which might balance out the rest of the organization which is not that good, but you know I guess it could still be better. So there's a promise out there really and we've got a top board representative of each minority group, so there will be somebody who represents disability, somebody who represents sexual orientation, so we have key people, really key people. It's amazing because when they show the video of the people signing the agenda, you look at them and they're all white male, 45+ or from certain universities and you're thinking 'yeah that's great ha, ha, ha', so... some staff see this as a bit of a joke. (Financial Sector)

Although employees are quick to read the implicit values that senior staff convey through their actions rather than policy pronounce-ments,[38] hiring practices are genuinely seen to be a key area where diversity issues can make a difference:

We change the universities that we're going to target or go out on our milk round to. We advertise in differing publications to attract different minority groups... It does affect how we market, it does affect the universities that we go to and it does affect the training we give our assessors, and the assessment process we put our candidates through. There was some talk in the past that we might have given a big focus on people who have had a year out and gone travelling and the experiences that they have had and how that adds to the application form, whether it's fiction or not but of course you'll get some eth-nic minorities who are very family orientated and therefore wouldn't have dreamt of having a year out and going off travelling somewhere, so haven't got the same experiences. So I know those issues have been taken into account so just to make sure that you're not disadvantaging a certain group of people. (Financial Sector)

However, the greater focus on the graduate leadership programme within this company, require them to be even more selective about who they hire. This brings into sharp relief the problem of diversifying the workforce, especially at senior levels. As the numbers of applica-tions grow as more people enter the job market with a university edu-cation, the pressure on companies such as this to screen out larger numbers at an early stage in the hiring process inevitably mounts. Consequently, any candidate that does not have twenty-two UCAS points at Advanced Level (equivalent of BBC) and an upper-second class degree will be immediately eliminated despite the fact that many non-traditional university students fail, especially at the first hurdle:

I think... it will change for next year... I think we will have to stick to the 22 UCAS Points and be more rigorous and maybe more ruthless around the entry requirements. Because if we're going to be looking for less, and we are wanting the best, then why are we wavering and doing what we do although we're trying to do the right thing by the candidates. (Financial Sector)

Therefore, while most employers presented the commitment to diversity and to hire 'the best' as a win–win scenario that enabled organizations to select from a broader range of applicants, there was also an awareness that these could be conflicting priorities. As an HR director in a major financial institution observed, 'Oxford and Cambridge still give you overall the best candidates. What it doesn't give you is diversity. And you can't do the two things.'

The War for Reputational Capital

Finally, the war for talent is presented as a rational response to the changing demands of a knowledge-driven economy. The basic message is that 'a talented few matter more'. This has led organizations in both the public and private sector to find ways of attracting and retaining the best talent available. Such ideas will be subjected to critical scrutiny in a subsequent chapter, but it is important to note that much of the behaviour of companies in respect to the issues covered in this chapter is irrational, in the sense that its relationship to raising productivity and profitability remains unclear, if not counterproductive. There is a herd mentality within graduate recruitment, as no company wants to risk losing out on a share of 'the best':

I think companies have got to feel that they are in competition. We are all out there for what people would see as the better/brighter graduates, we don't want the very top ones because we know we couldn't keep them . . . But on the whole if you take a generic group of companies and a generic group of grads, I think there will be a set in the middle there that we are all fighting over. I think more and more companies are now looking for that finite group of graduates although the figures are showing more people are going to university, in our experience there isn't a bigger group of people in the middle . . . and I think the smaller/medium sized companies also seem to be looking for graduates now. (Manufacturing Sector)

Indeed, investments in hiring have become closely related to the marketing and 'branding' of companies:

Did you see the Times top 100 graduate employers? We shot up the poll in that. Now whether that's a good thing or a bad thing, it's been bandied around internally as being a wonderful thing. I'm not so sure whether it is or isn't. We're in the top group and . . . if you look who was around us it tends to be the investment banks or the consultancies . . . That probably says something about the sort of people we're trying to attract. But then it also says something about their aspirations when they come here . . . You become really employable after two years. So you can leave if you want and go somewhere else although they don't, but they could. (Financial Sector)

Being an 'employer of choice' was seen as a way of branding the company as well as a way of attracting the best applicants. Yet, it was also acknowledged that playing this 'reputational' game in competition with other companies may simply up the stakes required to attract those defined as the best, while recognizing that this may do little to prepare the company for the future:

So there're all these reasons to join, but . . . does that meet our business needs going forward? Does it bring you the people that you're looking for as leaders or are you always trying to keep them with a different sweetener? I think the volume with which we recruit is just far too high. (Financial Sector)

It is also widely believed that many of those who connect to company websites may not finish up working for the company, but they may be future customers or clients. Where brand recognition is related to being a market leader, the best companies want to be seen to be recruiting the best talent, as these are mutually reinforcing. This represents a positional competition between companies that make it difficult for them to break ranks, apart from when they want to offer even more 'sweeteners' to the talented few. However, at least some employers question the over-the-top way in which some organizations were attempting to attract more marketable graduates:

We went for a very plain website this year, because last year we thought it was too much fun in a way. We went just for very plain, the black and white, and then the pictures so it wasn't all jazzy . . . Personally I . . . don't like the whole sort of, 'Come and work for us, we're crazy and here is a picture of us having a drink out together, we have fun.' Because to me that really turned me off and I would just want to know what's it all about, does it convince me? Is it professional? Talking to students, a lot of them said, 'We don't like the gimmicks.' We don't produce a flyer that is an origami swan . . . You have to unfold it, and to read it you had to turn it around and flip it over and people just said, 'You know, we don't want that, we are not that stupid. We know that it is still the same contents.' (Manufacturing Sector)

Managerial Talent: A Historical Interlude

Before concluding this chapter it is worth considering the historical legacy of the war for talent. In Reinhard Bendix's classic study of *Work and Authority in Industry* he examined the ideologies of management in the course of industrialization in England, Russia, and the United States.[39] In this study he drew a distinction between the ideology of the *entrepreneur* and the ideology of *management*. In the nineteenth century the entrepreneurial ideology in Victorian England was based on the pursuit of self-interest alongside the Christian virtues of hard work, frugality, and prudence. In many respects the individual was cut free of Feudal obligations to fend for himself and his family against a backdrop of harsh economic necessity. As Bendix suggested:

These virtues of moral self-reliance and self-development became a national creed where, as in the American environment, their practical application in the pursuit of material gain was readily identified with the conquest of a Continent. In the United States the businessman became a hero whose very material gain was celebrated as a moral victory. The people at large were admonished to emulate him, each man in competition with his fellows.[40]

Bendix argued that this ideology remained unproblematic so long as it did not have negative consequences for labour management. But with the rise of large-scale factory production, trade unionism, and the bureaucratization of business enterprise, new ways had to be found to buttress the employer's authority and to ensure the work efficiency of each employee. The answer was found in scientific management where the moral exhortations of the past gave way to scientific planning and the monitoring of employee behaviour. The craft knowledge of independent traders was transferred into the hands of managers, but at the same time the burden of responsibility for output and improvements in productivity also shifted from the individual worker to management.

The growth of personnel specialists reflected these changing responsibilities as managers became increasingly concerned with the emotional and social factors which affect an individual's outlook as well as his or her output. This led Antonio Gramsci to reflect on the way industrialists including Henry Ford had become increasingly concerned about the sexual affairs of their employees and their family arrangements.[41]

The shift from an entrepreneurial to management ideology did not extinguish the importance of individual striving, struggle, and achievement, which came to depend on academic credentials and progress within bureaucratic career structures.[42] But the public appraisal of the business leader had shifted from a celebration of individual human endeavour against all the odds, to the celebration of an economic system that enabled people to fulfil their opportunities and aspirations.

In these circumstances the ideal image of the entrepreneur as a risk-taker and innovator was gradually:

superseded by the ideal image of the manager as the skilful organizer of co-operative effort. And the fashionable vocabulary of motives by which the economic conduct of Everyman is 'explained' has shifted from competitive striving to the desire to stand well with one's fellows, from hard work as a virtue to work as a source of satisfaction, and from the desire for gain to the personal emotions and attitudes which underlie that desire.[43]

This discussion reveals that in many respects we have gone full circle. The WfT has much in common with the nineteenth-century entrepreneurial ideology. The emphasis on individual employability and talent re-asserts the importance of self-reliance based on hard work and moral exhortations, urging people to use their talents to the best of their abilities. The business leader as hero has also returned, as Tulgan extravagantly claims, 'The free agent is the hero of the new economy: She is adaptable, technoliterate, innovative, self-reliant, and entrepreneurial.'[44] However, the rugged individualism associated with the entrepreneurial ideology has been smoothed over. Hard work is not presented as a grim battle for economic survival, but a source of satisfaction and self-fulfilment. For those that can rise above the mass ranks of employees work is an expression of individuality. As we have noted the glittering prizes held out to the knowledge elite offer more than money and status, but rapid progression to senior positions are based on the development of leadership skills offering self-actualization.

Conclusion

In this chapter we have shown that the WfT presents a view of economic competition and corporate efficiency based on the assertion that human resources are a decisive facet of competitive advantage, and that there are significant differences in the contributions of members of the workforce that are reflected in their remuneration. The WfT takes human capital arguments a step further by suggesting that the efforts of a few matter more than ever and therefore companies should seek to identify outstanding talent and do whatever it takes to attract and retain it. In other words, the *technical* imperatives of organizations make it crucial to get the most talented people into key managerial and leadership roles.

While there is evidence of these companies sharing some of the assumptions of the WfT, such as the view that the human side of enterprise has become more important and that there is a restricted pool of talent from which to draw, there is also evidence that some of these organizations are aware of the downside of downsizing and revolving door employment policies.

The WfT reflects the major paradox that in the knowledge-driven economy recruitment depends far less on the knowledge of candidates. This is not because knowledge is unimportant, but rather because many more people entering the competition for managerial and professional jobs have met the knowledge requirements associated with a university degree.[45] As we will argue in Chapter Eight this has exploded one of the great myths of the age, that there is a limited pool of talent capable of advanced academic study or capable of managing in a work context. In theory, this should be a source of liberation for companies that are no longer restricted to recruit from the gene pool of previous elites.

But despite much talk about diversity being a new source of competitive advantage the discourse is dominated by the war for talent. Here, we can see how the idea of a knowledge economy points in two directions. On the one hand, it points to the need for diversity and to develop the talents of all, and on the other, to an even greater emphasis on outstanding talents, and the contribution and development of a few. We have shown that the latter informs the WfT. This has led to a focus on how to recruit and retain 'the best' and whether this can be achieved in a fair and efficient manner. It also leads to an examination of the secrets of success, focusing on the characteristics of those most likely to win the competition for elite jobs. These are important issues that will be addressed in the following chapters. But it is important not to lose sight of the broader significance of this discussion, as it raises issues about the way jobs are defined and opportunities and careers are structured. We need to challenge the cultural assumptions on which the WfT rests. This raises questions about the *positional* rather than the *technical* division of labour, that is how companies organize the workforce not only in terms of discrete tasks that need to be fulfilled but how these are organized, labelled, and rewarded. In the industrial bureaucracies of the twentieth century the pyramid of occupational status was based on differences in expert knowledge.[46] But as more people gain access to university credentials, the knowledge gap within the workforce has narrowed, and new ways have to be found to legitimate what amounts to increasing inequalities in the return on investments in education and training. The emphasis on outstanding talent, value-added performance, and market-driven employment that characterize the WfT can therefore be seen as an attempt not only to reproduce existing employment relations, but also to shape and legitimate new ones at a time when the workforce is becoming more 'educated'.

It can also be shown that employability for fast-track managerial jobs is shaped by the positional competition with other companies to attract, recruit, and retain the 'best'. Our argument is that the 'wft' is not the result of the poor quality of university education. The positional competition described in previous chapters is not restricted to individuals in the scramble for tough-entry jobs. It equally applies to leading edge companies in a bid to position themselves favourably in the competition for the 'best' graduates, that may have more to do with the 'reputational capital' of companies than issues of productive efficiency.

Here, we have examined the assumptions that shape corporate attitudes to human resourcing, why they maintain a fast track for some graduates even though there is a mass supply of higher educated employees. We have also explored why some employers believe that despite the rise of mass higher education the pool of talent from which they could recruit has not expanded. Our next task is to consider the techniques used by organizations to recruit onto the fast track and why the vast majority of organizations expressed considerable confidence in their select techniques based on an assessment of behavioural competence.

5

The Science of Gut Feeling

What counts can not always be counted, and what can be counted does not always count.

Albert Einstein

Introduction

Organizations are raising their expectations of what represents the threshold for entry into their workforces. There is general agreement among employers and governments alike that all workers of every age, race, and nation have to raise their game if they are to compete in the knowledge-based economy (KBE). Jobs in the twenty-first century, we are told, will not look like the jobs undertaken by our parents, or even ourselves just a decade ago. The majority, not just an elite few, are assumed to require a list of personal capabilities which in a previous life may have resulted in canonization.[1]

Not surprisingly, then, the stakes in managerial labour markets in the new knowledge economy are high. For those in the competition for tough-entry jobs these have been exacerbated by the seemingly assiduous shift in the narrative of employability away from what constitutes the *hard* currencies of employability, or formal badges of personal achievement and certification, to *soft* currencies of employability constituted by skills and capabilities of a less clear-cut, more aesthetic and performative nature. Substance is arguably giving way to form.

People no longer want to be managed, but led. Consequently, we are not merely looking for managers but for leaders. People have to be more than intelligent or well qualified, they need to be innovative and creative problem-solvers. Moreover, these new attributes need to be harnessed in such a way as to be enterprising or entrepreneurial within the context of the new economy. These changes represent the importance of not just knowing 'what' to do but also 'how' to do it. Employability, then, has become stylized, commodified, and ultimately embodied within individuals in such a way as to render the process of selecting individuals in the labour market process open to a new level of subjectivity. It remains unclear how this new subjectivity can be accommodated in the course of the acquisition, presentation, and ultimate evaluation and selection of these new capabilities.

Not that this new subjectivity has in any way dampened the ebullience of the recruitment industry. A vast array of methods and techniques are now deployed by the industry to ensure the accuracy, cost effectiveness, and above all else, the objectivity of the process of recruitment. According to some in the industry these new capabilities can be attested by an attitudinal test in as little as five minutes! Predilection to particular attitudes, ways of working, orientation to development, even the tidiness of an applicant's desk can soon be predicted with alarming accuracy and objectivity. Or at least so the rhetoric would have us believe. It is rhetoric organizations want to believe. It is not just enough to want to be objective in the business of recruiting new knowledge workers: organizations feel the need to be *seen* to be objective. In an economy where more applicants are eminently employable than ever before, hairs need to be split, and not just split precisely, but transparently and accountably. Thus, a new science of recruitment and selection is in the making: the science of gut feeling.

This chapter explores this new and evolving science of recruitment and selection against the backdrop of the contemporary knowledge worker labour market. Our focus is not with the actual process of selection decisions made by employers, which we explore in Chapter Seven. We are more concerned here with the perspectives employers adopt in relation to the methods of justification they employ for their hiring decisions. Our claim is that the competence-based recruitment and selection techniques utilized by organizations typically involve two related processes. The first is what we call *Pythagoras' Legacy*. Here, the narrative of employability utilized by organizations is based on the idea that managerial and leadership potential can be broken down into a range of behavioural competences that can be systematically interrogated in the recruitment process. Even those intangible qualities of character, drive, and interpersonal sensitivity can be measured through mathematical techniques, the recruitment literature confidently asserting that these techniques enable recruiters to reach accurate, objective, and above all else *quantifiable* projections of individual capability.

The second part of the process involves *'Making Up People'*.[2] It is not merely a case of individual assessors establishing what types of organizational and pre-ordained categories individuals fit into (e.g. 'fast-track' or 'graduate programme'). Rather, assessors create in their own minds, in many ways unwittingly, there and then through different narratives of competence, the very differences they ascribe to people, which in turn subsequently affect candidates' ultimate location into certain and—crucially—*discrete* categories (e.g. 'good communicator' or 'bad communicator'; 'employable' or 'unemployable'). The questions we ask here concern the legitimate foundations for fitting people into pre-existing categories established for them by recruitment specialists. How, for instance, does the new science of recruitment accommodate those individuals who do not 'fit' into these pre-existing categories?

Our contention is that employers 'make up' people in such a way to ensure their ultimate 'objective' location into the discrete categories the science of gut feeling has waiting for them. We conclude that the process of establishing a candidate's employability is not simply triggered by the 'observable' capabilities of individuals ticked off against the employer's list of required competences, but through the outcome of negotiation—tacit as well as overt—between candidates and selectors at recruitment events. We also suggest that candidates often do not play by the same rules laid down by the recruitment industry, opting instead to manipulate inherent inconsistencies to their own advantage.

Pythagoras' Legacy

We keep all the assessment down to all the facts, what we see, what we hear.

In contradistinction to the recent efforts of labour market analysts to highlight the social complexities of labour markets and the methodological implications of this recognition,[3] the recruitment and selection industry confidently claims the opposite is in fact the case. In the words of one consultant 'a test should measure what it is supposed to measure and predict what it is supposed to predict'.[4] Life really is presented as being this clear-cut. Validity, reliability, objectivity, accuracy, predictive measurement, and a whole host of other adjectives are utilized by those in the recruitment industry. Such a scientific approach can even apparently estimate the degree to which evaluations of candidates diverge. According to another consultant:

[T]he level of correlations between ratings given by different raters reporting on the performance of the same employees tends to only be of the order of 0.55 to 0.75, *which shows that a good deal depends on which rater is making the report*.[5]

Such subjectivity between selectors is glossed over, however. Listing the benefits of its services, one well known multi-national organization operating in over twenty countries points to its ability to provide 'independent reviews and assessments of individuals [which are] applicable when demonstrable objectivity is required [and] the process is open to outside scrutiny [and needs to be] seen to be fair and unbiased'.[6] Again, this standpoint is antithetical to the one adopted by the recent government-commissioned Policy Action Team on Skills which observed 'the relationship between skills and work is far from being a directly instrumental one'.[7] This suggests recruitment is far from being the accurate science of 'reading off' individual capabilities as it is portrayed to be by the industry itself.

The strength of the rhetoric surrounding the scientific and objectivity claims of recruiters may, in part, reflect their need to in some way distance themselves from the choices they ultimately make. Those charged with the responsibility of selecting for their organizations young graduates for training schemes are effectively dream-makers, representing the gatekeepers between young graduate hopefuls and the career sponsorship and development which awaits successful candidates. Organizations cannot claim to be anything else other than ruthlessly objective in their selection methods, especially when the current government takes seriously its manifesto 'commitment to combine a dynamic economy with fair standards in the work-place'.[8] It is no longer enough to justify why somebody has been hired; justification also has to be provided to placate the increasing numbers of individuals who have not been so fortunate. According to the latest data available, for every successful graduate hired, there are on average thirty-four other disappointed candidates.[9] Several of the HR representatives we interviewed alluded to this obligation now expected of them:

We needed to make a significant improvement on the recruitment processes we had been using in the past. It was really unscientific, with people selecting those kinds of people they thought we ought to be choosing without any real measurement or scientific approach. (Private Sector)

Yes, fifteen years ago we were doing assessment centres, and I am not sure how they were assessed. It was a lot more subjective in terms of the actual assessment. They probably were moving all the paperwork around, whereas we now have competencies on the forms. It was like the old interview forms, 'Do they sit this?' and 'Do they sit that?' without a lot of science behind it. (Manufacturing Sector)

Such claims of objectivity and fairness are, however, increasingly under threat, not because organizations are less scrupulous. Rather, it is the nature of the new economy and the demands it places on the new knowledge workers and, concomitantly, the recruitment process.

Selection of individuals has never been solely based upon relative levels of human capital. But in an attempt to cope with the explosion in newly qualified applicants, contemporary labour markets have moved even further away from formal qualifications, which to some extent explains the frenetic activity among academics, policy-makers, and organizations to define more clearly what capabilities individuals need in order to be 'employable'.[10]

This has been far from a straightforward process and has hardly captured the complexities of the new capabilities within the new and evolving knowledge economy.[11] These complexities take many different forms but aggregate around a clear recognition that 'doing business' does not simply involve formal qualifications but certain attributes of self presentation within organizations where individuals 'can present themselves through posture, gesture, use of personal space, facial characteristics and eye contact, for example, at interviews and during meetings'.[12] These 'new aesthetics' now represent the building blocks of employability. With new capabilities comes the need for new ways of evaluating candidates, or at least so one would think.

The recruitment industry thinks not. Far from the conception of new methods of recruitment, the industry relies today on largely the same techniques in assessment centres introduced before the Second World War by the German army and soon taken up by the British to cope with the dramatic upturn in applications for officer training.[13] Assessment centres were largely introduced as an alternative method or one that could be used in addition to interviewing. 'There is little doubt', claims one recent evaluation 'that the technique is superior to more traditional approaches for the assessment of managerial and profes-sional skills'.[14] We often heard powerful, yet contradictory rhetoric about how long such methods had been in use, while hearing about their contemporary scientific rigour:

We also test analytical presentation rather than just presentation abilities, but I did a group exercise, I did the one that we still use which drives me mad, the Swedish one. You would never guess that I did it 15 years ago—because I have been reminded every year since; it's terrible. It may well be that it is a good one, and it's fair, but it does get boring. So we still use that, I'm trying to think what else we could do, we obviously still have the basic interview that we do. (Manufacturing Sector)

The primary reason for the celebrated status of assessment centres lies in their use of behavioural evidence, as opposed to credentials and interviews alone, to ensure their accuracy. The problem with creden-tials lies in their inability to signal to employers certain innate or achieved abilities of individuals. Even when combined with one or more formal interview, it still leaves far too much to chance in the workplace in the eyes of employers, hence their utilization of behav-ioural evidence. In short, employers are seeking to predict how indi-viduals will perform or contribute to a particular role they are offered within their organization.

These are based on 'a thorough and accurate understanding of the nature of top performance' by those 'acting in accordance with the organization's values and strategic needs'.[15] Individuals are put into situations during assessment centres and interviews representing working situations and their behaviour and responses are observed. This behaviour is then matched with the behavioural norms of those who perform well in the role for which the candidate is being assessed. An indication of the alleged accuracy of this technique lies in the claim made by the 'bible of graduate recruitment' in Britain, the *Newcomer's Guide to Graduate Recruitment*, published by the Association of Graduate Recruiters (AGR) which points to the popularity of the method (some four-fifths of leading graduate recruiters currently use the technique). The justification for this approach is relatively straightforward:

The rationale behind the technique is that if a person behaved in a certain way in specified circumstances in the past, then they are likely to behave in a similar way, given a similar situation, in the future. If for example, in a simulated work situation at an assessment event, they show themselves to be able to influence other team members, then faced with a similar situation at work, they are also likely to display the same ability. *If* the ability to influence others is important to the employing organization, then this behaviour would be deemed to be positive, and would contribute in a positive way towards the overall assessment of the candidate.[16]

The behavioural methods utilized at assessment centres, then, are ascribed high levels of predictive power to estimate the likely future performance of an individual at work. Justifying the use of behavioural tests, a number of authors simply point to the long heritage of the technique, and a number of studies linking performance at assessment centres with later performance in work.[17] Claims are not just made about the predictive value of behavioural tests: they are also said to be objective, as a 'candidate's performance can be awarded a score, and compared with an absolute standard, or other candidates' scores'.[18] Awarding scores also enables such a technique to be 'fair to all candidates'.[19] We heard a great deal from employers about the objectivity of the techniques used, despite the obvious problems involved in the process:

It is the most objective system that we have got. When I first came in it was quite a subjective process and on occasions we had to re-interview people because there was always going to be personality clashes. It is a fairer system and it puts the responsibility into the hands of many, and more into the hands of the business, you can't blame an individual for getting it wrong and you've got a debate there. And you have people with differing views on what it is like for the business, so I think it is a very healthy approach and sometimes you are going to have the issues with different characters where you might have six or seven of you sitting around the table discussing a candidate who is academically brilliant but just will not fit into the culture, will not thrive. Now I would not want to make that decision on my own in case it was prejudiced, or seen as such, but when you have a lot of people making that decision and you can actually identify why and put your finger on it to make sure that that decision is a fair one. (IT Consultants)

Interestingly, it is the way interviews and group exercises are evaluated that are now seen to make the recruitment process more 'scientific':

It can be more of a science to be honest because I think we are better at it and we've worked with Saville & Holdsworth to come up with the competencies and how we rate them and they have done all sorts of research and proven things out.
Validation studies...
Posh word! So yes I think we've made it more of a science. Fifteen years ago it was an art but it is now a science.
We are definitely trying to get away from the approach where line managers say, 'oh I liked that person and they interviewed well, and I like them'. We're sorry but they didn't get through. 'Yes but they interviewed well', so we are definitely moving away from that.
They still try it but they don't get away with it anymore.
'He supports the same football team as me, we liked him'. (Manufacturing Sector)

Is graduate recruitment an art or a science?
We try and make it scientific but I couldn't sit here hand on heart and say it's scientific because I don't believe it is.
If you could quantify 'science', where is it from 0–100%?
Currently 80% at the moment … I think it needs to have the scientific edge to it for the consistency of the approach, the validity, being fair to the candidates, so it has to have that leaning but there is always this gut feel that actually we try and take out of the equation when we are assessing, 'I don't want to know about that, I want to know what you saw and what you heard on the day', although we do give assessors opportunity to talk about that but actually I think we have to assess on what we saw and heard.
Do you think you can take out the gut reaction?
I don't take it out, otherwise what we see and hear can be devoid of and be

very superficial and out on a limb and you don't get the rounded picture that you need to. But if we're talking about being as objective as we can be with human beings being part of this process then we need to keep in a lot of the evidence. However, I ask for them to back it up, but I do want to know how s/he made you feel. If they made you feel annoyed or you think they were sarcastic or didn't like the approach or, I need to hear that because that gives me the context around the evidence. Having the evidence on its own is, it can be great evidence but it can be portrayed in an awful manner. So it's trying to marry the two, which is why I think 80%–20%. (Financial Sector)

Again it will depend on the function because for finance people they traditionally are not overly chatty people and that hasn't changed over the years. You look at a number of finance people and they are going to show you fairly steady skill packs, but if that is the right skills for what they do, then fine. We do need them to be able to present and perhaps we do ask for a little bit more of that now but as a company we haven't changed the requirement, the emphasis might change, but I don't think we have put more emphasis on that now then what we used to do. As I said earlier we are now scientific about it and we are better at assessing it because we have now got some better tools in which to do it. (Manufacturing Sector)

For all of this scientific discourse, there are a number of issues surrounding the proclaimed predictive precision and objectivity of behavioural tests or 'tools'. First, we have already noted above Handyside's observation of the lack of correlation between the scores given for the same candidate's behaviour by two separate observers. At the very best, the coefficient scores referred to by Handyside suggests recruiters will disagree about the performance in these tests of one in every four candidates; and as often as one in every two individuals in the worst-case scenarios. With these statistics in mind, the aura of objectivity seems less discernable. Again, we heard clear evidence of such misgivings from employers who continued to maintain that their selection methods were both 'objective' and 'scientific' while having to, at the same time, concede the process was ultimately a subjective one. The metaphor of a jury used by one employer was telling:

It is because at the end of the day you have sort of got a jury system, you have your twelve men, good and true, deciding whether or not they are guilty enough. But you make sure that by having your assessment centre that they are assessed and each of the skills are looked at by a different person, and each of the skills is tested in a different way. You know, you are going to have personalities [that] you are going to have at [an] assessment centre, 'Well, I liked him and I didn't like her!' 'Why?' 'I don't know!' That is going to happen, we are all human, if it was a science I would just sit them all in front of the PC, given them tests and I would have a nice list of 400 people [from] 1,100 who I could give the job to. (IT Consultants)

But juries disagree, and reaching a unanimous or majority decision involves something more than the simple scientific measurement of individual attributes. Debate, and sometimes long and arduous discussions over particular individuals are not uncommon:

We have [debated] on occasions. Normally a wrap-up session will take 20 minutes. When you have got rid of the 1s or 2s you might be left with about 60% of them. Then the 4s and the 5s are off and then you are really debating ... the ones that sit in the middle and we have had maybe two hours tops on about seven or eight people. (IT Consultants)

This reference to debates when deploying the science of recruitment raises issues surrounding the lack of agreement between observers when converting observed behavioural attributes into ordinal scores

Constructive imagination. Freshness of approach. Intuitive originality

Text-books in his [*sic.*] thinking. Sticks to precedents. Applies old approaches to new problems. Tends to get into and 'stay in a rut'	Applies	Tends to	Neutral	Tends to	Applies	Comes up with novel ideas. Shows marked Originality. Has an 'intuitive' facility—gets 'feelings' about possible ways of tackling things
	☐	☐	☐	☐	☐	

Effectiveness with people. Ability to work well with others. Capacity to contribute to team effectiveness

Upsets people needlessly. Sours the atmosphere. Drains other people's enthusiasm. Damages morale and hinders team achievement	Applies	Tends to	Neutral	Tends to	Applies	An exceptionally good team worker. Wins respect for his [*sic.*] contributions and for his [*sic.*] ability to work cooperatively. People like to help and work with him [*sic.*]
	☐	☐	☐	☐	☐	

Fig. 5.1 Examples of conversion of behavioural attributes into ordinal scores
Source: Handyside (1989: 666–7).

(e.g. ranking a particular attribute from '5 = very good' to '1 = very poor'). Consider, for example, the two ordinal scales in Figure 5.1.

How exactly do we decide who has a more constructive imagination on the basis of these scores? How do we know it 'applies' to one individual, another 'tends' to be constructive, whereas another tends not to be constructive or imaginative? How do we 'see' people's 'feelings'? The second example referring to teamwork is arguably easier to classify, certainly at least at the negative end of the scale, although even here what is described as 'behavioural' remains enticingly ethereal: one observer's 'hindrance of team achievement' maybe another observer's 'enthusiasm'. And then there is the matter of deciding whether a particular attribute applies to an individual, whether their (observed) behaviour is capturing the essence of the candidate's employability. As recruiters often say to candidates, 'We can only measure what we can observe.' And yet, as we have seen above, classifying what people think they can in fact see remains highly problematic and ultimately subjective.

People clearly 'see' different things. This insight was provided to us by our attendance at a case study company's refresher training sessions for assessors. We were all asked to watch a video of a group exercise and mark the performance of individual candidates against the ordinal scales we were provided with. The discussion concerning the marks awarded by assessors afterwards served only to highlight further cracks in the science of gut feeling:

Assessor 1   'I saw a flicker of 3 behaviour'.
Assessor 2   *'If there's some 3 behaviour and some 1 behaviour, don't take the average, mark it as 1'.*
Assessor 1   'I thought we took the maximum behaviour we saw?'
Assessor 2   'No, you don't take the maximum mark, if you see more 2 than 3, mark it as 2'. (Public Sector)

One solution offered by assessors to the problem of variations in observed behaviour and its evaluation by assessors is to ensure the same individual is evaluated by different assessors, thereby reducing the subjective or unscientific tendencies, which are acknowledged to creep into assessment centres. We witnessed events where such practices were not employed, with assessors specifically focusing on the performance of one individual for the whole assessment centre. In their defence, employers suggested viewing the same individuals in different exercises enabled the 'true capability' of candidates to become apparent:

I think that is where your Assessment Centre comes in, that you test those skills in a number of different ways and I think yes you can learn how to behave at an Assessment Centre to a certain degree but your skills are all going to come out in the end if you are probed in several different ways. (IT Consultants)

The recruitment industry offers another scientific solution to the problem of subjectivity. Enter here the 'principle of vector addition'. Handyside provides an account of the problem and its scientific solution:

It is clear that simple addition of the scores on the [ordinal] scales is not a logically defensible way of arriving at the 'overall rating'; to do so would mean that one would be perpetrating such nonsense as assuming, for example, that high levels of drive and application compensate for deficits of such things as sound judgement and technical expertise—when clearly very energetic performance applied to ill-advised courses of action can be much more disastrous than less energetic application of ill-judged decisions.

To avoid this sort of nonsense which would be generated by simply adding up the component scores, one moves to vector addition. This involves the idea that conceptually independent aspects of performance can be treated as dimensions in a multi-dimensional space, and that what one wants to take as the 'overall assessment' is the total distance that the person is placed from the zero point—irrespective of the direction away from the zero point. The direction gives the qualitative answer, but the distance gives the quantitative answer.[20]

The deployment here of Pythagoras' theorem effectively treats an individual's employability as the missing third side of a right-angled triangle generated by the square root of the sum of the squares of the two sides, which are at right angles to each other. Handyside suggests this approach cuts through the complexities of observing an individual's employability as it:

means that when one has a lot of 'conceptually independent' dimensions one can arrive at a defensible 'overall rating' by regarding it as the zero point, i.e. simply by quoting it as the square root of the sum of the squares of the scores on the various aspects of [ordinal] scales.[21]

It is this conversion of 'conceptually independent dimensions' into ordinal scales where problems arise. It is easy to sympathize with recruiters charged with the responsibility of arriving at some form of logical—not to mention objective—evaluation as to the ability of a candidate in a particular attribute deemed important by the recruiting organization. Nevertheless, the conversion of, for example, an individual's level of 'constructive imagination' requires a certain leap of faith, which at best is highly partial, and at worst, frankly unacceptable.

The recruitment industry's rejoinder to this is that the ordinal scales ranking the observed capability of constructive imagination can be tightly defined and articulated. The use of the *Thurstone technique* can be used to make the metric or ordinal nature of the scale more readily apparent. This is achieved by using a substantial number of descriptive statements about an individual's capability in a particular skill and then ranking these statements in order, modifying and rejecting statements to arrive at an adequately defined metric (see Figure 5.2).

Whether the defined benchmark of 'taking action' represents an ordinal or another classic psychophysics technique of 'just noticeable differences' as the basis of measurement is not clear. And yet the distinction between these two techniques, although subtle, is nonetheless crucial. The distinction between the scales is not equal, underlining

1	No evidence of action. Blocks or inhibits the proactivity of others. Uses rules and tradition as a way of restricting the initiative of others.
2	Identifies or recognizes what needs to be done or changed, but describes only general intentions, superficial plans or limited action. Only responds to the initiatives of others.
3	Describes clear and specific action points, identifying what needs to be done.
4	In addition to the competence level (3) identifies actions to be taken by others, delegates or involves others in taking actions forward. Describes contingency plans to deal with possible setbacks.

Fig. 5.2 The conversion of behavioural attributes into ordinal metrics

Note: Benchmark: Taking action.

again the problematic nature of converting qualitative perception into numerical values. The key criterion is the accurate ascription on the scale to observed behaviour. We shall return to this problem in the next section.

We are informed, however, that good practice suggests 'for any important use of ratings it is almost always desirable to convert adjectival descriptions to numerical values.'[22] This still leaves us with the problem that while the adjectives in ordinal scales provide us with an agreed order, that is, 'very good' is better than 'good' and 'excellent' is better than 'very good' it would be nothing short of fallacious to suggest the number of differences between the steps is equal. This seriously precludes the use of arithmetical calculations such as averaging ratings by different judges or running correlations associated with cardinal measures, that is, equal differences between the steps on the scales.

The majority of recruiters observe this methodological qualification. Others do not, however, where once again a scientific approach for the conversion of water into wine—or, in this case—ordinal (scales) into interval (cardinal) data—is advocated. Again, we came across examples in our case study companies diverging widely from 'best' practice. Far from looking at the performance of individuals across isolated assessment centre events, one company simply added up their scores and utilized benchmarks to delineate the employable from the unemployable:

We add up all of the scores [...]. If they score between 101–115 we consider their suitability, although in practice we hardly ever offer them a job. We immediately make an offer to those who score 116 [or above]. Anybody with less than 100 we 'regret' [the term the company preferred for 'reject']. (Retail Sector)

At best this approach represents an indicative measure to evaluate the overall scores of individual candidates. At worst it represents what social scientists refer to as the 'epistemic fallacy' in which 'statements about being can be reduced to or analysed in terms of statements about knowledge'.[23] In short, social action or individual actions cannot be quantified, nor measured in such a way enabling the differences between the abilities of individuals to be calculated as in the natural sciences. In his exploration of skills and employability Holmes makes exactly this point in his critique of quantitative measures to evaluate an individual's various skills:

The 'skills' are treated as having some independent reality, capable (in principle) of being identified and of being causally related to performance in a variety of settings. Once they have been identified generally they can be identified in particular individuals; i.e. individuals can be assessed to determine the extent to which they possess such abilities. Find some way of measuring these abilities and you then have a way of recording students' transferable skills, to include on some form of profile or transcript.[24]

Looked at from this perspective this paradigm of recruitment and selection can be seen to have serious weaknesses. Nor is it just the quantification of observed behavioural aspects of individuals that is called into question. Serious questions also need to be raised about the deployment of psychometric and attitudinal testing, which deploy statistical techniques to allocate job applicants into particular groups and categories. While many employers suggest such methods should not be viewed as a panacea in recruitment methods,[25] a sizeable minority see them as providing a reasonably good and scientifically based predictor of subsequent job performance.[26]

We witnessed at one recruitment event the deployment of a particular psychometric test to apparently evaluate the 'personality type' of individual candidates. The test was set at the beginning of the assessment centre and was then utilized as part of the final interview with candidates at the end of the event. The interviewer effectively provided feedback about their performance in the test to individual candidates and asked them to comment. The problems began when individual candidates did not accept the descriptions of themselves provided by the tests utilized by one of the companies. These results would be presented in the form of a graph and behavioural descriptions of the behavioural tendencies individuals were supposed to have:

Interviewer: According to your [attitudinal test] scores you score average marks for confidence [...] and you are best described as somebody who is cautious and over-attentive to detail ...

Candidate: [*interrupting*] I don't think that's very accurate at all. I gained a lot of confidence from getting a First, which is probably why the questionnaire points to my attention to detail.

The interview continued with the candidate asked to describe whether she was somebody who conformed or not:

C: I am a creative person, but I could also be described as somebody who is a traditionalist and not fighting rules unless there is a very good reason for it. I like creative solutions.

I: That fits with what [the attitudinal test] got: middle of the range [in relation to conformity]. You are creative but like to set your own pace and prefer gauging your own success …

C: [*again interrupting*] Not especially, no. I like to have feedback especially!

Another candidate was more conducive to the results of the questionnaire, even though she had in fact scored very poorly. It was certainly evident to us that this candidate was not going to be offered a post. Far from offering the candidate the opportunity to challenge her performance on the questionnaire, or provide additional information for her consideration for an offer, the interview took the form of a process through which the impending rejection was legitimized in the eyes of the candidate by the interviewer. In the following extract from this conversation, the candidate in question was asked to comment on why she thought she had obtained very low scores in relation to her 'structural' tendencies, and in particular that her desk was typically untidy:

I: Do you not like being structured?

C: I am organised, but I like to plan as I go along. I am structured; I'm just not tidy! I'm always very organised, but I'm not sure anybody could just come in and take over my desk.

I: That's what the test has indicated [*showing her the graph*].

C: Yeah.

This invitation to accept the questionnaire's 'feedback' on the individual's performance was clearly deployed to ensure maximum acceptance of its results on the part of the candidate. The following extract again shows how the interviewer gently steers the same candidate into accepting the results, this time in relation to her 'conformity':

I: Our data suggests you are somewhat individualistic as opposed to somebody who is a team player?

C: Probably somewhere in the middle between the two, I think.

I: [*interrupting*] But towards the lower middle, suggesting more individualism than conformity?

C: Yeah.

The interview continues with the candidate laughing, almost parodying her poor performance on the test with the aid of the interviewer, who continually refers to the scientific accuracy of the test. Despite the candidate suggesting she herself is a team player and the test results suggesting not, the candidate still comments several times that the test itself is 'frighteningly accurate'. When asked to comment on her happiness with the (largely negative) feedback she is receiving, she simply says 'Yeah, frighteningly accurate'. The interview closes with smiles all around, with the candidate leaving the room happy with the scientific evidence suggesting she is at best in the mid-range, but more often than not in the lower end of the scores utilized by the test. She was not confident of being offered a post. Just a week later, during our follow-up interview, we learned of this same candidate being offered a post by an arguably more eminent employer. In just seven days, and one assessment centre later, what was 'frighteningly accurate' had been turned on its head.

Of course, the narrative used by the interviewer in the example above is not one of high or low scores. Instead, continua are used. One is either 'confident' or 'cautious'. One either 'conforms' or is 'creative'. While it is obvious at which ends of the continua candidates need to be at, the narrative of the interview is simply one of commenting on individual tendencies in such a way as to present them as not negative, but simply 'not something we are necessarily looking for'. Individuals may not, as we have seen above, necessarily agree with the categories they have been inserted into. Yet, faced with the scientific discourse of the psychometric tests flashed before them in interviews, it is difficult for individual candidates to feel confident enough about the information, or empowered enough by it to make the case for their employability. One employer offered their perspective for the scientific 'discourse of rejection':

You can't get rid of subjectivity. We've talked to the assessors about that but you've got human beings here being assessors and the candidates want to know, and when you give them feedback it's about what they said and what they did. 'You didn't get through because the evidence around x wasn't so good because you did *dddd*, and you said *dddd*.' So you've got to be factual with them. You can't say, 'Well, actually, when you came into the room we really didn't like the look of you!' So that's what we're trying to take away. Although there is an element of that, you do need—and I ask the assessors for this—but keep it separate from the evidence. Give the context, give a rounded picture. (Financial Sector)

Faced with such evidence, many candidates simply agree with the apparently 'objective' description presented to them. This brings us nicely to the notion of making up people.

Making Up People

In the previous section we suggested that the scientific methods used by recruiters to evaluate individual employability are far from robust. We also suggested a significant proportion of employers did not use these methods in isolation, preferring instead to adopt a combination of different methods of evaluating applicants. Behavioural competences are not only used to permit numerical results as a source of scientific legitimacy. They are used to enable employers to identify the various facets of what constitute the 'ideal' manager or organizational leader. Discussions about the employability of individual candidates are based on piecing together each area of competence to assess whether they fit the technical and social template of the organization. This is also claimed to involve a scientific approach where 'evidence of competencies will be tested for objectively'.[27] But here, too, there are problems with the process of interpretation used by recruiters to make decisions about people.

Classical philosophers drew a distinction between the process of measurement and interpretation. An argument based on measurement 'is one whose premises are claimed to provide conclusive grounds for the truth of its conclusion'.[28] If the argument can *demonstratively* provide conclusive grounds through measurement, that argument is said to be valid. Similarly, if through measurement the grounds for the argument are *demonstratively* weak, the argument is said to be invalid, there is no middle ground. Only, there is a middle ground: certainty is a chimera. Very little, if anything, can be proven with certainty.

The alternative, then, is to turn to interpretation whereby arguments are not certain or *demonstratively* valid. Their conclusions do not necessarily follow with logical necessity from their premises. No analogy is intended to be mathematically certain, valid or invalid. In short, 'Probability is all that is claimed for them.'[29] Thus, the conclusions we infer are not certainly, but probably true. Philosophers do attach a caveat to this form of logic, often overlooked by recruiters when justifying their methods of selection. In short, philosophers suggest 'the modesty of the conclusion relative to the premises affirmed is a critical consideration in determining the merit of the inference drawn'.[30] Or, more generally, the more one claims for their argument, the greater the burden of sustaining that claim.

For example, it is relatively easy for a recruiter to sustain the claim that, all things being equal, their observation of a candidate's teamwork skills enables them to *infer* they would make a good employee. To claim they can measure this observation, or, further still, to suggest a *demonstrative* and *predictive* capacity to calculate the later organizational performance of the individual in question is to make a bold assertion that the premises of the argument (e.g. observed individual behavioural characteristics) are not strong enough to support. Some of the employers we interviewed acknowledged this weakness in their method:

I think it's good to be passionate about your science. I think science will only take you so far and there is something in there about being passionate about your subject and enthusing, kind of showing that enthusiasm to your candidates. It's good to have something that is smooth-running and perfect in everyway. But if it's passionless, then that wouldn't be representative of our company. So for me it's having a process that is slick, that doesn't frustrate the hell out of people but shows that there is a human element to it as well. So I think there is a level of creativity in there. It's just interesting because it is really hard to be creative in graduate recruitment because most things have been done before. (Telecommunications Sector)

Employers claim to have a solution to this problem and seek to deploy it at their assessment centres. In short, when observing a group exercise against a benchmark of behavioural characteristics, assessors are instructed to write down as much of the evidence they can see during the exercise. After, and only after the exercise, assessors then have time to convert their observations into ordinal scales enabling them to reach conclusions as to how individuals have performed in a certain exercise against particular behavioural characteristics. Further discussion between assessors enables them to 'fine-tune' their observations and resolve any differences in opinion arising from the exercise.

This possibility of a difference in opinion between assessors sensitizes us to the conflation by this technique of measurement and interpretation. One cannot measure the extent to which an individual candidate, as in the example above (Figure 5.2), 'identifies or recognises what needs to be done or changed'; one simply *infers* this through interpretation and not via the deductive process of precise calculations by the 'reading-off' of observed behaviour against ranked metric scales. This ascription of scores to an individual candidate's perform-ance represents nothing more than the science of gut feeling.

This gut feeling takes on greater significance when the performance of an individual is less clear-cut, that is, in the case of the same example above, the difference between a 'superficial plan' and 'specific action points' makes the difference between a score of '2' or '3' crucial, the latter being employable, the former representing a failure to reach the required threshold. Hardly representing what Rorty[31] has described as a 'mirror of reality', this 'in-place metering device' to measure per-formance represents nothing more than the reification of reality, sup-plying rich narrative details, scientific facts and figures and references while forgetting the socially constructed context of the measures and scales of the narratives employed.[32] People do not neatly *fit* into these pre-existing scales: They are *allocated* and *shaped* into them, the scales representing the effective crystallization of the conversion of subjec-tivity into objectivity.

This observation raises profound implications for this element of prac-tice in selection and recruitment. Far from representing an accurate reflection of the abilities individuals actually possess, rating individual employability relies on little else other than on what individual assessors think they see, that is, what they *interpret* as opposed to what they *meas-ure*. It is what is 'seen' by assessors in real time that leads to the making up of people. Far from the possession of a particular set of pre-existing and fixed set of attributes awaiting their discovery or measurement by assessors, the employability of individuals comes into being at the same time as the measuring process, classifications, and categories themselves, each effectively emerging hand in hand, egging each other on.[33]

This enables us to begin to unpack why it is 'people spontaneously come to fit their categories'.[34] Far from being a static process whereby categories emerge from a painstaking process of our discovery of them (e.g. stars, bacilli, etc.), a dynamic process exists simply to do with possibility, or possibili*ties*:

How might a dynamic [process] affect the concept of the individual person? One answer has to do with possibility. Who we are is not only what we did, do and will do but also what we might have done and may do. Making up people changes the space of possibilities for personhood. [...] What could it mean in general to say that possible ways to be a person can from time to time come into being or disappear? Such queries force us to be careful about the idea of possibility itself.[35]

The most striking example of this changing in the space of personhood concerned an individual candidate who had excelled throughout his educational career. This individual had excelled in everything he had ever attempted: universal A* grades at GCSE, again in all five A-levels, graduating from Oxford with a degree in Politics, Philosophy, and Economics (PPE). The benchmark or employability threshold that this student had to reach was not necessarily higher than for other candidates, but he was expected to 'live up to expectations' that were different from some of the other candidates. After nearly all of the exercises assessors made the same comment:

I thought x was good but in some way I was disappointed. He didn't live up to his glittering CV I was expecting something more special, outstanding. He was okay, good even, but not *that* good. (Public Sector)

The claim made by assessors 'we can only record what we see' now takes on a different magnitude. What assessors may see may be the 'potential' in the future to develop into an excellent manager. Such evidence may be fleeting, or the status of such evidence among assessors may lead to disagreement. An assessor may 'see something' in a candidate that others do not. What is certain, however, is that most employers will not take a risk on a 'problematic' candidate:

How much faith do you have in the assessment centre procedure to enable you to see if some people have got what it takes?
A reasonably high level, it can never be absolute. We just never know if someone doesn't quite make it, we turn them down, they could have been real stars, we'll never know that. But what we do know is because our organization very early on expects our starters to handle some very tough examinations, which are demanding both intellectually and work related, that our examination pass rate is very high. In that respect we can say, 'Yes we are recruiting the right people, the right people are getting through'. But equally as well as the 'Would that person have made it had we offered them a job?' You have also got the opposite side of the coin where you offered this person a job because they seemed to shine in the process, but they have just bombed in their examinations. (Management Consultants)

Far from measuring an individual's observed behaviour during assessment events, assessors are now moving into a deeper realm of subjectivity regarding the future potential of a candidate. Consequently, not only are there serious question marks over whether assessors can in fact observe behaviour in the trouble-free way as the largely scientific rhetoric of the science of gut feeling suggests, there are now equally troublesome questions surrounding the accuracy of the inferences made by assessors when converting what they think they see into classifications of individual skills which ultimately comprise employability. Far from reading off individual employability, assessors construct accounts of employability to fit with their behavioural definitions of the attributes they deem to be valuable. These are then used to legitimate their recruitment decisions.

Hidden Persuaders

Finally the science of gut feeling stands or falls on its capacity to accurately differentiate between the performances of individual candidates during assessment centre exercises. But consider for a moment the ramifications for the validity of the scientific measurement techniques utilized by employers if candidates decided to 'play' the recruitment game by rehearsing narratives of employability that they think employers want to hear, rather than 'playing it straight' by giving employers a fair reflection of their strengths and weaknesses. What then for the scientific claims made by employers who advise candidates to be themselves? How can the science of gut feeling be described as objective or fair when some candidates who are being 'themselves' are in direct competition with other individuals who take it upon themselves to tell employers what they want to hear and present what they want to see in an attempt to give themselves a competitive edge over other candidates?

As Searle has noted, the integrity of selection and recruitment techniques depend on people being 'honest' otherwise the results are 'significantly distorted by faking and other less obvious processes'.[36] Recruiters like to imagine that they can spot those who 'fake it' but our evidence suggests that the science of gut feeling is not immune from this labour market strategy. Moreover, the logical consequence of increasingly congested labour markets is for more candidates to resort to player behaviour. To paraphrase Fred Hirsch, does playing offer to those individuals who dare to engage in such a process an additional opportunity to stand that little bit higher on tiptoes to see that little bit more? It is to these issues we turn in our discussion of Players and Purists in the next chapter.

6

Players and Purists

The people who do well in this new world are not necessarily those who were viewed as 'well qualified' in the traditional world of jobs.

William Bridges[1]

Introduction

The promise sold to graduates is clear. If you invest in a university education there are managerial and professional jobs waiting for you. Yet, at the same time individuals are expected to take responsibility for their own employability and to see their careers as a portfolio of jobs rather than a job for life. They are encouraged to develop their employability through greater attention to personal skills and self-promotion, alongside their academic studies, as employers are looking for people who exhibit drive, self-reliance, and charisma. These messages are widely circulated through the media, universities, and company websites. But how do those aspiring to the prize of a fast-track job understand and manage their employability? This chapter is divided into two parts. Part One examines graduates' expectations and views on the job market. It also examines some of the key factors seen to contribute to occupational success. In Part Two we examine the employability strategies deployed by university graduates in the competition for jobs.[2]

Part One: Great Expectations

The purpose of our interviews with graduates was to understand how those who had entered the competition for tough-entry jobs defined their career goals and managed their employability. Our evidence shows that virtually all those interviewed shared an expectation of work as a source of personal achievement and career development. In may respects work was seen as offering new learning opportunities and scope for responsibility that would take them beyond the world of formal education. They had bought into a view of work as challenging, exciting, and as a source of self-development:

Miriam: I see [my career] as on-going. It would be good to obtain a good number of skills in the initial years when you are developing and growing within the company. But I don't think training should stop there, I think you should be able to continue to learn. I think that life is a life-long learning process, so I think you should always have a chance to learn new skills.

Jonathan: Working for a good company travelling around, I'd like to be jumping around with my laptop from place to place doing stuff like that, but learning. I want to learn lots about how it all works the business world, just somewhere where I can feel a little bit more important than I've been, just build up some respect.

Sako: I want to be comfortable, get out of my debt as soon as possible but not really rich. I love engineering, I honestly do love engineering and I really do hope that when I graduate I get what I enjoy doing and I hope I enjoy it. We all spend most of our lives working so I would like to do something that gives me a buzz so it is not about money.

The reference to money in the above quotation was typical of the widely held view that money was important but not the overriding consideration. There was little evidence that these graduates were chasing the 'big bucks' although some did recognize that their earning power had significantly increased by going to a 'good' university:

Sarah: I wouldn't have any of the prospects I have now if I'd not gone on to higher education... Just having a university degree firstly gives you opportunities you just wouldn't have straight out of school. Secondly going to a good university, it's just stupid what I can potentially earn. I feel really bad in a way because I don't feel any more qualified than a lot of other people but there's just this assumption that if you go to Oxford or Cambridge that you're somehow a lot better. And maybe you're better at doing exams but I think it's dubious whether you're going to be better at doing a job.

For another graduate from a disadvantaged background, the value of his investment in a university education had an altogether different meaning:

Martin: I have a relatively poor background and I would like to be able to make sure that the rest of my very close family, my mum and my brother, more so my mum, would never have to be in a position where they'd have to worry about food or having a roof over their heads, but besides that, there're more important things in life than money. It's only a means to an end.

Higher Education, Employability, and the Competition for Jobs

For most of those we spoke to going to university was a natural progression. It was either taken for granted because it was the done thing within their family and school, or because of the stark realization that without a university degree they had little chance of finding interesting jobs:

Sako: To be honest I don't think I would have been able to get myself a job or anything. The main reason [for going to university] was to make myself more marketable. But at the same time it was the challenge of self-fulfilment.

Jonathan: I just felt that if I wanted, it's kind of a status in society now, it's a good thing to do and I've heard about the lifestyle and…people we respect and admire had all gone to university so its kind of inevitable really.

Angela: I guess I was a high ability achiever…I wanted to further my education if I was able to. I wanted to go into a career I suppose,—go into higher education and get a career, that was my main reason [for doing a degree].

But having made the commitment it was seen to put them in a better position than those without a degree. As the following comment from Peter revealed a degree was seen to spare graduates from the realities of routine work. Without a degree work was little more than an income where one had to conform to the agenda of others:

Peter: It basically helps you get further quicker, it gets you into a higher paid rung for a starter and it offers you more responsibility quicker which I think is good . . . whereas a lot of people who don't [have a degree] are asking to do call centre stuff like day in and day out and I can imagine that to be quite dreadful.

It was also widely believed that they deserved to get tough-entry jobs ahead of non-graduates, because they had superior knowledge and because they had made a significant personal investment of time, effort, and money to achieve a degree. But whether this was justified if they are doing similar work to non-graduates was less clear-cut:

Richie: If you've spent 3 years trying to educate yourself more, say I'm going in as an 18 year old, going into some medium size company, you think having invested your time and getting a bit more education that you should be on a little more than they are, not saying you've got to be better than them or whatever, but I would have thought you'd be on more. Whether that's justified or not, I don't know. But you have done 3 years, haven't you?

Although a degree was seen to put them in a better market position than those that had not been to university, there was also an awareness that their university credentials may not have the exchange value they previously assumed that it would. Graduates have become aware of increasing market congestion as hundreds of thousands of highly education people enter the scramble for managerial and professional jobs:

Peter: I think in today's day and age, if you land something or any kind of job with that company it's a bonus. Like you say getting 750 people down to 3 or 2 at the moment is bloody outrageous really. There's only so many companies that you can apply for because there's always going to be some people who don't get a job at the end of it so it makes you think why have they spent 3 or 4 years doing a degree and what has it all been for. I mean, that's the way my girlfriend is looking at it at the moment.

Jonathan: I was always told and I always thought that all you need to do is get your degree, get a good degree and you will just walk into a job. But it's not like that at all. All the degree really does is maybe get your application looked at a bit longer than everyone else's, but it's no guarantee.

Despite much talk about the global economy few of those we interviewed believed that they were in competition with graduates from other countries, although many expressed an interest in working overseas, but this was usually understood as gaining international experiences with the organization they hoped to join in the United Kingdom. Tom did however recognize that there may be international competition for prestigious jobs in the financial sector:

Tom: I know when I went to a leading retail bank there was a guy from France, a guy from Canada and a couple of people from this country as well as a girl from America who was working in London on the day I was there. So those jobs are quite prestigious jobs and maybe have more allure for foreign people, whereas these sorts of accountancy jobs or for pharmaceuticals, I'm sure there are similar positions in Germany or France.

What no one doubted was that having a degree, even from an elite university, was no longer enough to secure a fast-track appointment. It was widely understood that they would be judged on their personal qualities and experiences beyond the lecture theatre or the examination hall:

Jade: Because everybody's going to be coming here...with a good degree, good set of A Levels etc, etc, which is why I think they want to know so much about you and your experience, because that's going to be the only thing that's going to differentiate 600 other people who are going through this process, because you could be the brightest person in the world, but if you haven't got any ideas or experience or you've no interpersonal skills, you're not going to get anywhere at all.

How then did these graduates respond to increasingly competitive market conditions? What, if anything, are they doing to demonstrate their worth to employers and why they are more employable than their peers? Before addressing this question we need to consider who is perceived to have an advantage in the selection process and what factors truly count.

Some are More Equal than Others

While most of those we interviewed had reached the final stage of the job selection process, most were aware that some were more equal than others. This was not only a matter of what university one went to or of academic grades, but there was also an awareness that physical appearance, accent, gender, ethnicity, and social class, may all have an impact on future job prospects. Most of those we interviewed believed that 'looks' made a difference in the competition for jobs. They understood that employers expected a certain look that conformed to the image of the organization. It was also widely recognized that attractive people tend to be at an advantage, although this was not seen as a legitimate basis for deciding the merits of individual candidates:

Sarah: There's this City law firm, I'm not joking all the people I know who've got in...are really good looking. In presentations everyone's good looking and the whole company seems to be. I'm sure they can't go out of their way to discriminate against maybe not so good looking people, but it is bizarre how many good looking people are in the company. So I think some of the big firms are quite into their looks and things.

Jonathan: I think the last thing an employer wants to see is someone coming in with various bits pierced and messy hair—just a mess. I think it is important because even if you could argue that that person might be Einstein underneath but I still think especially for the type of work I'm going for which is client focused as well where you're going to meet people, you're representing the company outside, so you've got to look the part.

Douglas: Yeah I think attractiveness is important, but then I don't rate attractiveness just on physical appearance; I look at the all round person, and the persona that the person's got, because you might come along and you might...say a girl's gone for the job and she was the most absolutely stunning girl you've ever seen in your life, well if that girl can't count to three its not going to count for much, so I think it comes into play to a certain extent.

Accent was also recognized as having an impact on the way candidates were perceived by employers although it was seen to depend on the organization in question. Some of those interviewed thought that accent was an important indicator of 'social fit' with future work colleagues and clients. They also felt that some people with regional accents were at a distinct disadvantage although it was also pointed out that within the media 'it's become quite cool to have a different accent', but this was a minority view:

Catherine: I think it probably depends on different organizations...I've got a really middle class accent and I do think that that affects the way people deal with me...I really hope not...It's like the thing with acne isn't it, it would be wrong if it did but at the same time...it all boils down to the sort of 'old boys network' doesn't it; if somebody speaks in the same accent as them.

Gail: I remember once . . . I was meeting somebody quite influential and I tried to make a really good impression and I went around saying 'chick-in' rather than 'chicken', and that was quite sad and of course trying so hard. So yes I am so aware of it, definitely.

Teresa: I was quite pleased that I lost my accent actually because when I was in London people couldn't tell where I was from and I suppose that's probably worked to my advantage, and when you go to talk to people who've got a Black Country accent you can quickly pick them up . . . I must admit that when I've been around say in the City, I've only heard one person with a Birmingham accent in a pub or a bar, so I definitely do think there's a big thing about accents.

One of the most significant changes since the data on graduates and corporate recruitment collected by Brown and Scase a decade ago was the dramatic shift in women's career expectations and job opportunities at least in terms of access to fast track management training.[3] The following extract neatly captures the confidences of some female graduates:

Do you think you've got the same chance as a male who's got the same skills and qualifications?
Sarah: Completely, I never even think that, it's really weird I can't imagine there ever being a time when women felt that they couldn't compete equally because when I go to interviews I almost feel I have an advantage over some of them.

In what sort of way?
Sarah: Girls are a lot more easy to get on with a lot of the time and probably come across better in interviews quite often . . . and however bad this sounds, there's a huge advantage because a lot of the interviewers are male and if you're a female without doubt it puts you at a slight advantage.

In what sort of way?
Sarah: Well, male interviewers feel a lot more inclined towards the female candidates and a lot more friendly and easy going and they almost still have the stereotype that girls won't be as capable as the guys because they're a lot nicer and then realise that you're . . . quite a good candidate.

Interestingly, for reasons that will be apparent below, Karmel believed that women were at an advantage in the selection process because they were able to play the game in adjusting to the requirements of the situation. The only exception was when men where motivated by amorous intent:

Karmel: Men are really one track really, they have loyalty and everything, but they . . . they're very honest in terms of their expression sometimes . . . while as a woman they can adjust themselves, they can tailor it, you know. I think men are very open... you see them when they talk, they're just the same with everyone, how they talk, unless they have a sexual interest, that's a different thing!

There was also a view that women had an advantage in those occupations that have traditionally recruited large numbers of men such as engineering. As a male candidate observed 'with engineering companies I would say 9-out-of-10 she would get it... there is an awful lot of discrimination'. But other candidates were quick to point to some of the harsh realities of 'real life' labour market outcomes:

Angela: Anyone who says sexism is dead isn't living in the real world. It's still there but whether the recruitment process overcomes that I don't know.

Liz recognized that the discrimination confronting women was less noticeable after leaving university, but would become more of an issue when women confront the issue of balancing work with the realities of having children:[4]

Liz: I think that certainly in the future we'll have more hassles than a bloke because I think there's always the thought that if we employ this woman at 29 or 30 she's going to go off and have kids in 2 or 3 years and I think you hit a bit of a glass ceiling, but I think that at graduate level I don't think it is an issue. We're a bit younger at the moment and I hope it doesn't affect me but I can see why it would in the future.

Most of those we spoke to were ambivalent about the impact of race and ethnicity, despite evidence that shows that some, although not all ethnic minorities, confront significant discrimination both in access to elite universities and managerial and professional employment. There was a general view that racial discrimination had become less important as companies recruited more people from different ethnic backgrounds. Indeed, Jonathan believed that he was now at a disadvantage as a 'standard white English type':

Jonathan: If you're just the standard white English type maybe it does slightly disadvantage you these days. Employers want to be seen as having equal opportunity and being global as well I guess, so maybe it does. But, as I say, in my little world it's all fair and equal.

Much of the discrimination confronting those from ethnic minority backgrounds is 'institutional', for instance, there is a higher preponderance of Afro-Caribbean students in so-called new universities that makes it more difficult for them to survive the initial screening process used by the organizations in this study, even if they apply.[5] But one of graduates from an ethnic minority background did reveal evidence of direct discrimination although this did not involve any of the organizations in this study:

Miriam: I had applied for a position and my CV was good and everything. It was for an agency so...I applied for a position and they told me to come down to the agency because the agency people wanted to like, see how you are and screen you and decide whether they are going to let you go through to the assessment centre stage. And I went down, had the interview, they asked me questions, I answered them and everything. Then I got some feedback...they said that some of the feedback was good and relevant, they said that I had seemed a bit unsure over something, which I knew was true, but they also said that I wasn't of the right culture and I found that quite offensive.

When asked about the importance of social background, many of those we spoke to felt that it had an important impact on job opportunities. This was invariably seen to favour those from middle and upper-class backgrounds although as Jonathan told us, if there is any question of introducing positive discrimination he's 'got a big thing against it, but that's probably because I'm a middle-class male'. But the advantages of coming from a privileged background were widely acknowledged:

Angela: If they come from a family that's a high class family and everyone's already done a degree and everyone knows the system and everyone's in good jobs...and all that carry on, then it must influence you in social skills I guess. I mean you must be in a better position than someone who comes from a very working class background, whose family have never done a degree and have all had working class jobs, and you're the first to do graduate recruitment like a fish out of water, and even though there's a lot of facilities at the union like careers centres, you would still not be in a strong position I think.

The following quotations makes a similar point but links a 'bad' background with that of a Birmingham accent that is seen to compound the disadvantages of social class:

William: It's imperative. You're average interviewer is possibly going to be a partner or senior up in the company, perhaps say, gets someone from the same area as me with a really bad Brummy background, who's had to work really hard and made a lot of debt at University, perhaps don't dress themselves as well as me, they come in, they don't speak as well. They are going to be at a disadvantage to me. He may well be brighter than me, you win some, you lose some, occasionally. Obviously it might not matter, you might find some employer who sees you for the potential of the company rather than if you look the part, but its going to happen.

The influence of social class differences on access to the personal, cultural, and social capital valued by fast-track employers is clearly articulated in the following statement. But Kate also recognizes how hard it is to be an equal opportunities employer when the social 'product' derived from the privileges of class is precisely what employers are looking for:

Kate: I do think specifically for me the example of the public school is quite a relevant one for me...because someone who's been to public school has developed social skill, they might have mingled with their parents' friends and be used to mingling...it gives you more confidence, and you see a lot of public school people who are very confident come across very well. I'm sure employers can see through it if there's nothing behind that but I think that's the presentation aspect and the kind of communication aspect can often have been greatly developed and given a real head-start and it takes a longer time for people to catch up maybe. You hope that at university those kinds of things would start to even out anyway, that people would hopefully develop social skills. And I do think it's really hard to be completely equal opportunities employers, because how do you do that if someone's developed better social skills because of their background, and that's what employers are looking for and they don't see it as discrimination because that's the sort of person they want and that's a difficult one: how do you say to someone you're discriminating only for them to say, 'no, that's what we want.'

Part Two: The Games People Play

Notwithstanding these similarities in the career expectations harboured by those we interviewed, there were significant differences in the way they understood and managed their employability. To capture these differences we identified two 'ideal types' called 'Players' and 'Purists' (see Figure 6.1).[6] Ideal types are useful analytical tools, but we should avoid the tendency to assume that they mirror empirical realities.[7] While many of those interviewed gravitated towards one or other 'type', there was a lot of fuzziness in the middle. Some expressed comments that were difficult to categorize. There were statements that clearly fitted into one type but the same person could also make statements that seemed more appropriate within the other. This caveat is important because we are not suggesting that all those we interviewed could be neatly labelled as one or the other. This does not pose a major problem for us here, as there was no intention to quantify the numbers of Players or Purists. However, we are frequently asked what proportion fit into either category. Our crude response is that approximately a third gravitate to each category while the remaining third were somewhere between the two.[8]

Before we detail the differences between the Players and Purists some further clarification is required. First, the distinction between the Players and Purists does not reflect differences in ambition, motivation, or a willingness to make an effort. They all want to give it their best shot in trying to gain the vocational prizes they are contesting. Some of those at both ends of the continuum had a clear sense of vocation, for instance, in wanting to be the CEO of a large company, a management consultant, or a research scientist. Others within both categories lacked a clear sense of direction beyond getting onto a fast-track management programme.

Again, the difference between them is not the presence or absence of a clear vocation or career goals, but the way they understood and

Approach to employability	Players	Purists
Competition rules	Market	Meritocratic
Task	Win positional game	Technical puzzle
Self-development	Expressed through work	Work expression of self
Career strategy	Maximize market options	Maintain-career integrity[a]

[a] Integrity is used to imply coherence at the same time as being true to the 'self'.

Fig. 6.1 The social construction of employability

managed their employability. Players who adopt a 'scattergun' approach saw this as playing the market to assess what was out there, and to assess their position in the market place. On this basis, they assessed their tactics to ensure that they sold themselves in the appropriate way in line with what employers in different organizations were seen to want. Indeed, the fast track was a means to rapid advancement, so the important thing was to get access to elite training programmes and add value to their job resumè, in some cases irrespective of the employer. In contrast, the Purists saw a scattergun approach as a way of assessing where their strengths lay. It was a technical puzzle of finding the right fit between themselves and an employer. Recruitment was seen as a meritocratic competition that enables both parties to find the right match in terms of knowledge, skills, and self-identity.

Second, the way people understand and manage their employability is an ongoing social process rather than a once in a lifetime decision or event. We should not rule out the possibility that some of those labelled as Purists may come to see that the only way to succeed in the scramble for tough-entry jobs is to engage in Player behaviour. As one of the male Purists confessed 'If they asked me to wear a dress, if they paid me £50k a year, or if I was only to wear a bra and suspenders, then I'd do it'. Equally, some of the Players may discover that their attempt to play the market does not work to their advantage and decide to be 'themselves' regardless of the market consequences. It is also likely that those who were difficult to categorise will quickly learn that they need to get their 'act together' if they are to find suitable employment.

Finally, it does not tell us who will be successful. For instance, a Player who does not fully understand the rules of the game or who leads recruiters to believe that they are 'faking it' has virtually no chance of being appointed. We will, however, go on to explain why the Players appear to have a positional advantage if they understand the rules of the game and have been properly coached.

Players: If at First You Don't Succeed, Play and Play Again

Players understood employability as a positional game, with its own set of rules. They recognised that there were other well-qualified competitors looking for the same jobs so the aim was to adopt tactics that gave them a competitive edge. For them it was more than a 'merito-cratic' competition based on ability or technical expertise that led to achievement within the education system. In the job market you had to market yourself in ways that conformed to the broader require-ments of employers. The Players spend time learning the rules of the game, including the requirements of potential employers to maximize their chances of success.

They used the university careers service, employer websites, and social contacts to help them 'decode' the winning formula. They attended workshops that simulated group exercises at assessment centres and practised psychometric tests. They read books on how to 'reinvent oneself' for success along with those that tell you how to answer difficult interview questions. They understood the importance of developing a narrative of employability that mirrored the require-ments of the employer. Acquired skills are repackaged for consumption within the recruitment arena through a combination of social net-works and an understanding of how to convert their economy of expe-rience into tangible job offers. The following extracts provide insights into the lengths to which Players go in order to package themselves accordingly:

Gail: For the most recent company I found out all about the project that they were running, found out the philosophies that they had, found out through people that had already worked there, were they male or female? What panel would be interviewing me? And I really geared it to that, went in there saying that I couldn't work for a company that didn't have the philosophy that they had...so really just covered all my thoughts and beliefs on the sheets that they provided and I asked them to provide me with the literature and they did so and I just looked at it and went in there to be that person that they wanted. But I didn't believe any of it...

In another part of the interview Gail told us:

Again it depends on what job, if it is management then I am very much into martial arts and if it is a management position I'm a 'go-getter' and I put things like that on there. If it is dealing with vulnerable people in mental health then I take that off, so yes that changes as well...It is great that you don't have to tell people the truth because you lie so much at interviews.

Simon: You learn the best way to sort of sell yourself. Especially when you speak to them and realize what they're looking for and I think a lot of them...you sort of, you find out what they want to hear and then you learn to tell them what they want to hear...I try to come across nicer than I think I really am.

Playing depended on good preparation and tailoring one's experiences to the requirements of employers. This preparation included taking advantage of practice sessions run by university careers advisers:

We were talking earlier about preparation for interviews, what kind of preparations do you think you'll do?
Kate: I'm going to go to the careers centre talk on preparing for interviews. I was given advice from someone about that and also...I watched a video about it in the careers centre about assessment centres—basically they were saying that you need to make a list of all the things that they want. In the literature they give, it's true they say, 'These are the qualities we want', and then, 'Make a list of examples of how you've shown those qualities in the past'. So they would say in an interview situation, 'We've said that we need people that can adapt to *x* circumstances. How can you show that you've done this?' Then I've got an example in mind because when you're asked that, you're nervous and when you're ill prepared you come up with stupid things. I've known that from my previous interviews, she'd ask me questions and I didn't have a clue and then a couple of days later you think, 'Oh I could have said that, I could have said that!' So you need to be prepared, so that's what I've started to do; and I'm feeling much more confident about it already. I know what they're looking for, I've got specific examples I can say, 'Oh yes I'm good at that...So I think preparation's really important. I've watched a video on an interview—that was it. There was a guy sitting there, and there was a guy interviewing him and this woman and it was really surreal he'd ask a question and this guy would go, 'Um ...' and he'd stumble, just like I'd imagine I would do! He'd falter or he'd say something really not very good and this woman [careers advisor] goes, 'Stop!'—it was really surreal, like freezes in time, and goes, 'That's not what this guy wants [to hear], can you think of an example?'

These extracts encapsulated the strategies Players engaged in, but we are not suggesting that the Players deliberately lie, but they are economical with the truth. The moral consequences of these strategies are discussed in the final chapter but here we focus on the nature of Player tactics. After all, anybody can read material sent by employers conveying the skills they require, just as anybody can visit their web pages and familiarize themselves with the list of desirable personal qualities organizations are looking for. Players, however, devoted time prior to attending recruitment events to construct an appropriate narrative of employability as they understood that it is not enough to possess the desired skills, it was how they were embodied and conveyed that really mattered:

Zoe: I always look through the module that I did last year with all my examples and all my achievements documented in it. I always look through my CV and the application form. I always go to the company website and see if I can get some sort of idea from that of the kind of specific qualities that they're looking for in people, and often you can get that from the literature as well. If they're particularly keen on people who are—for example Unilever: they were keen on people who were innovative and could think up new ideas—so you can get some sort of idea of what they want you to say from the literature.

Rose: I think employers prefer to see that you've got lots of different things rather than the same example for everything and I think a lot of my friends are struggling because they don't have the examples to call upon that I do. I find like its quite scary when I go to an interview and I can't actually get everything that I do into the interview, I've got so many now...I know it sounds, 'Oh gosh I'm so wonderful, I've done lots', but it is quite nice because I don't worry about interviews as much as people who sit and think, 'Oh gosh I've got nothing to say',—I've got a lot of things I can call upon and I do think it's paying off.

The Players understood that the value of personal capital depended on the very language people use, its style and mode of delivery—whether spoken or in written form. Consider, for example, some of the strategies adopted by the Players in our study:

Victoria: You've got to talk a bit better and you're a bit calmer. You don't treat them the same way as you treat your friends.

Rob: You always want to try and write using the past verb—'organized', 'was involved', use strong words; instead of 'responsible for', 'controlled'; trying to make it all sound more powerful...it is something that I've worked on a lot and obviously seems to be paying off.

Jonathan: I may put on a slightly more public school voice, I don't know.

You've got a neutral accent, though?
Jonathan: I think I have—nobody knows where I'm from. I guess I maybe tend to use less slang, more formality, I'm often attempting to match the person that I'm talking to.

The last statement once again raises the issue of accent that was widely recognized to influence one's chances in the job market. Issues of accent and self-presentation are also important issues for the Purists, but as we will see the latter will always try to remain true to 'themselves'. Yet, many of the Players understood these issues well before they started applying for jobs. While at university they sought to add value to their *curriculum vitae*. Voluntary work or extensive extra-curricular activities such as being a club captain, society treasurer, or charity organizer, were deliberately undertaken as a way of sending the appropriate messages to employers, demonstrating drive, self-reliance, and 'get up and go'. We are not suggesting that the Players undertook extracurricular activities purely because it would look good on their CVs. Many social activities involve mixed motives such as wanting to contribute something to the community by undertaking voluntary work with deprived children but also recognizing that this could add value to one's CVs. The Players were acutely aware of the importance of this economy of experience.

They do not shy away from self-promotion they embrace it. It never hurts to exaggerate a previous experience if it contributes to the packaging of the self, as the situation requires. Hence, what defines a Player is not only someone who sees employability as a market game but also someone who is willing to 'act the part' with all its theatrical connotations.[9] They constructed story lines that conveyed their competence and promoted their employability:

Sarah: I have a set few examples that I use, say Junior Common Room secretary, Boat Club secretary, organised a big cocktail party and raised £1,000, so that's always good, delegating [of] work or whatever. I have about five situations that I can apply to any of the questions they ask, so I just try and integrate those because I like giving different examples. And usually they ask the same questions 'give an example of where you've found an innovative solution to a problem, etc'.

Rose: I have to admit you go for a job interview and they say, 'Are you doing this? Are you doing that?' and I think all the way through I've thought, 'Oh gosh you've got to have more because everybody's going to university now,' and I've felt from day one that you need to stand out, you can't just come out of uni with a 2.1 and nothing else because everyone's got that. Whereas if you can say 'I've been to America for a year, I've been doing this, I've been doing that—employers go like 'Wow'! How has she been doing all that and got a degree?' And although I have to admit, like every day I'm running around and totally busy, I actually think that's part of the experience because what else would you be doing—watching telly?

Not everybody had such a vast array of experiences that they could call upon in order to differentiate themselves from other candidates in the recruitment process. Some had more 'experiences' to cash-in than others. Some candidates also lacked the specific personal skills deemed appropriate for the job for which they were applying as we noted above in the discussion about social background, gender, and ethnicity. But all the players recognised the need to be economical with the truth that placed demands on the self in a context of intense market competition:

Do you think you can be yourself in interviews or do you tailor your answers in terms of what kind of person they're looking for?
Zoe: Well obviously I don't lie and I do try and impart some of my personality in interviews but I think to some extent with interviews you have to play the game and you have to point out to them that you have the skills that they are looking for, so perhaps you might have to emphasise a part of your nature that isn't . . . make it more of a part of your nature, if you see what I mean?

Do you think you can be yourself at assessment centres and interviews?
Gail: I don't know, I think some firms will actually disregard you if you are . . . With interviews and jobs you have to say the right things . . . for some of the interviews and some of the jobs, they are not going for the true person, they are getting what they want to hear and because we know what they want to hear, we are telling them that . . . you don't expect to be yourself in interviews. You don't want to . . . it's not there for you to be yourself, it's there for them to judge you on certain competencies. I mean I've had a laugh in interviews and I didn't get the job. So my feeling is no, you don't be yourself.

They also used existing contacts or develop new ones that could help them once they entered the job market. In short, they did whatever it took to win an advantage in the competition for a livelihood. The perceived need to go to such lengths in order to differentiate their *curriculum vitae*, together with a need to exploit personal connections, opens up a different stratum within the labour market that is simply not open to all Players or other graduates:

Did you use any of the pamphlets from the careers centre or anything like that?
Sarah: No, it was just family because they'd all done them and knew what was involved. And then the last one was an interesting one because they actually

phoned me up. They had employed a recruitment company...and I got a phone call from them and they got my name from being on the Junior Common Room exec, they had an exec list—they were looking for good graduates and they were phoning Oxford and Cambridge and London and Nottingham and things, and they said we were also looking for something else so then they found lists of sports captains or executive committee members and things like this and then they narrowed it down, I assume by choosing maths and economics because all the people at interview were mathematicians and economists.

Another defining feature of the Player was that she or he was sceptical of employer claims that they could 'see through' people who were play-acting rather than offering an authentic rendition of who they really were. In some respects they saw through the veneer of objectivity espoused in the recruitment literature. There was an implicit recognition that it was social 'form' rather that technical 'substance' that was being used to separate candidates who met the basic requirements of the job, and that these intangibles were difficult to authenticate. Therefore, there was plenty of scope to put on a performance that at least for Gail was unrecognizable from the real person:

Gail: I was studying psychology and doing a lot about communication and personality types and so you were aware of yourself. I decided not to use any of the psychology...but every week the Guardian puts a little section about how to get on and presenting your CV, covering letters, interview formats. It is very good and even that tells you...you don't have to be yourself. It almost tells you not to be yourself because I think that was what is reinforced. I had to put a different head on to walk in there [interview] and that is why I never socialise with any of the people I have worked with because they would just think 'that is not the same person that walks through this room'.

Players recognized the task as one of learning to be competent at being competent. They responded differently to the experience of initial failure. For them, employability was a learning process. If at first they fail they seek to learn from their mistakes and repackage themselves in ways that can contribute to success in the next contest. They were willing to work on their tactics and to treat previous assessment centres as recruitment training:

Peter: It's a game you learn, don't you? Just like they catch you out in the interviews, you learn what to say, don't you?

Beckie: It's having the knack and knowing what they want and playing the ball...If you've done them enough times then you know what to expect and then you can prepare yourself better and jump when they jump.

Victoria: I think the first few [assessment centres] I didn't know quite what to be, so I was me, and now I sort of tailor myself down slightly. Yes, it's me, so if I really have a strong thought on a certain answer, then yes I'm me. If it is a really strong point about should we do animal tests or what have you, and I have a really strong view on that, and so the answer will be like—that's my answer. Whereas I think with some answers you can be quite broad, so that you are not: 'She's a definite no'—because I think if you have a too strong, sensitive mind, then especially for the management schemes, I don't think they like you. For the management schemes you have to be that sheep that they can, you know, they can cut your wool off you to make you into what-ever sort of shape they want.

Rob: They often highlight skills that they use, so I try and look through the information they provided. This company have got quite a good, compre-hensive one, that I've actually based quite a few of my applications on. They talk about the main issues, such as competencies which is business-sense, drive, initiative, working together, influence and thinking—things, basically every time I give an example of something I've done. I try—when they ask a question, I try and think straight away which competency are they looking for here, and then I try to give an example of that to illustrate it, emphasizing how I've shown them. I don't make up examples, although you might glorify things a bit. Because I don't know, I mean some of my friends have made things up.

The last two quotations highlight a degree of ambivalence that explains why some of those interviewed were difficult to classify as either Players or Purists. The degree of unease expressed by some of the Players reflected the fact that they are not shallow people, but rather that they were doing what they felt was necessary to get ahead. Often under considerable family, peer and personal pressure to 'succeed', or at least to fulfil the high level of expectation that many of these grad-uates carried with them for as long as they could remember.

The extent to which some of the Players were willing to go to get ahead was however again illustrated by Gail. She felt that it was important to demonstrate her background credentials to prospective employers in a way that showed that she was from a successful family. This led her to omit the very existence of her mother because she lived in a council house and worked as a care assistant. When discussing her social background she only talked about her father because he owned his house, drove a flash car and was in the right sort of job:

Gail: When I go for interviews if they ask about family...I seldom mention my mum at all and in fact I just tell them that I have been brought up by my father and I don't even mention that my mum ever exists, because if they then quiz me about my father I know everything he has done is acceptable. He owns the £200,000 house, he drives flash cars and he is in the right job, but my mother lives in a council house and is a care assistant and I know that wouldn't go down too well. So I just omit the fact that she exists.

The Players, however, recognized this commodification of the self and family background as packaging that was distinct and distanced from the authentic self:

Sarah: I think [group exercises] are dreadful. I think they're really bad, because if you were in a situation at work where you were in a group, then firstly you would all enter the room with your different roles, you would know that someone was the manager and someone else was—you would all know where everyone stood and what was going on. Instead you get thrown into something where you haven't really read the data and everyone is trying to think what the assessors want you to do. No one's ever honest, honestly portrays themselves, and there's little key things that everyone has to get in like 'I think we should break down the time' or 'I think we should do this' and everyone's trying to do that, and I just don't think they see the right side of people. Because I also think people try too hard—I think if people were just themselves—they never really get an honest picture of people.

Gus: I think about what I'm saying a bit, I don't think about the accent or anything, because if it is something that I can do then I can twist up so that it actually sounds a bit more, a bit posher let's say, but I can also do it the other way as well. It depends on the company that you are in. [...] So, for example, when I had that *Bank* interview that was a situation where it needs to be very proper because the people you are speaking to are, they are your ex-public school boys. It is very important to them that they work with people that are that way, so I suppose you sort of become that way.

The problem is that although they may initially see this as a game it quickly becomes a way of life. The Player and the person dissolve into one. Some Players can handle this particular requirement of the recruitment process. When asked if they could be themselves at recruitment events Players adopted a different, more employable persona:

Zoe: In the group exercises…my personality is that in a group discussion, perhaps I would listen for the first 5 or 6 minutes, sort of get the general mood of the group and clarify my own ideas. But I don't think that's necessarily the best way of being noticed and standing out so perhaps you have to sort of jump in and take charge early on when that isn't perhaps part of your nature.

Gail: I would love that…the ultimate job would be really to be able to be yourself in that environment…But I go out every once in a while and get absolutely ruined with the girls and have a good laugh but when I'm at work I just sit there looking at journals and I would never let on that I'm a party animal…in fact I think I would be totally embarrassed if some of my managers that I work with came out with me. I think they would sack me the day after, it would literally be that bad.

Playing could enhance the employment opportunities for the individual concerned but playing badly, such as when employers suspected that you're faking it had the opposite effect. In another example, Jodi tried to convince us, as well the recruiters concerned, that she had a genuine commitment to working for the public sector:

Jodi: Basically I want to be in something that is quite worthwhile, sort of dealing, I know this sounds like I'm doing the whole interview thing, but I'm quite genuine about why I want to do this, I really do want to be challenged and involved in world affairs and important events, and I would not be happy doing a banking job. I mean I really want some broader scope to what I'm doing.

Will you apply for something in the private sector?
Jodi: It's not that I don't want to apply for anything in the private sector, I don't kind of block that out as a possibility, but it just depends on what happens here.

Players may never get the option of being themselves at work. Indeed, this may be a luxury that very few can afford in an environment of doing more with less, meeting tough deadlines, and engaging in career networking. They understood that in congested markets the self must be presented as an expression of work. You had to convince employers that work *is* life. For some, the results of this packaging were stultifying and negated the opportunities for individual personalities to shine through:

Victoria: They always say, 'We are looking for someone who will fit in with the team', but sometimes when you see the people that are successful, you wonder whether that's true because quite a lot of them have no personality.

Do you think they are looking for clones?
Victoria: Not so much clones but just, because a friend has got on one, and she is one of those people that she doesn't stay herself—depending on who she is with, she'll adapt and take on their characteristics and I think that is why she got the job.

Rather like a deep personal relationship one had to convince recruiters that one was sold on the company. More accurately, it was more like a theatrical farce where both parties made promises that they knew they couldn't keep! We will return to this issue in the next chapter.

Where career progression was an overriding consideration, playing the market was the price of success. This should not be understood as self-alienation, as many of the Players viewed it as challenging and exciting.

Zena: I don't think people want jobs for life now; I think its quite fun moving now. I think one of the nicest things about it if you get stuck somewhere you can move. I think, one of the things... about no job for life is that you take responsibility for your management skills and like one company I know have found, they call them 'Seagull Managers'—they fly in, shit on you and fly out again, and I think that is a very interesting concept because what I would like to do is go into a company for a time to treat it like my degree—as a learning experience and not a stepping stone.

They also welcomed the opportunity to pitch themselves against the best in a competition for some of the top vocational prizes. For those with the appropriate personal capital it was a source of individual empowerment that enabled them to trade off flexibility in the job market to hike up salaries and other benefits. Hence, the Players had taken the new 'realities' of employability and self-reliance to heart, as the current social climate encourages all to 'play the game'.

Venessa: I think the trouble is now that if you're at a company where any minute you could be made redundant you therefore can't help the fact that you're always then not loyal to them—and it is all swings and roundabouts.

If you're somewhere where you don't feel very secure and you don't feel happy you're not going to do very well because you're just not feeling like the company really wants you. […] It is hard I think now. I do get the impression that people are just assets. They're not people anymore, employees are just people that do a job or perform a function and its gone really more away from the positive side of people, having an affiliation to your company and being loyal.

Consequently, in the same way that many companies emphasized shareholder value over the welfare of their employees, the Players have come to mirror the cynicism of companies who espouse that their most important asset is their human resources. They have embraced short-term expedience and speculation over long-term commitment and loyalty as a survival tactic in an overcrowded and intensely competitive labour market rather than a moral creed of market individualism.

Purists: The Truth, the Whole Truth, and Nothing But the Truth

Samuel: The only strategy I've got is to be me and if they don't want me then I don't want to work for them.

The Purists lived by the meritocratic creed that informed public ideas about personal success, social justice, and economic efficiency for at least half a century. The goal was not equality but the right for all to have an equal chance to be unequal. The meritocratic race must therefore be organized so that its outcome, whether in the form of credentials, jobs, or wages, reflect differences in individual achievement based on our efforts and innate capabilities. In these terms education is viewed as the progressive unlocking of human potential. Over time talent will be revealed as the knowledge requirements of advanced study are shown to be beyond the capacity of most people. The problem for the Purists today is that the acquisition of the knowledge, skills, and know-how that are a prerequisite for managerial and professional employment, are no longer restricted to a small elite.

Consequently, the Purists were aware that they were in a competitive situation but still believed that if they were good enough they would get a good job. This view was illustrated in the following quotations about whether assessment centres favoured particular kinds of people:

Sako: I believe these assessment centres...favour the people that deserve it, if you do well then you are the person they are looking for so, if it favours them then fair enough.

Maureen: Yes I do think they favour people with relevant degrees and the relevant subjects. Not unfairly, I think that's just life.

In the following transcript Martin expressed some uncertainty about whether the academic pecking order was meritocratic, but he also felt 'to be honest' that it reflected the relative worth of credentials from different universities:

Martin: If they see application forms from candidates with the same grades from Cambridge or Middlesex University, they'd think me more than the other guy, which is quite crap, but to be honest we did do more work, because to be honest that's how it is, it's because they do work you hard, and I think it is a shorthand, rightly or wrongly for certain things which employers may well be looking for.

Other Purists believed that using this 'shorthand' was unfair because people should be judged on what they know and their academic performance rather than the reputation of the universities where one studied:

Do you think employers judge graduates differently depending on the university they attend?
Miriam: I don't think so and I would hope that they don't. I think that it doesn't matter where you have studied, whether you have been to Oxford or not. I think that your grades are going to be important and what you know, but it is not always the case where someone who has been to a top university is going to be the best person, do you see what I mean.

Notwithstanding these differences in views the Purists exhibited a high degree of faith in the job market to serve as a fair and efficient means of matching the right people to the right jobs. Assessment centres were a necessary addition to the traditional job interview as employers tried to ensure that the best person for the job was identified on their competence. Therefore, while they were aware that the process was far from perfect there was an underlying belief that organizations could overcome such problems ensuring a fair system. Purists believe in the integrity of the recruitment process:

Douglas: Assessment centres get more out of people than one interview. You can blag an interview I think, that's the best way of putting it, if you want to. You can come across all rosy but in an assessment you come across as your real self, you're not given the time to do anything else, you know, you do come across as your real self.

Olivia: I think it is an excellent idea. You are daunted when you go in there as a candidate hoping to get a place, but it kind of sorts the wheat from the chaff if you know what I mean, because a lot of people...I've met quite a few people now working in this organization who talk a very good talk, so to speak, but do they have the some knowledge and do they have a degree of not just education but also common sense? Things like that are really important when you work in that organization...Anyone can talk the spiel, but can you actually deliver the goods? And I think that the management training scheme looks to seek those people out. And I think it does it very effectively.

Jahangir: I suppose it gives you the best indication of success and future career I suppose—it's the closest you can get to a working environment and to judge competencies...on the assessment centre, on the whole it can be quite successful and a good indication of which job is best.

They understood that the use of assessment centres reflected the changing nature of managerial roles that required employers to find out much more about job applicants that their list of academic and other achievements. But it was also recognized that the use of assessment centres were a response to the growing numbers of qualified applicants that made it more difficult for employers to determine who were the most employable:

Miriam: I think that it helps them to get a picture of what the candidate is like, what the candidate can do. It helps the candidate as well to see what the company is like, when say they do presentations, and you learn a bit more about that company. Also I think that sometimes when you have positions and you have so many applications, when you hold assessment centres and you get to see the people for yourself you can decide, it makes it easier selecting people as well.

Do you think they are effective?
Miriam: I think they are.

Do you think they favour certain kinds of graduates or do you think they are a fair way of finding the best people for the job?

Miriam: I think that sometimes with say, for example, with the tests and things, sometimes I think that they are not fair in the sense that there could be, say if there are 10 people, well they'll use it as a means to eliminate, and sometimes it could be a case whereby a candidate is capable of doing the position, so I think sometimes you shouldn't judge a candidate on whether or not they can do a position by the results of like a general test, if you see what I mean. I think you need to speak to them, if there is an interview that would help as well...I think they are good but I don't think that companies should always consider the results of like a psychometric test or something.

Do you think they're fair?
Liz: Fair? I don't know—life's not fair is it?

Let me put it another way—do you think they favour certain kinds of graduates?
Liz: I don't know, really. I guess people that are quieter would probably find them [more difficult] but I would have thought that the company that was doing the recruitment would tailor them to suit the people they were looking for.

There was also a minority view that the assessment process was moving away from the principles of meritocratic competition, that companies had moved the goal posts. And in doing so assessment centres were judging 'form' over 'content'. These male candidates clearly felt that modern selection techniques were inappropriate:

Simon: I've got a Chemistry PhD! Doesn't that tell you that I have skills?

Martin: Well I can see why they use [assessment centres] in most industries, and they're obviously incredibly fake, like get people to sit round and do a group exercise. You all know you're supposed to act like you do in a group because you're applying for a job that would pay you *x* £ thousands per year... don't know how good [recruiters] are at telling whether people would be good for the job. I personally dislike the whole idea, because I think it does make me like a rat in a cage and looked at and prodded which I find quite disheartening and a bit unpleasant.

This view was not widely shared by the Purists for whom individual employability amounted to a 'technical puzzle' of finding a job that offered the right fit with their knowledge, personality and aspirations: a little like fitting square pegs into square holes. This is akin to the use of academic examinations to evaluate knowledge and ability. The recruitment process amounts to a technical matter of measuring up to specific occupational roles.

So what are you expecting from the actual assessment centre itself? You said you worked out exactly what's going on: how do you feel about it?

Maureen: Its quite exciting actually, well as I say, there is an element of 'personal PR', you can go there, not exactly show off but really do your best and show what you can do and really try to impress, but be yourself, so if you do get the job then you know that it's your sort of a job, you're not just randomly picked, it's not a lottery, you're just not picked by the fact that you've got good grades, but because you genuinely will be the right person for the job.

Purists with a clear sense of vocation confronted the task of demonstrating to employers that they were the 'right' person for the job. Whereas for those that lack a clear sense of vocation, the application process was a voyage of self-discovery. It told them important things about what was a suitable job for them rather than lessons in how to play the game as understood by the Players. This voyage of self-discovery involved the search for a job profile that closely mirrored that of their interests and personality. It involved getting a better understanding of what organizations were looking for and, crucially, whether they felt they had the right competencies. Purists read background information about the organizations they apply to, but what distinguished them from the Players was what they did with that information. Unlike Players who tried to fit their narrative of employability to the competency profiles of prospective employers, the recruitment process for Purists involved finding the right match between themselves and an employer's stated requirements, as Miriam told us:

Miriam: I always try and make sure that I am myself. I don't try and be something that I am not. I want them to have an honest picture of me and I would like to have an honest picture of the position as well.

This is one of the reasons we used the term Purist because the recruitment process was seen as a 'pure' relationship, in that they expected recruiters to judge them according to a set criteria that assessed their competences to undertake the job in question irrespective of wider considerations such as gender, race, age or social background. Again Miriam, who is of Asian decent, raised the issue of accent when being interviewed for jobs:

Miriam: The way I speak is just how I am so I don't think a person should speak a certain way or be a certain way, you have to be who you are. When you are in the environment and you are working with them that is how you are going to be and I don't think that an employer should judge someone on their accent. I don't think it should affect that, it should be your ability that counts.

This required a high level of self-disclosure for recruitment experts to assess whether they were the right person for the job. Hence, their whole approach to employability was characterised by 'take me as I am', which in turn involved the presentation of the 'authentic' self as opposed to the 'competent' self packaged by Players.

Purists tried to present themselves in a good light to employers while maintaining a sense of who they are. They played it straight. It was important to be prepared but this was a question of giving a good account of one's self. They often recognized that it was difficult to be yourself at interviews or at assessment centres, but this was because the situation was artificial or nerve-racking. What distinguished them from the Players was a willingness to try to convey a true sense (as far as it was possible) of who they are and their genuine suitability for the job. The following extracts were typical of what we heard from Purists:

What do you think you'll need to succeed in your career?
Douglas: Ambition, determination, honesty, 'get up and go', you've got to be yourself really. If you try to be something that you're not in a job that is only suited for you whenever you're not your actual self, you'll find difficulty in succeeding, because you'll be constantly hitting a barrier against what you're actually like, so I think it's about getting a job that's completely suited to you.

Did you compare yourself to the other candidates there?
Teresa: Um, no, not really ... you have to just be who you are really. And if they are not looking for someone like you then well that is the best way to go into it I think. Just be yourself; there is no point on trying to model yourself on someone else you have met or whatever.

Did you feel you were able to be yourself when you were there?
Teresa: Yes pretty much so.

Do you think anyone goes there you know with not being themselves and trying to be somebody else? I mean have you come across anyone?
Teresa: Well I think that some people go in there with a kind of over inflated version of themselves. But I don't think I have ever, ever met anybody who I thought was playing or play acting, making themselves something that they are not. I think that if you do, if someone like me can see it, then the assessor can see it.

Angela: I get quite nervous [about recruitment events] and I find the whole situation very intimidating.

Do you think you can be yourself in them?
Angela: I guess you ought to be but you also get this overriding feeling that you ought to 'perform' somehow. I find them quite false as well, when you get someone sat there reading out set questions it's not, it doesn't feel natural, all very forced, so you feel like you're having an out of body experience almost.

In interviews do you think about how you're speaking, is that something you're aware of?
Angela: I try and use long words, not as in Queen's English, but I guess I must sound intellectual and then sometimes you get yourself tongue-tied and you think, 'Why didn't I just say …!' So I guess because I've got interviews coming up I'm thinking about it a lot. Maybe it would just be easier to speak normally and get the message across rather than try to speak intellectually. I try and construct my sentences carefully—economically—whereas if I were just talking to a friend down the pub I wouldn't bother.

This 'self' integrity along with an ultimate faith in the assessment process to weed out anyone who tried to 'fake it' limited what the Purists learnt from their labour market experiences. They used their experience to increase their confidence or attempted to improve their self-presentation skills but they were reluctant to change their basic game plan of finding the right job for themselves.

Sako: You can't really practise to present yourself in a certain way, if you are a certain person that is the way you are but I think the only thing you can build on is your confidence, maybe that is what really puts people through. I believe with the tests a bit of practise would really help. As regards interviews I think being confident helps more.

Martin: I don't think you can learn to be good at assessment centres, you can only learn to be yourself. To be able to adapt well, that is all I can say.

They viewed the 'acting out' of the Players not only as cheating, but also as industrial sabotage that undermined the integrity of the merito-cratic process. Although some of the Purists such as Simon were aware that this gave Players an advantage if they could get away with it, despite their faith in the selection process:

Simon: I think there are a few repugnant people who are managing to pick up decent jobs out there. You know, they can put on a mask and pretend to be something they're not really.

Part of wishing to maintain an integrity of the self was the idea of the 'productive' individual. Marketing oneself and personal PR was seen to obscure the real value of 'knowledge' work. But some of the Purists also believed that even if it was possible to 'fake it' and get offered a job, there were long-term personal costs that many of the Purists were not willing to countenance at this stage in their careers:

Martin: To some extent I want them to judge me as I am really, but I'd like them to see me and obviously I will, you try and put a certain—you do try to give them what they want to some degree. Equally I don't want to get a job just because I've managed to act out a role for a day, it's not in your own interests in the long term.

Do you think people do that?
Martin: I don't know, I'd be surprised if people didn't ever because underneath people just want a job so they don't really think about whether they want that job and therefore if they pretend or put across a certain persona, it's going to be terribly hard in the long term to keep that persona up.

Rose: I stick to being myself basically at every assessment centre. I've been unsuccessful currently but in a way I've been totally myself and when they've given me feedback in a way they've been totally right; I wasn't into that company and I think that's much better to be yourself because if you got the job based on pretending to be something you'd be miserable.

However, this aversion to 'cheating' was not a defining feature of a Purist, as some maintained their approach to their employability simply because they had not woken up to the realities of labour market competition, or because they believed they do not have what it took to 'act the part':

Simon: I found the application form really hard to complete. They ask you loads of questions about what you've done, you know, the certain situations you've been in and how you've been influential in running things. I just hadn't done any of that, although I'm sure I could do if I'd had the opportunity. I just haven't had the time because my degree has taken a lot out of me. I could have lied and just made up my application form but I would have been found out, wouldn't I? I thought being at a good university would help my applications because everybody says they look at A-level scores rather than your actual degree. I got ABB and I'm going to get at least a 2:1. That's what employers want.

While no less ambitious than the Players, these Purists wanted to avoid the schizophrenic lives of the former. Work was an expression of the self. They wanted to keep a balance between work and non-work that offers the potential for self-actualization. They saw a continuity between education and work in terms of further self-development. They were more likely to believe that once in a job they would be able to show how good they were in a meritocratic competition, leading to career progression within the firm, although if there was inadequate scope for career development they may consider shifting employers. Purists who fail to get a job they wanted may resign themselves to the fact that they lacked the appropriate skills, or that they were simply not good enough leading them to reconsider other career options. But we should not rule out the possibility that they will come to recognize that they will not find a decent job unless they resort to Player tactics!

Conclusion

This outline of Players and Purists presents a view of individual employability that is far removed from human capital theory. The concept of self-identity is, for instance, clearly important when it comes to examining how individuals construct and manage their employability. How an individual approaches the labour market is intimately linked with their ideas about what kind of person they think they are and the kind of person they want to become.[10] The chapter also highlights how those at the top end of the labour market have responded to changes in employer recruitment practices and to intense market competition. It offers an insight into the personal concerns and consequences of the changing relationship between education, jobs, and rewards.

What it also highlights is the cultural confusion that has engulfed middle-class students and families. While they share certain similarities in wanting good jobs that are both personally and materially rewarding, increasing labour market congestion has heightened ethical tensions about the legitimate route to success that reflect changing cultural values of British and American society. The meritocratic ethos remains deeply ingrained in the middle-class psyche, in the sense that what is achieved should reflect individual efforts and abilities. But the conflicting interpretations of individual achievement that have been bubbling below the surface for decades have become clearly visible. While some believe that achievement within meritocratic competition is based on the unfolding of innate capacities that individuals must make an effort to develop, others view achievement in market terms, as a Darwinian struggle for positional advantage based on the exploitation of all the resources an individual can muster—intellectual, cultural, social, if not sexual. This includes buying a better education, using personal networks or tailoring oneself to the perceived requirements of employers. This chapter has demonstrated that this cultural confusion has not been resolved and is manifest in the way employability is understood.

We should, however, remember that there are major differences in market power that make some more employable than others, irrespective of whether they are Players or Purists, recognized by many of those we interviewed. There are important 'within type' differences in personal, cultural, and social capital that have profound implications in terms of labour market outcomes. But this chapter does raise the issue of whether these contrasting approaches to employability privileges Player behaviour in the competition for tough-entry jobs. Does Player behaviour lead to a competitive advantage or are the Purists equally able to demonstrate their future productive worth? In the final analysis, it is the employers that have the last word in who wins and loses in the allocation of life-chances. It is to an evaluation of 'picking winners' to which we now turn.

7

Picking Winners

> If unacquainted with the individual, observers can glean clues
> from his [*or her*] conduct and appearance which allow them to
> apply their previous experience with individuals roughly similar
> to the one before them or, more important, to apply untested
> stereotypes to him...However, during the period in which the
> individual is in the immediate presence of others...many crucial
> facts lie beyond the time and place of interaction or lie concealed
> within it. For example, the 'true' or 'real' attitudes, beliefs, and
> emotions of the individual can be ascertained only indirectly
> through his avowals or through what appears to be his involun-
> tary expressive behaviour.
>
> *Erving Goffman*[1]

How then, you might ask, do employers go about selecting those
workers with whom they wish to carry out future knowledge-
intensive work? This chapter sets out to answer exactly this question,
capturing as it does our experiences and observations of employers
as they conduct the actual process of recruiting graduates.
Overwhelmingly, the majority of work in this area fails, rather ironi-
cally, to unpack how employers *actually* recruit workers, opting
instead to record what they *say* it is that they are looking for. In
Chapter Five we moved beyond this shortfall within the literature,
exploring the different discourses offered by employers to justify the
processes they utilize to make decisions about candidates. In this

chapter we move into new territory, this time exploring what is said, about whom, why, and the ultimate effect these discussions have on the perceived employability of candidates. We are, effectively, watching the judge and jury at work as they pick the winners in the graduate labour market. What follows is split into two parts. In Part One we present and evaluate the official discourse of recruitment used by employers to capture the skills and attributes which they think signal an individual's employability. We argue that the public *rhetoric of competence* obscures the realities of what employers are actually looking for. This boils down to a threefold criterion of employability (suitability, proactivity, and acceptability) that are remarkably straightforward and represent the touchstones through which candidates are judged and employers legitimize their decisions.

In Part Two we bring the selection process to life by drawing on our observations at assessment centres. For the first time we move beyond the rhetoric of what employers say they do, and how they claim to do it, to observe what it is they actually say about individuals during recruitment events within the confines of the confidential 'washing-up' sessions used to make their final recruitment decisions at assessment centres. We conclude with an insight into who is more likely to be seen by employers as 'winners' and, by default, those who are more likely to 'lose'. We then turn to the burning question for all knowledge-workers, young or old: is there a magic formula that can be used to 'play' the knowledge-worker labour market and 'win'?

Part One: The Rhetoric of Competence

We have to stick to these competencies and avoid gut reaction. (IT Consultants)

The last decade has witnessed an outpouring of research dedicated to establishing the skills that comprise employability. League tables of skills abound. In one survey alone, no less than sixty-two different skills are arranged into rank order to display their level of importance to employers.[2] By 1997, sixty-two skills had become just four 'key' skills, identified by Dearing in his wide-ranging review of higher education in

England and its relationship with modern workplaces.[3] These skills were closely aligned with those continuously topping the league tables in analyses conducted by researchers and the media who identified communication skills, problem solving skills, numeracy, and an ability to learn new material.[4] Our contention here is that little has, in fact, changed throughout this debate with regard to the overarching competencies organizations are looking for from new knowledge-worker recruits. Indeed, little appears to have changed since one of us last examined the graduate labour market a decade ago. Still in place are the employer recruitment strategies discussed by Brown and Scase.[5] There have, however, been slight modifications in what constitutes these different criteria of employability, which we summarize in Table 7.1.

Two observations need to be made in relation to Table 7.1. First, the criteria are not mutually exclusive. When combined they represent the complete personality package sought by employers. The relative importance of each will fluctuate in different organizational and work settings. Our contention here is that within knowledge work settings individuals have to demonstrate a relatively high level of performance within each to be perceived as employable. This level of perceived competence changes in line with the expectations of different organizations. A second observation relates to the application of these criteria beyond the graduate labour market. The same factors are also being used by organizations to recruit knowledge workers of all ages. Indeed, this is one of our main findings: that where there was once a certain level of latitude afforded to graduates to 'grow' into a knowledge work job, this luxury has now been removed. Graduates, like the older knowledge worker, have to be proficient from day one, and they have to be able to demonstrate this, or face rejection at the first hurdle.[6]

Suitability: The Commercially Savvy Self

As in the 1990s, *suitability* is still primarily about an individual's capacity 'to get the job done'.[7] The rhetoric now, of course, is one where the ability to get the job done means meeting the ever-growing expectations of employers as to what the threshold of employability actually constitutes. Two developments appear to be significant here.

The first is the apparent eclipse of the primacy of technical skills. Let us be clear about what we are *not* saying. There are still jobs, even

Table 7.1   Employer's selection criteria of employability

Criterion	1990s	2000s	Main reasons for change
Suitability	The basic competence 'to get the job done'. In some jobs an almost exclusive emphasis on personal, transferable skills, even within more 'technical' fields. Technical competence no longer 'enough'.	Remains essentially the same although with a greater emphasis on 'readiness' or the 'commercially savvy self'. Individuals have to show greater levels of business awareness and acumen alongside the personal and social skills that are necessary to get the job done.	Highlights the continuing tension within modern organizations between the management of talent and short-term profitability. Greater emphasis on cost cutting and 'quick wins' leads to a focus on 'oven-ready' graduates who are 'billable within six months'.
Capability to proactivity	*Capability*—about the identification of future leaders and individuals who can 'add value' through their 'raw talent' and 'charismatic' personality.	*Proactivity*—the demonstration of raw talent is no longer sufficient, although it remains important. They also want people who have demonstrated the capacity to get things done. People who have lots of 'get up and go' tailored to the competence profile of the organization.	Highlights the paramount importance of individual performance and contribution to the bottom line. As for suitability it also reflects the importance that is now attached to hitting the ground running.
Acceptability	Emphasis on the 'social fit' between the individual and the organization.	'Social fit' and 'personal chemistry' include a focus on clients and customers, along with colleagues. Also more emphasis on an appropriate narrative of employability.	Highlights the increased emphasis on client focus and customer information. It also reflects the importance of networking and managerial activities beyond the physical confines of company premises.

within the highly fluid and arbitrary world of the knowledge economy that require a high level of technical skills and knowledge. What has changed, however, is not so much a downgrading of technical skills but an insistence on their increasing synergy with the more aesthetic and social skills relating to the personal characteristics of the individuals competing for jobs in today's knowledge-worker labour

market.[8] Consider, for example, the specification for technical competence by one of our case-study companies, a leading IT consultancy:

Understands and Applies Technology Commercially: Demonstrates a working
knowledge of basic techniques and technological concepts. Keeps abreast of
and uses the latest technological, professional and business developments.
Continuously improves knowledge and skills specific to own field, seeks
advice and expertise where appropriate.

Logical Evaluation and Analysis: Displays an analytical and objective approach
to problem solving. Views problems from a number of different angles.
Analyses information accurately and develops themes to generate workable
and innovative solutions to business issues.

But technical prowess is no longer enough. This must now be coupled
with business acumen set at a level far higher than in previous generations of graduates entering the knowledge worker labour market.
Technical skills have to be coupled with a 'client focus' and a high
degree of 'business awareness' enabling technical issues to be *applied*
to different business settings:

I think as the company grows, and has grown, I think we look for a bit more
business nous and awareness from students and more client facing skills, I think
that has been more important for us recently. I mean ultimately we look for the
technical skills, because…they could be on a job from their second week, we
don't give them an intensive three week technical training course because we
expect them to have done that at university. So the client facing business and
interactive skills, yes always have been important but more so because I think
the client expects it. They don't expect, you know even with young professionals, they expect them to be able to go out into their business and conduct themselves and understand and have the listening skills rather than this is just our
graduate training, that is not in this industry anyway. (IT Consultants)

Crucially, this is still not enough. Suitability requires a second attribute. To be seen as a suitable candidate technical skills and 'commercial
savvyness' have to be combined in such a way as to convey the individual self as the 'finished article'. This involves being 'more ideas oriented than task oriented' but these ideas need to be related to the
'commercially savvy self':

We look for people who really present themselves well on the application so
that they have a knowledge of all this IT stuff, but you can get a technical

application that is just a list of jargon. So they have to come across well and they have to be able to demonstrate to us that they understand what they are doing and it is not just technology for technology's sake, it is technology in order to solve a problem, so they have to be very specific because they have to be able to sell their skills in the context of, you know the application of them. (IT Consultants)

A recruiter from the retail sector bemoaned to us how rare this level of savvyness in candidates actually is in today's graduate labour market:

It's nearly always, 'just point me in the right direction, tell me what to do, I'm ever so enthusiastic and would work hard at whatever it is you want me to do' never, 'I've done this, I can do that, I can offer this.' We need people who can hit the ground running, add value from day one and be an asset to us, not a liability...They don't even appear to have actually thought about what it is they *can* do. They seem to be incapable of applying anything to our world or the world of work more widely...It's hard to articulate what I mean...it's about being commercially savvy, worldly wise, having a head for business. (Retail Sector)

All too often, candidates who looked excellent on paper, were unable to convince employers of their 'suitability'. The candidate under discussion in the following example had excelled academically and in extra-curricular activities. But converting all of these attributes into a convincing narrative of employability presented a major hurdle:

I didn't think he was that good, especially because of his educational background. His prose were very clear and precise, but he had little in the way of tangible evidence to support his case. He couldn't express his own ideas in our terms; he somehow seemed uncomfortable. Disappointing really. (Public Sector)

Proactivity: Don't be Backwards in Coming Forwards

When she was in, she was in. And when she was out, she was out. (Science Sector)

While intellectual ability and potential remain important, it needs to be grounded to meet the pragmatic and strategic needs of the organization. Having a brilliant CV and commercial savvyness may meet the criterion of suitability but it does not necessarily demonstrate the 'drive' and 'get up and go' that organizations demand. One of the most significant recent developments has been a shift from an over-arching sense of *capability* to one of *proactivity*. In the War for Talent (WfT) discussed in Chapter Four we heard much talk about the need to recruit the 'best of the best' and 'tomorrow's leaders'. What is seen to set them apart is that 'extra something' that comes from a deep hunger or drive for achievement and success. But many of those recruited onto these management training programmes are not only being trained for middle or senior management but are expected to fill certain functional roles within the organization that require a high level of personal initiative and drive. The emphasis is on a certain attitude or approach to working life that is seen as worthy of recruitment. This is not only true of leading corporate leadership recruitment programmes, but in hiring the foot soldiers of the knowledge economy. In both cases candidates are required to demonstrate a high degree of 'get up and go'.

In an increasingly competitive economy one has to combine suitability with self-determination or 'drive' linked to clearly defined targets:

Organises own and others' activities to ensure optimum use of time and resources. Personally monitors performance against objectives; takes responsibility for achieving desired results in a timely fashion. Flexible and adaptable when personal, or project, plans need to be changed. Initiates action and drives projects along. Overcomes obstacles and shows determination to achieve or exceed targets. Demonstrates optimism and enthusiasm; energetic and persistent. Keeps difficulties in perspective. (IT Consultants)

Another example, this time from our retail case-study company want candidates who can demonstrate a heady cocktail of commitment, tenacity, self-motivation, and self-confidence:

Drive & Commitment: Someone who loves working on the sales floor, is totally committed to it and will put in that little extra effort when needed. Tenacious and self motivated. Not constrained by self-doubt or lack of ambition. Keen on self development. (Retail Sector)

Although organizations in the public sector are not driven by bottom-line profit, their performance is subject to various performance measures and external scrutiny. We found very little difference in emphasis but as public sector organizations are expected to do more with less resources they need highly 'proactive' managers. An example came from a public sector management training scheme that preferred to talk of *drive and values*:

[B]eing determined to succeed, highly motivated and clear about what you want and why you want it. (Public Sector)

We continually heard employers referring to proactivity during their discussions about their observations of individuals' capabilities during assessment exercises. The following extracts from the public sector highlight how some students fail to demonstrate their proactivity during the recruitment process, while others are seen to evince what it takes:

I'm not sure about him. He would just sit back; let others take the lead. He never seemed to once take the initiative. (Public Sector)

The way he highlighted the fact that he felt he would reach his full potential via the management training programme impressed me. (Public Sector)

She said she was not getting any job satisfaction in her present job and would rather do long hours for us than in the private sector because this would be more rewarding. (Public Sector)

Part of being proactive involves selling your soul, but this is precisely what employers are looking for. Being proactive means going that 'extra mile' on behalf of the organization you are hoping to work for. This not only requires commitment or a willingness to work harder than anyone else, but about channelling your energies to the maximum relevance, and consequent advantage, of your employer:

He was under no illusion about our management training programme and how hard it was going to be. He was not frightened to address his weaknesses. He has clearly done enough to warrant a 4 [the maximum score] because he has taken action and improved himself in key areas relevant to our cause. (Public Sector)

Proactivity in today's labour market is essentially about the regulation of oneself through making a career. Crucially this is achieved, 'through the creation and maintenance of a particular career mentality... to accomplish a "subjectivity base" for the right kind of action, including whatever is in line with the image, rhetoric and orchestration of social interaction deemed to be appropriate'.[9]

It is here where the now clichéd year-out experience, work experience, and extra-curricular activities come to the fore. Where it was once enough to have simply suggested one has travelled the world and been subject to different cultural and personal experiences, the onus is on the individual candidate to demonstrate how these experiences have developed him or her to such an extent that they have the necessary 'experience' and 'initiative' to make certain social situations work in their favour. Where it was once enough to simply state that one had canoed up the Khyber backwards, one now has to demonstrate the individual competences, which have been acquired and developed through undertaking such an exercise, *and* how they relate to the required competencies being sought by the organization one was hoping to work for. This is not always an easy task. Assessors are often able to see through candidates who overuse or stretch just a little too far certain previous experiences:

He's had quite a narrow experience of life thus far, hasn't he?

I agree. We've had just about all of the mileage out of his cricket club that we're gonna get, and, frankly, it's not enough. (Public Sector)

There was a definite tendency for him to focus on his time with Goldman Sachs. He used this in all of his examples and he was only there for three months of his life. It's all too structured and narrow for my liking. (Public Sector)

Failing to exude the appropriate level of proactivity at an assessment centre does not mean individuals are not proactive. But, as the often-used slogan suggests, employers cannot evaluate something they cannot see. Candidates have to demonstrate the 'right' qualities. You have to push yourself forward, be proactive, 'pushy' even—and this favours people who are seen to possess such qualities, and disadvantages those who do not:

She didn't understand what impact and influence was about. She thought it was assertiveness, which for her means *having* to stand on people's toes. There was very little evidence to demonstrate how she would be assertive and have an impact or any influence. She thinks it's about being aggressive—and she doesn't want to, I don't know what it is, she wants to 'belong', or something. There was no management or career drive—she just wants to 'find herself' on a management scheme. (Public Sector)

She thought more about others in the group than about herself as an individual. This was a real weakness. (Public Sector)

She looked to others to make the running.
Yeah, I was a 2 or 3 [out of 6].
I'm reluctant to hammer people in the first exercise, but... (Public Sector)

It is here where one's economy of experience can come back to haunt individuals if they cannot adequately construct a narrative of employability which conveys their proactivity. Many candidates make the mistake of turning up and thinking they merely need to list their extra-curricular activities: that having done them was enough. This strategy had a detrimental impact on their chances of success in the eyes of recruiters:

The whole year out thing is her weakness. Surely you'd know what you wanted to do after this? You wouldn't just stay in the UK: you'd bugger off and find yourself. She just hasn't demonstrated any drive. It's just not there. She doesn't know what her goal in life is or how to achieve it. She's had a whole year out and—na, no chance! (IT Consultants)

Acceptability: The New Body-Vocational

In knowledge-intensive organizations much of what they do is uncertain and difficult to evaluate, this is equally true for the way organizations identify managerial talent.[10] Organizations are simply left with the prospect of using 'surrogate indicators' to measure the qualities of their performance, and the attributes they require of individuals. Much of what knowledge workers do is highly symbolic and fluid in nature. Given the absence in many instances of any tangible output with measurable characteristics, many turn to the 'social fit' of the subject as opposed to what they produce or what they do.[11] Indeed, as we have already argued the way things get done is inseparable from the end product. This raises the importance of what Michel Foucault describes as 'the technologies of the self', one of which:

permit[s] individuals to effect by their own means or with the help of others a certain number of operations on their own bodies and souls, thoughts, conduct, and way of being, so as to transform themselves in order to attain a certain state of happiness, purity, wisdom, perfection, or immortality.[12]

It is how individuals use 'their own means with the help of others' that has preoccupied us during our analysis of assessment centres. A crucial and under-researched influence on the outcome of the decisions made by assessors revolves around the so-called labour of aesthetics in which organizations take an increasing interest in the management of feeling achieved through the selection of individuals with certain dispositions by paying special attention to their personal and emotional characteristics.[13] These attributes of people are captured by focusing on their social behaviour, which, in turn, is shaped by their embodied dispositions—how they speak, stand, walk, think, feel, or look.[14] The premium placed on social capital in knowledge work—our networks and trust with clients—also increases the importance of having those embodied dispositions deemed *acceptable* in the conduct of performing knowledge work:

What we want now is someone who is very bright. To be a partner you can't just be bright academically you have to be very commercial and go out there and win the clients. So what I am saying is what we are looking for now is we are trying to up the ante of quality of graduates we get through the door. But to be partner track you would have to be able to get your clients, keep your clients and have that 'umph' that you can't actually just find. (Accountancy)

Organizations are effectively recruiting a particular aesthetic experience for their colleagues, customers, and clients by paying a premium for the appropriate personal capital. The way somebody looks, thinks, talks, walks, and acts in certain situations, and, crucially, embodies these dispositions are precisely what assessment centres investigate. Having the 'right' personal capital is crucial to organizations engaged in knowledge work as its management involves little, if any, direct control. Those involved need to have internalized those forms of cultural and disciplinary conduct and self-control viewed by knowledge-based organizations as essential to be a modern-day and team-based knowledge worker.[15]

Acceptability involves recruiting those types of individuals who best 'fit' with the social norms or ethos of the recruiting organization. Due to the ambiguity of knowledge work it is crucial to regulate the identity of workers as those who can 'cope with the strains of—and exploit the possibilities associated with—the indeterminacies in this kind of work and organization'.[16] Moreover, one has to be able to convey 'that something rational, sensible and valuable is being accomplished'. Such symbolism involves certain personal skills that exude competence and instil a feeling of security within the hearts and minds of those purchasing the knowledge work on offer. It is about personal confidence in certain, highly pressured social situations. One has to embody and 'perform' the new *body-vocational*. One of our recruiting companies put this succinctly:

You have to remember that these people are walking into organizations and asking for hundreds of millions of pounds in investment. If they are tongue-tied, lack social skills, cannot handle themselves in certain situations, you cannot expect potential clients to be instilled with a great degree of confidence in what they are seeing and hearing...You just have to have the right kind of social skills to bring these kinds of deals off. You've either got it—and we'll see it—or you haven't...I cannot define it. You just feel it, sense it. You know it when you see it. And you know when it's not there, as well. (Pharmaceuticals)

An instinctive sense of whether a candidate is acceptable was not uncommon among the employers and recruiters we spoke to:

Isn't it funny because most people you ask in this business will say to you and they fully believe that when they walk in the door I know the good ones, and people from the business will tell you this as well. Why do we go through all this business [assessment centres]? I know them as soon as I meet them—the good graduates—and there is a small part of me [which thinks] that if you are experienced enough instinct goes a long way and it has got something to do with cultural issues as well you just have an innate sense. (Retail Banking)

Despite this emphasis on instinct or personal chemistry employers denied they were recruiting in their own image or that those from lower social economic background or ethnic minorities were less acceptable than white middle-class men or women:

If people from the sort of ethnic minority groups have this perception that basically the management scheme is for white males who have been to Oxbridge, then that is bad news because they are going to select themselves out, and we want the best people from the minority communities to come in. We don't actually have a problem and we get loads and loads of good female applicants from Oxbridge and other places. (Public Sector)

Within the same organization it was, however, recognized that some ethnic minority applicants were less acceptable because they relied too heavily on their academic achievements, and therefore failed to manage their employability in an acceptable fashion:

I have certainly found that amongst ethnic minority candidates that they tend to think that, or put it another way, they tend to feel that having brilliant academic credentials is all they need. I mean, this is probably changing but certainly if you go back five years then that was a very prevalent view that as long as they had got their straight A's then they thought that was their passport and as we know lots of studies have shown that actually that is just your entry ticket into the parade and it is then what you do with those academic credentials that counts. (Public Sector)

It is, perhaps, not surprising that one of the assessors in a different organization told us 'ethnic minorities in management still find it a hostile environment'. Most of the employers rejected any reference to cloning or recruiting in the image of senior managers. Over the last decade organizations have become more politically sensitive about issues of cultural diversity that has led to a relative reluctance on the part of employers to explicate the dimensions of acceptability in the same way as they do for the other criteria of employability. As a leading business consultancy observed when asked if they recruit in their own image:

It depends on whose image, but if you mean in the image of the senior people in terms of basic ability and competencies, yes, but we would be missing a trick if we were not recognising the rate of change that faces us in our commercial market and the different array of clients we have to face. (Business Consultants)

Our evidence would lead us to doubt that issues of diversity are leading to a transformation in the kinds of people who are socially acceptable for these kinds of jobs. But several employers believed that things had changed. They were willing to admit that they used to recruit on whether their face fitted with the organization, whereas now they stick to measuring the appropriate competences:

People like us sort of syndrome...we are trying to do a lot to get rid of the blue eyes, or the people like us factor, maintaining the old school. (Public Sector)

We've been quite strategic now and actually sat down and talked about what we are looking for and how to identify it. Last year we said we'll just take you in if we like you. It came down to the partners interview . . . I was saying 'she's so nice and everyone really liked her' and the partner I was doing it with said 'but that is the whole point of doing this because we wanted to get away from taking on people we really like and having people that can do the job as well as be really nice.' (Accountancy)

Despite the rhetoric of competence, issues of appearance, social fit, and personal chemistry have, if anything, become more important. While there is much anecdotal evidence in the recruitment world that is suggestive of the importance of social fit and although employers played this down we have enough evidence to suggest that such social considerations remain the defining feature of acceptability.[17]

One leading public sector organization explained why many of their best candidates came from Oxbridge. They are not just intellectually able but also receive the appropriate social education. It is also felt that those candidates with the same 'package of skills' from other universities are more likely to be attracted by the glamour and glitz of the private sector:

There is a very high intellectual hurdle that everybody has to get over in order to get into Oxbridge so almost everybody gets straight A's at A-level to get to Oxbridge and the ones who come to us, very rarely have less then a 2 : 1, even though we only specify they need a 2 : 2.

So there is undoubtedly intellectual quality but over and above that in order to get to Oxbridge these days, they have also got to have very good personal qualities and Oxbridge is one of the only universities that still does the interview system to get people in the first place. So they are not only intellectually good but they are also highly selected in terms of the other criteria that we are looking for as well, so they really are a good group of candidates.

Now, obviously you get some candidates at other universities who have got that package of skills and competencies but there aren't as many of them in the other universities and my doubt, and I have got no evidence for this other than hunch, and I think this applies to candidates from ethnic minority backgrounds too. The very brightest of those from the non-Oxbridge universities tend to go for other careers which are perhaps more established professions like the obvious ones, medicine, dentistry, law etc etc. or major public companies that they have heard of and like the sound of, in the business world, lots of money, expense account, that sounds good to me!

Such views confirm the importance graduates attached to university status, social background and social confidence in the competition for jobs whether Players or Purists. They were also correct in recognizing the value attached to appearance, accent, and appropriate behaviour. Far from shattering the urban myth surrounding self-presentation, we want to underline here its importance. For example, in the retail sector companies graded individuals on their *first impression, such as* 'Well groomed and smart personal appearance'. But this is not restricted to retail:

I thought it was a very nice, new M&S suit and he'd also bought some very nice new shoes—the first day back at school routine. (IT Consultants)

In terms of acceptability recruiters also had to make decisions about candidates that did not match up to the appropriate dress code:

If it's something we can fix like their tie is squiffy, or they've got an earring then we would put on the form, 'Needs to work on appearance, but this can be fixed.' If its more difficult to fix we tend to say no. (Accountants)

Finally, here is another example to provide a flavour of what we saw, heard, and smelt!

This is the guy with really bad BO. I found the smell unbearable. Somebody is going to have to tell him about personal hygiene in the feedback. We can't put him in front of a client smelling like that. (IT Consultants)

Part Two: Winners and Losers

While the rhetoric of competence offers an insight into the way employers understand and evaluate the strengths and weaknesses of individual candidates in the recruitment process, we have so far limited ourselves to general accounts by employers rather than to the workings of the recruitment process. In the following discussion we get much closer to what actually happens at assessment centres, and how the employability of individual candidates comes to be judged in different ways. Much of what is presented below is derived from our detailed observations of assessment centres, and especially from the 'washing-up' sessions at the end of the processes when assessors spoke

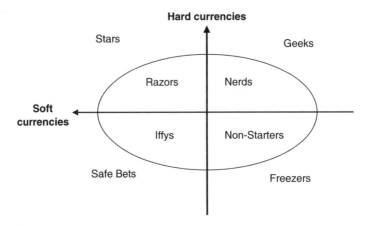

Fig. 7.1 Employers' mental constructs of employability

candidly about the performance of individuals they had been asked to observe.

Figure 7.1 illustrates the different categories into which employers allocate candidates during an assessment centre. We do not lay claim here to being able to look inside the minds of employers. These categories simply capture the conversations and notes made about individuals we have heard and read during the assessment centres we attended. The terms used here are not necessarily the same as those used in any systematic way by assessors. Rather they represent our attempt to capture the mental constructs through which employers judge the performance of individual candidates relative to others.[18]

Some further explanation of Figure 7.1 is required. The vertical axis represents employers' evaluations of candidates' hard currencies of employability—educational qualifications and formal achievements. These observations are principally made before meeting an individual at an assessment centre, whether in relation to the short-listing of the candidate or immediately at the start of a recruitment event to enable assessors to establish the formal achievements of an individual. This often takes the form of a potted summary of a candidate's *curriculum vitae* covering education, employment experience, wider interests, a summary of their referees' comments, and perhaps other additional information, which usually comprised of a short summary evaluating the contents of the *curriculum vitae* against the competencies sought by the selecting organization.

The horizontal axis represents employers' evaluations of what we have referred to as the soft currencies of employability that relate to the personal and aesthetic skills of candidates. In the *Science of Gut Feeling* we showed that these evaluations cannot be presented as anything but subjective. Far from an objective 'reading-off' of individual employability, this evaluation relied heavily on the expertise and experience of assessors. As described in that chapter extensive notes of the observed behaviour of candidates are made during assessment centre exercises by the recruiters. These summaries were then transferred onto a summary sheet reviewing and highlighting the views of the assessors of a candidate's performance against specific competences deemed important to the recruiting organization.

By way of an example, *Stars* are those candidates who are viewed as having high levels of ability and individual achievement (hard currencies of employability) typically high grades at GCSE and A Level and a minimum of an upper-second degree, together with a rounded education with a number of wider experiences (e.g. captaincy, senior student, debating society chair, sporting achievements, international travel, etc.). Stars are also seen as having excellent soft skills—evinced by their interpersonal sensitivity, persuasiveness, emotional resilience, personal presence, management of people skills, teamworking—to name some of the soft currencies our case study companies were evaluating. The Stars are, therefore, defined as offering the complete package that employers are looking to identify. Whether a candidate is defined as a Star rather than a *Safe Bet*, a *Razor*, or a *Freezer*, will depend on this combination of hard and soft skills. It depends on how employers 'make up' an overall picture of the individuals, including an evaluation of each candidate's authenticity.

The inner-circle in the centre of Figure 7.1 is our way of highlighting the fine line between success and failure. The distinction between a Star and a Razor illustrates how easy it is for potential Stars to be defined as too pushy or wanting to stand out from the crowd at the expense of others. They may be seen to put themselves forward in ways that are judged to be detrimental to the performance of the group dynamics: to be 'too sharp for their own good', hence the label Razor. Whereas Non-starters are negatively judged as out of their depth often leading to complaints from assessors that they should never have been invited to an assessment centre, the Freezers represents a charitable interpretation of poor performance. These candidates may have said little or been 'fazed' by the event due to nerves or lack of experience. Either way Freezers and Non-starters will not be offered employment. We will now illustrate each of the categories identified in Figure 7.1 to elucidate how it is that some win while others lose.

Stars—Reach for the Stars

It seems appropriate to begin with the success stories! Stars are individuals with good, if not excellent, educational biographies. They combine this high level of hard currency with an abundance of soft skills. Crucially, they are able to demonstrate their employability with plenty to spare. The Stars have it all:

> She's sensitive to others, has energy, enthusiastic, meets deadlines and achieves where others might think she is weak. She develops herself in perceived weaknesses incredibly well. She explores data in depth, shows sound judgement and is persuasive in group discussions. (Public Sector)

Their high levels of hard currencies more than demonstrate the formal aspects of their suitability. Consider, for example, the following educational biography of a Star candidate:

Education & Work Experience
- 10 GCSE passes, 9 at A*
- 5 GCSE A Level passes—all at grade A
- Economics (*Cambridge University*)
- MSc Political Economy (London School of Economics)
- Placement with leading merchant bank
- Excelled in sporting achievements at county standard.

The right qualifications are not enough to be a Star. You have to be able to 'talk-with-competence'. For employers this means living up to their expectations of you in person, which, as we have seen, can be artificially inflated for those with better hard currencies than most. A primary hallmark of the Star, then, is effective communication:

> I thought his communication skills were excellent. He asked, 'Can you understand that? Am I labouring the point?' He was making sure I could understand him, that he was being clear enough. Really good, a pleasure to talk to him. (Public Sector)

He said that he would look to develop his communication skills by obtaining feedback from his mentors and line managers to enable him to develop more quickly. (Pharmaceuticals)

He was very coherent and very strong analytically—the LSE's influence. He was very good on the topics I hit him with. I enjoyed having the conversation with him. (Public Sector)

Of course, communication skills are not simply about what you say. They are also about how you listen, what kind of impression you give to the assessors when you are listening to others—assessors or candidates— when they are speaking:

She always contributed, listened, never interrupted, nodded, smiled. She could challenge people, but in a nice way. She was always ready to compromise. (Public Sector)

Stars are also exceptionally adept at conveying their proactivity. As we have already seen above, this does not mean demonstrating simply how hard one will work for an organization. It is about commitment and channelled energy that reveals a certain rational approach to career management:

He was also proactive because he applied not just once but twice, having been rejected first time round. This shows real commitment and drive towards achieving his career. (Public Sector)

Many organizations now focus heavily on the commitment of an individual to their cause. This was once the hallmark of public sector organizations keen to establish a sense of commitment to the 'public cause', or within medicine or the law, where long and arduous hours of study over many years test the conviction of even the most focused of individuals. For private companies, commitment was largely in relation to the burning issue of employee retention. Faced with a large bill for first recruiting and then developing an individual, the last thing these organizations wanted was for an expensively acquired and trained individual to go and work for the competition. Stars were very good at conveying this level of commitment—even though we will never know if it was genuine!:

She really wants to work for us; it's obvious. She's done her homework, knows all about us and has thought very seriously about what she can offer to us. She hasn't just turned up and rattled off her skills list. She's weaved her way into our way of doing things. (Pharmaceuticals)

Shines in personal skills and amazing drive. Twenty hours a day is nothing to her. (Public Sector)

This proactivity could also be seen within interviews during which it would be discussed how candidates felt they had performed during assessment exercises. Individuals are even allowed to make mistakes in these exercises—shattering a popular myth many have about these events, providing that they recognize those mistakes on their own initiative and, crucially, say how they might go about rectifying those mistakes during interview:

He said that if he could do anything differently in the group exercises he wouldn't have sat back quite as much as he did in the first exercise. He already knew this, he didn't need prompting. (Public Sector)

She does not see failure as failure but as a learning opportunity. (Public Sector)

The best examples, however, were still to be found in the public sector where genuine commitment and a high degree of personal proactivity are demanded. While there is room for errors, only a certain degree of latitude is afforded to candidates who ultimately have to demonstrate they understand the *modus operandi* of the organization they are applying to:

At the end of the day he has clearly demonstrated that he understood that delivering an excellent service and benefiting others is what it's all about. (Public Sector)

He has it all really. He knows the discourse because he's worked for [us in another capacity]. He will hit the ground running. He's very strong analytically, and he's even practiced his numeracy for a year to make sure he got a 3 [out of 4]. He was very strong on impact and influence and managed to take set-backs during the assessment centre but just got on with it. He's got plenty of drive and wants to work in the public sector. (Public Sector)

The combination of excellent hard and soft currencies of employability enables Stars to construct excellent narratives of employability. It is here where Stars excel in their ability to combine their hard and soft currencies in such a way as to weave a narrative that speaks the language of the employer. In the following example, we see the discussion about one individual who amazed the assessors with her ability to 'tick-off' each of the organization's required skills in her descriptions of her university experience. But first her actual answers to some of the questions:

Can you provide me with some examples of when you have been in team situations?
Quite a few times, actually. In rowing I was 8-coxing. There is no one person in the team. I know it sounds corny, but ultimately if you don't work together you may as well not be there. This taught me how to trust other people. People have to do what they're responsible for. I can be responsible for myself and for them, and they have to be responsible for themselves.

Tell me about a time when you have faced a major challenge.
Living abroad. I had nothing planned. I had a tiny place and I wasn't in halls. I was living in this eight metre-squared box with dubious hygiene standards. I did not receive much in the way of constructive help from Cambridge. It was really difficult to get a student card because it's so bureaucratic in France. I had to face the bureaucratic challenges of living in France, and getting used to the attitudes of the French. It's quite scary because they have a go at you if you don't know what it is that you need to do. I can just remember saying to myself, 'Well, I've got this far, I'm not going back home without my student card.'

Just how impressed with these answers, and others offered by this candidate, are captured in the following extract from the discussion of her performance by assessors during the final washing-up session:

She's a bit of a star. She has good interpersonal skills with plenty of evidence to support this in her rowing, singing, employment. She can adapt in her coaching skills. I have 5's [out of 6] for everything, for drive—she decided against her school's advice, she adapted to life in Paris and coped with the ferocious bureaucracy there. She admitted to doing too much. She's one of those 'The more I do, the more I can' kind of people. She is very reflective, very self-aware, sees her own development and prioritises developmental issues. Outstanding. In fact, she is clearly a 6! She simply has a great story to tell. Singing has been her life. She throws herself into things—whether it's singing, rowing. If that's not drive I don't know what is. She loves change and can adapt to new things effortlessly, and she's completely committed to the public sector. She's a 'straight-6' candidate.

Razors: Too Sharp for Their Own Good

She came over wanting to be the one who just *had* to be 'The Boss'. I could see her walking around with a clipboard evaluating everybody and winding them up no end! (Retail Sector)

Razors epitomize the thin line between success and failure. They often have hard currencies similar to the Stars, but the Razors were seen to be 'over the top'. They were judged to be arrogant, pushy, or as trying too hard to impress. Assessors often referred to them as 'liking the sound of their own voice', dominating the conversation, and precluding the development of group exercises, designed to evaluate not just their skills, but also those of other candidates. In many ways the Razors exemplified the socially constructed nature of assessment centres—the performance of one or more candidates may be facilitated, or in this instance, precluded by what was seen as the over-domineering presence of a Razor.

Assessors looked at the way that candidates dealt with the competition between candidates that was bubbling under the surface, but often became visible during group exercises. The Razors were those who misjudge this competition, seeing group exercises, even interviews in some cases, as all or nothing social contexts during which they must 'win' an argument. The emphasis on winning at any cost did not go down well with assessors, especially when Razors effectively did the same to them as well as other candidates:

He didn't listen to anyone else at all. He closed me down during our one-to-one and returned to his own main argument. (Pharmaceuticals)

I had him down as a downward 3 [out of 6]. It was always, 'my perspective', 'I was advising', 'I advised'. There is a hierarchy with him at the top. (Public Sector)

He always kept to his brief but he was a bit brusk. He never checked to see if other people agreed. I had him down as a 2 [out of 6]. He tended to repeat what others were saying rather than changing track.
'Yes, I had him down as a 2, too.
'Very brusk—2. (Public Sector)

He should go into politics: far too opinionated and over-bearing. He had to say his piece, you could see him working up towards it. (Retail Sector)

He was just one of those people who had to say something before anybody else. (Retail Sector)

Despite their obvious intellectual abilities and personal achievements the Razors failed to demonstrate their interpersonal sensitivity or team approach that led to their rejection. The same abruptness with colleagues, clients, or customers was seen as counterproductive, hence their location within the inner-circle of Figure 7.1:

He rather abruptly asked people to restate a point.
Yes, I marked him down for that. I thought he was quite harsh.

He got quite agitated. 'Right', 'Right', I counted, I don't know how many times.
His work on his brief would push me up to a 3, though.

But he was stifling debate.
He contributed but he showed irritation when interrupted with 'Rights' peppered everywhere.

Two things made me like him, though. He contributed, and at times he clearly got them there. Otherwise the rest of the group wouldn't have stood a chance.
Just too abrupt with other members of the group. (Public Sector)

Did you notice how when somebody else tried to say something he would just raise his voice to block off any interruptions? The rest of the group clearly found this very irritating! (Pharmaceuticals)

If pushed we would be tempted to suggest the majority of Razors are in fact male. Nevertheless, we saw instances of women doing exactly the same, albeit less often:

I counted five different interruptions. Most of the time it was Crispin she interrupted, but it was just too much for me. She flatly interrupted him. Yes, she was almost taking advantage of her gender. He would give way to her for fear of being seen to talk over her, but I felt that she abused this on more than one occasion. (Pharmaceuticals)

One of our personal favourites was one individual, male this time, who had clearly decided the whole assessment process was scientifically flawed. While we were sympathetic in many ways to his obvious frustration with some of the techniques being used to differentiate himself from other very similar candidates, his insistence on arguing with the assessors did not leave him in a very good light with those who would be making decisions about his future professional career with the organization in question. During the final washing-up session the comments from assessors about this candidate were unforgiving:

He didn't agree with the [attitudinal test's] findings. He said he likes to be organized [the test had suggested otherwise] and that he was professional.
What about his resilience score?

Under pressure he pointed to his PhD supervisors asking him to present findings. He agreed he was tough-minded.
Oh my God! You mean he actually agreed with something we said?!

He's very goal oriented, probably to the cost of other things. He isn't terribly adaptable though. He was better yesterday than today.
Yeah, he compromised, but only on a very few occasions.

Agreed, he appears to abandon all reasoning under pressure. Everything goes out of the window!
It's been tough on the others in his team. He's been driving his own answers to the cost of everybody else.

[...]
In communication I thought he was good and clear, although he tended to interrupt a lot, and pointed to people all of the time, which really annoyed the others, and me.

Yes, he is very clear, but he doesn't listen, does he?
I thought he was patronising.

I thought he was a weak three [out of 5].
Yes, acceptable, just!

[...]
In teamwork he just didn't want to ask other people for help.
What was his team type?

He came out as detached—developer and a good analyser [according to the attitudinal test].
I would disagree with that! His participation was high, but it was not of high quality. He just tried to dominate the exercises.

He was totally against the [attitudinal test] during the feedback. It's the first time I've known anybody to disagree so openly with the results of the [attitudinal test]. He was very argumentative about it.
So we don't think he can handle the work place here? He hasn't got the skills to work here? No. I would not be happy with him working here. He sat there drilling into me with his eyes. He didn't smile, did he?

No. He'll just antagonise people.
Okay, a decline, then.

Safe Bets—The Bottom of the Top

In making their final decisions about who to appoint, the 'wash up' sessions where often dominated by those who fell in the lower-left hand quadrant of Figure 7.1. This included many of the candidates on the border line of employability. Most organizations are not only looking for the stars of the future, but a 'safe pair of hands' who will do a decent job for you and possibly shine in the future. As one graduate recruiter put it:

We are not just looking for the best out there. We also need solid people with solid jobs who can do a sterling job for us for the next 25 or 30 years at say £25,000 per year, max, before pensioning them off with a golden watch to say 'thank you for your service'. (Pharmaceuticals)

This is especially true in organizations selecting large numbers of graduates where employers do not want all of them clamouring at the door of the boardroom.

The Safe Bets were not viewed as the brightest and the best even though many of them went to 'good' universities. But they were viewed as competent. They had weaknesses as well as strengths but, overall, they were seen to be *employable* individuals able to carry out the work the organization required of them:

She was very much at the bottom of the top. She was pretty much 3s [out of a maximum of 4] right the way across the board. Anybody with a mixture of 3s and 4s would be above her. She was below the line numerically, but she was aware of this. She was insightful about what it entails to move from being a student to work and had a maturity that was more 'work' than 'student'. She wants to work for us. She will need help and career advice but we'll take her. (Public Sector)

Every one of her scores was above the threshold [of 3]. She got a 4 for the group exercise, although her in-tray exercise was too sweeping; she would have been better saying more with less. She interviewed very well, although she had a tendency to tear herself to shreds, very self-critical. She was incredibly nervous, and at one point when she was speaking she was close to tears but she is recommendable. (Public Sector)

The Safe Bets involved employers taking a gamble, but only when the chances of fulfilling the basic requirements of the appointment where judged to be high. The source of concern about the employability of Safe Bets was their uneven performance, where they exhibit strong performance on some measures of competences such as communication or analytical skills but at the same time fell down on others such as resilience or as lacking the necessary 'get up and go'.

Therefore, despite the rhetoric surrounding the war for talent, many organizations are still looking for people able to get the job done even if they are not judged as high flyers. Ultimately, whether somebody qualifies as a Safe Bet is epitomized in the following discussion of Jonathan. The deciding factors in appointing him to a managerial position were a good brain, evidence of potential and crucially, his perceived willingness to be 'one of the lads'. In other words he could fit into the organization without 'pissing off' colleagues, clients, or customers. Here is the exchange between two of the assessors (underlined and normal text) and umpired by the moderator (italicized).

What about Jonathan?
Not a bad interview.

I thought he just sat in the exercise and took notes.
Was he nervous, or above it, or couldn't be bothered?
I don't know.

He made just ten contributions in a twenty minutes exercise. I make a point that they should all be equal in terms of contribution, and he was well down. In many cases this is down to Steve dominating the group. I thought he'd have a lot more to say.
Technically sound; a good technical interview.
He's 22, got a First and has work experience at Rolls Royce.

I think he needs to get out more.
Smart lad.

I'm quite happy not saying anything in meetings. Maybe he's just happy to do that. I could give him the benefit of the doubt—it depends on what you want.
The fact we've got here 'A sound understanding,' may well have it. We'll never know unless we try.
He has the potential, then?
He's quite happy being 'one of the lads'.
A 'yes', then?'
Okay.

Spotting the Stars and, as we shall see below, the *Non-Starters*, is a relatively straightforward task for assessors. The majority of candidates, however, fall somewhere between these two categories. Many are seen as 'solid people' who can do a 'solid job' for an organization. For assessors, the task is one of deciding whether a candidate has the right combination of suitability, proactivity, and acceptability, which turns on a candidate's combination of hard and soft currencies. Ultimately, however, it comes down to how many vacancies remain compared to the number of candidates. The Safe Bets highlight the fact that employability is relative. A strong field of candidates would probably mean many Safe Bets would not be offered employment—and the downturn in graduate vacancies in recent years has probably exacerbated this affect. Nevertheless, in the good times, or at organizations perhaps not as glamorous as some of the traditional and well-known graduate recruitment opportunities remain.

It also depends on perceived performance on the day:

Difficult to get information out of, although technically, he's the best I've seen today.
He's a 'no'. He only scored three out of fifteen for his test: ninety out of one hundred would do better than him.

He was very quiet.
A 'no', then?
Agreed. (Pharmaceuticals)

This extract highlights how a number of candidates can demonstrate what assessors refer to as 'flashes of types of behaviour'. Sometimes this can be positive, sometimes negative. In the above example the student's technical ability is highly rated. The clinching attribute, once again, however, was not an objective measurement. In this case it was the candidate's lack of vocality—which is perceived as a lack of proactivity. It is this lack of theatrical persuasiveness that tilted the assessors one way as opposed to another. This example, and the many others like it which we saw, demonstrates just how fine a line some organizations draw when determining an individual's employability, which in some instances may turn on a 30-min exercise.

This may also help us to understand why some of the Players are at an advantage when small differences can determine whether one wins or loses. The Players are more likely to be attuned to the 'types of behaviour' employers are looking for and, therefore, more likely to exhibit 'flashes' of the appropriate behavioural competences. But an interesting question is whether these 'flashes' of employability are more likely to be interpreted in a positive light if exhibited from a women rather than a man, a white rather than black candidate, or a middle-class rather than a working-class contender. This is difficult to evaluate but when most candidates meet the technical requirements of the job, whether one is judged to be a Safe Bet often boils down to personal chemistry.

Iffys—So Close but Oh So Far

The Iffys represent a significant category as it incorporates many of those who lost out in the selection process. They were often judged to have clear strengths that brought them into contention as Safe Bets or even potential Stars but failed to convince assessors as 'you have to be across the board and not just clever'. Some of the Iffys were also seen to lack commitment, business awareness, or sufficient 'horse power':

His lack of knowledge reflected a lack of horse power, intellectual ability. He had not been bothered to find out and this lack of curiosity suggests that he is not up to the job. I couldn't see him with a group of senior colleagues, he wouldn't survive. (Public Sector)

This failure to convince employers of their employability was often interpreted as 'waffle'. While they could initially appear as plausible candidates, as group exercises unfolded it soon became apparent that some individuals simply had too much to say and what they did say 'did not add up to much':

Waffled too much. Always said the first thing in his head. (IT Consultants)

Too inclined to talk at length.
Yeah, he takes a breath just before the end of one sentence before launching into another.
He just repeats the same things but in different ways.
He was slightly persuasive but everything is done at length. (Public Sector)

There is a lack of conciseness which reduced his persuasiveness for me. (Public Sector)

Sometimes it was *so* long-winded, I couldn't actually follow the point that she was trying to make! (Public Sector)

I really liked Crispin. He listened to people. He was very sensitive to issues such as diversity. His main problem was that he just took up too much time. He was something of a nightmare to control in group-situations. It wasn't fair on other group members. (Public Sector)

You could see people switching-off as he talked, as the steam came out of his ears! (Public Sector)

His favourite phrase was, what was it, I've written it down somewhere, here it is, 'Let's find out, then. We need to find out. Shall we find out, then?' I would have just kept quiet had I been him! (IT Consultants)

What about her *persuasiveness* scores?
She didn't explain her main thesis. Dead bizarre! I didn't understand her, and nobody else did.
Between a 2 or 3 [out of 5], then?
I had a 3.
Me too. She didn't run with her ideas.
I liked her picking up what Robert had said.
Well, I'm sorry, but she waffled on a bit for me, so I'm a mean 2. (Pharmaceuticals)

Being defined as Iffy, in many ways, captures the different narratives utilized by employers to describe those individuals who were not just seen to be 'playing' the market place, but were seen to be playing it badly. They were trying to convey a narrative of employability that was simply not convincing. Or in some cases, led to a sufficient level of uncertainty that led assessors to conclude that the risk of appointment was too great. Iffys could not carry off the image or sense of self they were trying to portray to assessors. This failure to demonstrate one's employability manifested itself in many different ways. For example, a key stumbling block was that of a claimed commitment to the organization hosting the recruitment event through which employers tried to detect those who were genuine commitment from those who were 'faking it':

'I'm totally committed to you', she said, and then said she's applied for other different schemes. (Public Sector)

When I asked her what she might do to improve her performance on the basis of how things had gone she simply said she'd wait for the feedback from the assessment centre. There is a focus on what we do to some extent, but I felt there was very little depth to what she actually had to say, and there is so much more she could have said had she thought more deeply and clearly about what she might do. She hadn't in any way thought about what she would do after her training—it was all just aimed at getting the job and then doing something. (Public Sector)

What do you know about [IT Consultancy]?
Not as much as I should know. I was reading your web page yesterday.
So why apply? (IT Consultants)

You're not getting on with somebody at work. What would you do about it?
I'd speak to a manager.

But you're the manager. What would you do about it?
I'd speak to my manager.

And if that didn't work?
I'd speak to the person causing the problems. If this didn't work I'd meet up with my manager in private.

But if this person on your team is lagging behind and damaging your project what would you do?
Try and assist them, if it's possible, making sure it doesn't affect my workload, or speak to a manager.

So, what you're saying is that you, yourself, would do nothing, have no strategies for managing people, you'd just talk to your manager and expect them to sort it out?
Er, yes. (IT Consultants)

For the Purists the problem was a failure to convince assessors that they were the right person for the job, based on the presentation of oneself in the best possible light. The problem for the Players was a failure to sustain the personal 'self-image' or narrative of employability they had previously rehearsed. Instead of demonstrating 'consistency', employers saw flashes of what they were looking for but this was not sustained.

A favourite example of ours was the case of an individual candidate attending an assessment centre for a well-known retail store's management training programme mentioned in an earlier chapter. One of the assessors intimated to us that she was 'not convinced she was genuinely retail', had not done her research and was effectively 'trying to persuade us she's into retail when she's clearly not'. The assessor had decided to focus her hour-long interview with the candidate on establishing the candidate's level of commitment to the retail sector. The interview did not go well for the candidate:

So what makes you suitable for a job in a [Retail Company] store?
My own initiative, desire, ambition. I can give total commitment and enthusiasm, to put 110 per cent into the job.

Okay, but 110 per cent into what, exactly?
Er ...

What do you know about [Retail Company]?
You're a large department store, all around the country.

Anything else?
Uum...that you have been very successful of late.
[...]

Do you think you will be able to work on the shop floor?
I don't mind that. Ultimately, I want to work for a prestigious company that will push me forward, that I can make a contribution to. Some people just do their jobs and go home, but I won't.

What will you do?
Er

What would your ideal job be?
A [university] lecturer.

Why?
You get constant stimulation, there are always new areas opening up before you.

And how do you think [Retail Company] will deliver constant stimulation and new opportunities?
Erm
[...]

Do you have any questions?
What can you do for me?

What do you want us to do for you?
Er, development...and stuff. (Retail Sector)

Being Iffy is also manifest in the eyes of employers when confronted with candidates who deployed certain player strategies when they lacked a satisfactory answer to a question posed to them:

So what do you do at [current employer]?
I'm currently doing placements, but I cannot tell you very much for security reasons.
Okay, but how, then exactly, are you going to sell yourself to me? (IT Consultants)

In many ways he came over very well; I couldn't shut him up. He's been up Kilimanjaro, BAe are interested in him. He's not brilliant, bordering on solid. I just felt he had nothing original to offer to the exercises or conversations he was involved in. He just seemed to summarise what other people were saying and he talked over people a lot, not rudely, just because of an inability to remain silent. (IT Consultants)

The Iffys often had good social skills. They were often viewed as personable and well liked by others. Their problem was that they were judged to lack substance. They cannot evince the proactivity and commercially savvy attributes for which employers were looking for explicit signs. They were seen as reactive, lacking the knowledge required to make a contribution to a particular discussion in the same way as Stars or Safe Bets could. They often contradicted themselves in answers to successive questions deliberately designed to examine an individual's capability to be flexible and 'think on their feet'.

A telling example was a female Player who appeared to have it all: an upper-second class degree from Edinburgh University, schooled at an expensive private institution, Lacrosse team captain, experience of life in France, Spain, and India, spoke three languages, and had work experience at the British Broadcasting Company and the United Nations. She got off to a good start:

personable, smily...aware of the confidence and privileges of her background, but what we do is comment on what we've seen...the BBC stuff is all broadening her experience. Conscious of the public school background she wants to broaden her experience. The travel is not only done for family reasons but part of her, she needs cultural diversity.

But the female chair of assessors decided that 'she is terribly good at being able to present herself, rather than thinking on her feet'. The other assessors then began to focus on her analytical and teamworking skills. After the next group exercise negative evaluations came to the fore:

Maintained good eye contact, but at times confrontational...you can see the same evidence and come to different conclusions.
Obstructed the group a bit. Slow and repetitive when she got into things.
She is not happy about persuading on ideas rather than herself.
Appears not to be thinking on her feet. Her judgement is occasionally degraded.
I give it a 4!
What you describe there was more of a three [out of five].

In the final analysis this candidate was judged to be Iffy—a near miss!

Personal resilience good but intellectual resilience no.
She would be good in meetings but not able to write policy papers quickly, but I thought we might disagree about her...I think she would be very frustrated if she did join us.

Why this candidate was regarded as too risky was not altogether clear, as she appeared to meet virtually all the usual criteria for recruitment. There was however a feeling that she was a player whose career ambitions would lead her to leave the organization before the completion of the initial two-year training period.

But this example also suggests that coming from a privileged background did not give her an advantage. What sounds impressive on the surface is, in actual fact, discounted by assessors if it is nothing more than an account of where they have been or what they have done without being able to closely relate these experiences to the specific attributes recruiters are examining during the assessment centres:

She's been to Africa, nursed the leopards and has experienced life. But it's not as spectacular as it sounds. It's hardly as *Born Free* as it's cracked up to be. I found it quite hard to get tangible things that *mattered* out of her. (Public Sector)

I was disappointed with her account of the last 24 hours as she'd experienced it. When asked what she would do next she indicated that she wouldn't worry about the numeracy test or group exercises, even those things hadn't gone very well. She didn't relate her answers to her experience of the last 24 hours. (Public Sector)

In another example the candidate's social class experiences were defined as too narrow:

Some good work, but over-shadowed by his under-performance in relation to his curriculum vitae. He's not quite there on people skills and it is only in the analytical categories where he's done well. It all just seems too narrow, too well-schooled. (Public Sector)

Finally, some of those defined as Iffy also fell into that category because they were not sufficiently 'oven ready'. They come across as naïve or too idealistic. Waffle sometimes served as a code word for a lack of experience or confidence in self-presentation. It did not mean that they would never be employable like the Non-Starters. Some were judged to have the potential but were not sufficiently up to speed or lacked the 'across the board' competences that employers were looking for:

There is absolutely no way he is ready to work for us. He's a very big fish in a very small pool. He recognizes he needs more experience but he doesn't know what it is he wants to do. He knows what he doesn't want to do. It was summed up for me by his response to when I asked him why he wanted to work for us. He just said it was because he thought his friends would think it would be a laudable thing to do. He just shrugged his shoulders when I asked him about his management experience and what he might have to offer... He needs to go away and travel for a couple of years, acquire some experience and then come back to us. It isn't enough to have excelled at everything that has been imposed on him. He needs life-experience, people experience. (Public Sector)

It's a pity that the two people we've spent most of our time focussing on have really strong things to offer, but this is the fast-track and we do have standards. We'll suggest to both of them that they could re-apply in a couple of years' time. (Public Sector)

She has shown us evidence, and she has thought about what she'd do if she didn't get onto our management training scheme. But she's not at the stage of being able to reflect upon her experience. She's got potential; she's just a bit green. She simply fell down on her inability to reflect on the process individually.

Geeks—It's Cool to Be Geeky!

In many leading organizations being seen as a geek was far from cool, if fact you had no realistic chance of being appointed. But there are management jobs in the knowledge-based economy that do require a high level of technical ability where no amount of personal charisma will suffice. There is a market for *Geeks*—those who are passionate, one might even say obsessed with keeping up to date with the latest developments in information technology, or another chosen technically based subject area such as engineering, science, or mathematics. While not everybody recognizes what Bill Gates has done in terms of legitimizing the social acceptability of being a Geek, one of our case study companies, an IT-based consultancy, was unequivocal about the need for technical expertise:

First of all they need to have the technical skills, they need to have an academic grounding. Again because we are project based, we are different to most, we need an academic grounding, and I mean one in IT in specific. *You mean competence?*

Yes in IT. There we differ say from someone like IBM who will look at an academic level and then train them, because they will take a lot of technical people but they will also be more diverse at the disciplines they recruit from, but they operate internally in a different way. First of all they have to have that, for I would say 90 per cent of the positions. We do take some of what we call 'potentially bright bunnies', who might go into the UK Services where they might come from a business, management or marketing background and their roles would be more client facing straight away and more about understanding business straight away but that would certainly be 10 per cent. The other 90 per cent have to be technical because it is very likely that they will be programming, developing, protecting, or integrating software systems as a first role. That's the number one. (IT Consultants)

This organization clearly practised what it preached. During a discussion in a final washing-up session the assessors from this organization debated whether Dave, viewed as something of a 'boffin', was employable or not. As you will see, *Stark Trek* fans everywhere can rejoice:

He was very nervous during the interview.
Bit of a 'boffin', I thought.
He wasn't very good in interview, either.
I have a bit of a problem with him because he barely said anything to anyone during the coffee breaks.
His tutors say he's going to get a First and that's pretty much shown up by his 'Fast Track' performance scores.
He did okay in the group exercises, but he had his hand over his face all of the time. He was very nervous. But he's done okay, I *suppose.*
He could learn about the business, he's young.
Al, what do you reckon?
I have to admit, I asked him *the* 'boffin question'.
Oh, oh [*lots of laughing around the room*]
He's into science-fiction in a big way. I asked him 'What's the best between Star Wars and Star Trek?'
And?
He's a "Trekky".
[*jokingly*] He's in!
We'll come back to him.
No, let's give him the benefit of the doubt.
Okay.
Okay.
He's a 'yes'. (IT Consultants)

As if to prove this was not merely a one-off example, the very next candidate under discussion exemplified how some organizations at the technical end of the knowledge economy continuum require Geeks, and it also serves to highlights how employability is understood across different economic sectors:

Okay what about Dan then?
He's in the 96th percentile for his fast track exercise.
His interview by Al wasn't good though, was it?
I tried several avenues to try and get into business as well. He's a very technical person, but was clueless about business.

Tends to work alone, doesn't he?
He's 21 and young.
'Works with minimal supervision' according to his reference.
What's his degree in?
BA in Computer Sciences at Oxford. Straight A's at A-level.
I found it difficult to assess his exercise, though.
Technically very competent though. I'd have him.

What about if your bonus rested on him?
Oh, that makes me think! Technically he's very good. He's one of those you'd lock up in the cupboard.
Technically very good, but a bit of a risk.

But we need people who can churn out software.
What's he been like in the coffee breaks?
Not the most confident, but he's chatted.
Talk to Al in the morning [who by now has left the room], and I'll keep his folder here until you've spoken to him. He's a 'yes' unless Al convinces me otherwise. (IT Consultants)

These examples highlight again just how much leeway the assessors, themselves, have in making the final decision about an individual candidate's employability. In the first example, the individual is given the benefit of the doubt. The second example highlights how important technical skills can still be, but also illustrates the point we made above concerning the shifting balance between the hard and soft currencies of employability. Dan clearly has the technical skills required, an important point not lost on one of the assessors. The decision over the candidate's ultimate employability does not rest on his test scores, however. It comes down to his performance in coffee breaks, the impressionistic opinions assessors have formulated about his aesthetic performance during their brief encounters with him, or even watching him from afar. Ultimately, the decision will come down to whether one of the assessors, when asked the following morning, can think of a reason why he may not be acceptable. He is clearly suitable, proactive to a limited extent. But his employability turns ultimately on his social acceptability in the eyes of one of the assessors.

Nerds—Lock Them Up in a Cupboard

Nerds: an enthusiast whose interest is regarded as too technical or scientific and who seems obsessively wrapped up in it. A lack of social skills. (Oxford English Dictionary)

Underlining the importance of social acceptability is an additional category of candidates we heard about very rarely yet nevertheless, are alive and well and found in today's knowledge worker labour market. *Nerds* cannot be explained without reference to Geeks. Where the latter is seen as highly competent in a technical sense—gifted, even—a Nerd is simply somebody whose lack of social acceptability will preclude his or her ability to function within the highly team-based ethos of many IT or research-focused firms:

I think [an important issue] is, 'Will this person work well in a team?' If he or she—and you can have personalities which are very learned, or very strong opinions and the right opinions—they can be the brightest person in the world, but if they are going to piss somebody off on the team then you don't want them on it, because it just won't work. There are a few jobs where you can lock them in a cupboard and shove them a cord and bring it out at the end, but not that many. (IT Consultants)

Of course, the temptation is to simply point to a lack of social acceptability on the part of Nerds but this should not overlook the fact that they are also seen to lack suitability. Far from requiring just the technical skills to thrive in a highly technological-based environment such as the one presented by our IT Consultancy case study, suitability is also about business acumen. Nerds spend time in front of computer games, master programming, and a vast range of technological skills we could not even imagine, but they are seen to lack the ability to apply this very highly specialized knowledge to the business requirements of the organizations to whom they hope to sell their labour. This lack of commercial savvyness manifests itself in all sorts of ways:

He really does have an amazing brain on him.
Yes, agreed, but he's good at everything apart from the application of technology.
What was his degree in?
Maths and Astro Physics at Cambridge?

Great, but the only thing he could probably do for us is load *Microsoft Office* onto a machine.

He's scored well in terms of his CV, but failed on everything else, which is a bit surprising for a Cambridge graduate.

(IT Consultants)

What about John, then?

No.

No?

No.

Another classic case of a lot of ability and no application.

Freezers—Ah Bless

Returning to the final quadrant of Figure 7.1 we find the Freezers and the Non-Starters. Both were losers in the selection process. Freezers were the candidates who, with the best of intentions, did not perform at the assessment centre they attended. For some it was because they were very nervous, and to be fair to recruiters, they expressed sympathy for these individuals who just 'froze' on the day. In these circumstance there was little assessors could do because the whole rationale of the assessment process was based on observable behaviour. If there was little to observe there was little to judge, and as one assessor told us 'you can't conclude that they can't do it, only that they didn't do it'.

This does raise very important questions about the pressure young people are now being placed under; pressure which is being intensified by the increasing investment they and their parents are making in their university education, the value of which turns on the outcome of the recruitment events we have observed. Of course, employers simply suggest new recruits have to adjust to the stresses and strains of the pressures of working in a modern knowledge-based economy. But this is little compensation to those individuals to whom we spoke. We saw tears, frustration, and in some cases, real anger. But for the most part, Freezers were identified not by an outpouring of raw emotion, but by their inert body language:

He just curled up in the corner and said nothing. (Public Sector)

I can't say anything other than negative remarks because there is nothing to comment on. He contributed nothing to the exercise. (Retail)

She twitched a couple of times, but beyond that, nothing, really. (Public Sector)

Part of the problem for Freezers is the very language they used was interpreted as acquiescent and as evidence of a lack of resilience in difficult circumstances, such as 'I don't know, I could be wrong' or 'you don't have to agree with me but...' Far from exuding confidence, proactivity and commercial savvyness, Freezers lacked the social confidence that was an essential requirement for success. All of this did not go down well with assessors at recruitment events, who have little else to go on:

He was very quiet. BCD for his A-levels, so not so hot. A 'no'. (IT Consultants)

She was good yesterday, but she switched off today.
Yes, I've made that point too. She was good but just fizzled out for some reason. (Science Sector)

Perhaps she was tired or flagging? (Pharmaceuticals)

She's definitely not graduate training programme material.
Agreed, she didn't see herself as introverted when I talked her through the [attitudinal test]'s findings. But she, like a lot of others, just cannot see that her personality renders her completely ineffective in a work setting. She's very introverted. (Science Sector)

A bright chap. Just the communication problem. (Pharmaceuticals)

I thought she was very shy, so my feelings about her are mixed, she was very difficult to mark... She was initially interrupted—and then she didn't get her point of view across [and] she tended to be disregarded by the rest of the group. (Public Sector)

Non-Starters—Not at the Races

The Non-Starters have been included to complete the picture. This category refers to those who 'weren't at the races', they were never serious contenders. They were few in number and often led assessors to bemoan the fact that they had been allowed to proceed to the final stages of recruitment. Much of their behaviour resembled that of the Freezers but assessors were less charitable as to the reasons for their poor performance. The one exception that we witnessed during this research was a male candidate called Frank who decided to have a few drinks at the evening dinner with the female lead assessor and a senior corporate manager. A number of the candidates met in the bar an hour or so prior to the meal and during this period Frank consumed at least six pints of *Stella Artois*. At dinner he refused to drink the wine provided by the company in preference for eight malt whiskeys. After the dinner we all sat in the lounge where Frank regaled some of his fellow candidates with stories of his previous exploits when the lead assessor announced that she was retiring to catch up on her beauty sleep. Frank immediately turned and announced 'God, you should have gone hours ago!' Recognizing that this was not the most appropriate response he bent on one knee to propose marriage! Although candidates were told that the informal dinner was not part of the formal assessment, Frank's antics were circulated to all the assessors the following morning and he was labelled as a 'bit of a nutter'—a Non-Starter. In the absence of this misdemeanour he would probably have been recruited, as he performed well throughout the assessment centre exercises themselves!

Conclusion

There seems little doubt that the quality of decision-making in the graduate labour market has improved with the introduction of assessment centres. There are genuine attempts to relate candidates to predetermined behavioural competences, that move away from simply recruiting on the basis of the old school tie or family contacts, although these still have a powerful influence within elite labour markets. At the same time candidates are getting smarter at understanding how to play the recruitment game and we have clear evidence that the ability of recruiters to identify those who are 'faking it' is far from foolproof.

What is also striking about this analysis is how small differences, such as the way a candidate phrases a response to a particular question, can make the difference between success and failure. The sense of a lottery reflects our observation that many of the candidates were likes peas in a pod. There was often little to choose between them, despite the fact that some excelled and some froze. As previously noted most of the social selection had taken place at earlier phases in the selection process.

As the recruitment industry has become increasingly sophisticated it has done little to change the fact that winning depends on whether your face fits. Not withstanding all the talk about the lack of graduates with the appropriate skills, assessors often found it difficult to judge between candidates and no matter how much they try to dress up their decisions in the paraphernalia of science it often boils down to a subconscious feeling for which candidate one would rather work or socialise with. These subliminal inequalities lead us to connect with some people and not with others. And the tendency to recruit people who appear to be like ourselves, even if not in our own image, remains strong and always will do because work is a social context.

This reminds us that those candidates that seek to play the recruitment game will only succeed if they are able to make social connections with those assessing them, above and beyond their well-rehearsed narratives. And this usually depends on the same cultural props of class and ethnic privilege that characterized social elites in the past. The major change, if not minor revolution, in the graduate labour market has been the success of women from mainly privileged backgrounds to give their male contemporaries some serious competition.

Finally, what this chapter highlights is a new technology of rejection. There are now almost infinite grounds on which people can be legitimately rejected, in the face of serious market congestion where only a minority of highly qualified young adults can achieve the kinds of jobs that are the focus of this book. In the next chapter we examine these conclusions within a broader discussion of the management of talent in the twenty-first century.

8

The Wealth
of Talent

When one reads the speeches and reports of executives about the type of man that is required, one cannot avoid this simple conclusion: he must 'fit in' with those already at the top. This means that he must meet the expectations of his superiors and peers; that in personal manner and political view, in social ways and business style, he must be like those who are already in, and upon whose judgements his own success rests. If it is to count in the corporate career, talent, no matter how defined, must be discovered by one's talented superiors. It is in the nature of the morality of corporate accomplishment that those at the top do not and cannot admire that which they do not and cannot understand.

C. Wright Mills[1]

Introduction

This chapter will challenge the core assumptions that underpin the war for talent (WfT). The promise of greater organizational diversity and efforts to exploit the talents of all employees is not being met. Contrary to the view that organizations seek to exploit the talents of all their employees, more resources are being attached to a small minority of recruits destined for senior and executive management. They are given access to additional training, mentoring, and career opportunities that are denied to other well-qualified people even within the same organization.

Our conclusion is that many companies have yet to grasp the full implications of mass higher education, or in some cases, the requirements of knowledge-driven productivity. The major problem confronting organizations today is how to educate, select, and develop the wealth of talent now entering the job market with close to two decades of formal education.

It will be argued that the WfT is based on vestigial thinking associated with outdated views about the pool of talent. It privileges a Darwinian model of charismatic leadership where performance rather than knowledge or expertise is used to legitimate existing authority relations and the huge wage inequalities found in many American and British companies. This is despite the fact that a growing proportion of the workforce has professional credentials. The focus on recruitment and the talents of the few, rather than the training of the workforce as a whole, also underplays the importance of work context and the contribution of all employees irrespective of their position in the corporate pecking order. As O'Reilly and Pfeffer observe:

the unfortunate mathematical fact is that only 10 percent of the people are going to be in the top 10 percent. So, companies have a choice. They can all chase the same supposed talent. Or they can...build an organization that helps make it possible for regular folks to perform as if they were in the top 10 percent.[2]

Moreover, the WfT mindset cannot be explained purely in terms of ignorance or cultural inertia, it is also driven by 'positional' considerations within and beyond the organization. Elite recruitment strategies are fine-tuned to reputational concerns. Leading organizations not only want to recruit the best talent, but that they must be *seen* to recruit the best because it supports their claims to brand leadership. To understand why much of the wealth of talent lies dormant also requires an understanding of the vested interests of those in positions of power who have most to benefit from existing arrangements, which makes it difficult for organizations to break the mould.[3] Consequently, the corporate rhetoric of recruitment for diversity sits uncomfortably with the underlying cultural assumptions of many organizations.

Fundamental change will only be possible when these cultural and social barriers are challenged and overcome. The real WfT is how we make better use of the wealth of talent that is now being produced. This is not to ignore the huge waste of talent in Britain and the United States where around a quarter of children are living in relative poverty, but here our focus is on the fortunes of the fortunate. There needs to be a cultural revolution in the way talent is understood and how it is nurtured, along with a recognition of inherent limitations on its early identification, that casts considerable doubt on the rhetoric of scientific objectivity within the recruitment industry.

The elaboration of this argument is organized around four core assumptions that inform the WfT. We begin by challenging the view that organizations rise or fall on the contribution of a small cadre of top performers.

The Wrong Metaphor

Assumption 1:   The need for innovation and competitive advantage makes it even more important for organizations to recruit outstanding talent to contribute to the future leadership of modern organizations. The identification, recruitment and retention of outstanding talent has become a major source of competitive advantage.

A sense of crisis is typically evoked in an attempt to capture the attention of human resource professionals, battered in every direction by the protagonists of some new idea to win their organization a competitive advantage. The WfT is no exception.[4] In an earlier chapter we described how consultants at McKinsey's resorted to Churchill's war rhetoric, 'never in field of human conflict was so much owed, by so many, to so few'.[5] This they asserted was analogous to organizations in the twenty-first century, whose fate was in the hands of a few and to whom the majority of employees owed their economic welfare. Priority is given to getting the right people in the right places, adopting 'revolving door' employment policies. Corporate efficiency is achieved through the workplace equivalent of musical chairs. It encourages organizations to look for their salvation in astute hiring decisions within the wider job market rather than through the development of those already in the organization. This reflects the disease of short-termism, where the emphasis is on the maximization of share-holder value, rather than building competitive sustainability. It encourages the view that there is no time to cultivate anything, including what they espouse to be their most precious resource—people. It is not surprising, therefore, that companies such as Enron were used to exemplify 'best practice' from a WfT perspective. This is because it was blind to much of what is important within organizations such as integrity, trust, and loyalty.[6]

While it is true that companies in many sectors confront more international competition and the pace of technological innovation shows few signs of slowing, this does not in any way make it inevitable that companies need to shift to revolving door employment policies. What it does mean is that companies have to get smarter at using the talents, knowledge, and skills of the whole workforce in ways that enable them to remain flexible and innovative. This study highlights a major tension between the celebratory rhetoric of market individualism that drives the WfT, and the needs of businesses (rather than financial markets) to develop the productive capabilities of the workforce.

Many companies have become increasingly aware of the downside of downsizing and the market-driven workforce. There was a high degree of scepticism among those employers we interviewed about buying in able managers and executives as and when required. Most of the organizations we spoke to saw the importance of having a management team that was committed to the organization and that looked beyond the short term. In companies concerned about succession planning and the value of growing their own talent, the free agent mindset is an impediment to organizational performance. The metaphor of the WfT misrepresents the real issues for most organizations—how to nurture the talent that already exists in organizations along with the growing supply of highly educated labour.

This does not negate the importance of recruiting people with the appropriate skills, knowledge, and motivation to drive the organization forward. However, the performance of organizations is not only shaped by the calibre of employees but by the way organizations are structured. People can be institutionally encouraged or discouraged to develop or use their capabilities. If the bulk of the workforce is distrusted by senior management and given little discretion over their work, it is unlikely that these employees will demonstrate initiative and creative flair.[7]

However, the shift from a bureaucratic to flexible paradigm of organizational efficiency offers new opportunities to redefine cooperation and the foundations of trust relations in fast-moving, knowledge-driven organizations. Cooperation in high performance companies depends on the 'collective intelligence' of economic actors, as intellectual and emotional intelligence becomes a key feature of the learning, innovation, and productivity chain. In a knowledge-driven economy, characterized by rapid change, adequate job performance cannot easily rely on external controls, as people need to be proactive, solve problems, and work in teams that depend on institutional trust.[8]

There is a growing body of literature which suggests that in circumstances where employees are given room for individual discretion and see some point in what they are doing, they will show a strong tendency towards cooperation and competence rather than resistance and resentment. Daniel Goleman noted that the single most important element in what he called group intelligence was not the average IQ in the academic sense but social harmony, 'it is this ability to harmonize that, all other things being equal, will make one group especially talented, productive, and successful, and another—with members whose talent and skills are equal in other regards—do poorly'.[9] Talent has to be translated into high performance, it is not automatic. Companies, therefore, need to recruit good people but this is only a part of any success story.

Such evidence raises serious doubts about the WfT and its impact on the priorities for human resource professionals. As Jeffrey Pfeffer has noted:

companies that adopt a talent war mind set often wind up venerating outsiders and downplaying the talent already inside the company, set up competitive, zero sum dynamics that makes internal learning and knowledge transfer difficult, activate the self-fulfilling prophecy in the wrong direction, and create an attitude of arrogance instead of an attitude of wisdom.[10]

Talent: A Limited Commodity?

Assumption 2: There is a limited talent pool capable of rising to senior managerial positions that inevitably put companies in fierce competition to recruit the best'. Therefore, a key task is to make one's organization uniquely attractive to talent.

Not all employers subscribed to the view that there was a limited pool of talent, but it is a key assumption that underpins the WfT. To make sense of this view takes us beyond issues of organizational efficiency, to those of culture, authority, and legitimacy. What constitutes talent is always historically contingent. Like the concept of employability it depends on how one's talents are judged relative to others. It rests on being seen to have a special aptitude, skill, or asset that others do not exhibit. In an earlier chapter we showed the difficulties management theorists had defining talent, although this did not prevent them extolling their brand of management leadership.

A further problem is that talent has little meaning in the abstract. When we think about a talented footballer we do not focus on their kit or appearance but draw conclusions based on performance—the ability to play football, although this does not stop people spending hours in bars and cafes engaged in heated arguments about the relative merits of individual players. Such judgements are compounded when thinking about managerial talent because it is a team game with hundreds, if not thousands, of people involved in multiple functions.

What we understand as managerial talent has also changed as a result of organizational restructuring and changing business priorities. Consequently, we have shown how many organizations have become 'impatient'.[11] They want more than someone with potential; they want people who can 'hit the ground running'. They want people who can add immediate value. This may limit the talent pool for no other reason that many graduates may not be as 'oven ready' as companies would like. This is a rational approach in companies that adopt revolving door employment policies, where there is little consideration given to the medium-term requirements of the organization. But where issues of talent management are taken seriously it makes far less sense.

The changing definition of managerial talent also reflects the rise of mass higher education. In post-war Britain under 8 per cent of young adults entered higher education. These graduates were, by definition, regarded as a talented elite that reflected the limited pool of innate ability within society.[12] The education pyramid mirrored the separate streams within the corporate bureaucracies of the day. Hence, the jobs pyramid had distinct entry routes and career structures that were justified in terms of the manifest talents that university graduates had demonstrated in the education system.

The 'knowledge gap' between those recruited into managerial and professional jobs and the rest of the workforce legitimated differences in income, training, and career opportunities. But a paradox of the knowledge-driven economy is that recruitment depends far less on the knowledge of candidates as this gap has narrowed. This is not because knowledge is unimportant, but rather because many more people have entered the competition for these jobs and meet the knowledge requirements associated with a university degree.[13]

For the proponents of the WfT, the expansion of higher education has not increased the supply of talented managers because of the greater demands on managers and leaders in leading edge organizations. To admit a wealth of potential talent would raise questions about what organizations are doing to harness it. It would point a finger at organizations rather than individuals, and in a political climate where responsibility for employability rests squarely on the shoulders of individuals; it is not a view to be encouraged. It would also raise doubts both about the appropriate selection criteria, and what is being judged. Within Western culture inequalities based on natural differences are always easier to legitimate than those based on social circumstances, despite the fact that elites are not born but made.

At least some of the blame for graduate under-employment is directed at the universities who stand accused of failing to teach the appropriate employability skills or for 'dumbing down' their degrees in order to attract growing numbers of less able students.[14] While there are reasons to be concerned about the role of higher education, it would be ridiculous to argue that mass higher education amounted to the wholesale dumbing down of society. A more plausible alternative is that organizations have extended and widened their barriers to entry, in ways that go well beyond the requirements of the many jobs.

The rise of mass higher education has caused a legitimation crisis. The increasing proportion of the workforce with experience of higher education casts considerable doubt on innate explanations of managerial talent.[15] As a much larger proportion of young adults gained university qualifications, it has exploded one of the great myths of the industrial age, that there is a limited pool of talent capable of advanced academic study or capable of a career in management.[16] This suggests that what separates the winners and losers in the competition for tough-entry jobs are differences in social and cultural experiences and in the way they manage their employability. This raises awkward questions about the nature of managerial talent and what is it that makes those who are successful stand out from the rest?[17]

This should be a source of liberation for companies that are no longer restricted to recruit from the gene pool of previous elites. Yet, despite much talk about diversity as a new source of competitive advantage the discourse remains dominated by enduring concerns about the paucity of talent.

This returns us to the issue of positional conflict. What constitutes the best talent reflects the market considerations of both senior managers and organizations that are far removed from human capital accounts of the relationship between skills, jobs, and rewards. A further paradox of the knowledge-driven economy is that as the supply of knowledge workers increased the wage differentials between managers also grew. Flatter corporate structures should not disguise the fact that rewards are spread unevenly, with executive pay racing ahead of other categories of professionals and managers in many organizations. Arguments supporting the contribution of star performers are crucial to the legitimation of wage inequalities. Equally, the 'quality' of new appointments at all levels of the organization reflect the market power of those already in post. Where there is fierce competition from high calibre applicants it is seen to enhance the bargaining power of those already in the organization, who may be keenly aware of the need to optimize their job prospects beyond their present employer. Attempts to increase diversity will be resisted by existing employees when it is seen to dilute their labour market status.[18]

Contemplating the wealth of talent may, therefore, not only be bad for the wallets of senior managers and executives but also bad for their egos! Occupational elites have grown up believing that they are part of a cognitive elite. They have got to the top because they are brighter and better than the rest. To acknowledge that there is a much larger talent pool challenges their claim to elite status. Lasch claims that 'although hereditary advantages play an important part in the attainment of professional and managerial status' the new elite have 'to maintain the fiction that its power rests on intelligence alone. Hence it has little sense of ancestral gratitude or of an obligation to live up to responsibilities inherited from the past. It thinks of itself as a self-made elite owing its privileges exclusively to its own efforts'.[19]

The pool of talent is also artificially limited by companies for reasons of market reputation rather than limitations on the supply of able employees. Recruitment issues have become more important as organizations seek to benchmark themselves against their competitors. This has become a feature of the way companies 'brand' themselves, especially when they attempt to highlight the quality of their products. In many knowledge industries, including management consultancy, financial services, or IT solutions, the calibre of the workforce is an important indicator of its brand and reputational capital. It may be difficult to judge the quality of the service, but the perceived calibre of the consultants, and whether they are on the same wavelength as their clients, is an invaluable part of the knowledge and status claims of leading edge companies.

In such circumstances market leaders must be seen to attract and recruit the best talent. Despite the rhetoric of diversity, recruitment gets restricted to a small number of elite universities because they are assumed to have the most talented students. Elitism in education and the job market are mutually reinforcing as top universities report the labour market successes of their students to highlight the value of their credentials, which in turn is justified by the imputed quality of the students that attend that university.

At the same time some of the non-elite universities have introduced the most innovative curricula in line with business demands to enhance the employability skills of graduates, but as a recent report on such initiatives understates, 'paradoxically, those institutions at the forefront of employability development may be ignored by the larger graduate employers. It is true that recruitment practices are beginning to change, but higher education and employers still need to work together to overcome residual biases'.[20]

This is more than residual bias; it reflects the very essence of the new economy of knowledge. The wealth of talent is under-utilized by organizations for reasons that have little to do with the employability skills of individual graduates.

Companies are constantly alert to the manoeuvres of their competitors in the competition for the best candidates. These reputational considerations lead organizations to fish in the same ponds, despite the sea of talent that exists throughout the higher education sector and beyond. The reality is that many companies question the fast track but it is maintained more for positional rather than performance reasons. This leads to an absurd situation where companies are trying to outbid one another with promises of limitless opportunity, fun, and self-development that seem far removed from the realities of working life, even for those in privileged jobs.

Talent Spotting

Assumption 3: Modern recruitment techniques allow them to predict the star performers of the future.

A major problem with any form of early selection is the problem of assessing potential rather than actual performance. The fast track is justified because scientific recruitment methods enable them to identify the star performers of the future. This view is difficult to sustain for the reasons outlined in previous chapters. Basing recruitment on the behavioural evidence of people at the beginning of their working lives is ultimately inefficient and unfair. It extends the idea of employability from that of having the skills, knowledge, and commitment to do a particular job, to include the capacity to develop in ways that will also make them employable for senior managerial positions in the future. This has its legacy in the psychology of intelligence testing, where it was assumed that the 'educability' of an individual could be assessed at an early age through formal testing such as that previously used in Britain at the age of eleven. This assumes that people are hard wired in ways that are difficult to change, and therefore future potential can be predicted. It is wise to be sceptical about such ideas.

The productivity of employees depends on work context, which is difficult to predict before entering the workplace. Ghoshal and Bartlett point out that there is a high failure rate among managers in adapting to new job tasks in restructured and re-engineered organizations that underlines the importance of identifying selection criteria to help to predict success.[21] The problem is that these are very difficult to identify. They suggest that a universal 'leadership competency profile' does not adequately capture the range of abilities, skills, and work-styles required among different managerial functions such as operating-level entrepreneurs, senior-level developers, and top management leaders.[22] However, all the organizations involved in our study adopted very similar management profiles despite claims that they were based on the specific requirements of their organizations.

Ultimately, management is a concrete activity that involves communicating and working with others. In Robert Kelly's study of 'star performers' he argues that it is not high IQ, social or political skills, or even motivation and creativity, that held the key to successful performance but differences in the *way* we work.[23] It is how we adapt and develop the skills of teamworking, networking, and perspective that appear to stand out.[24] Again Ghoshal and Bartlett observe that even among those who seem ideally qualified in both personal qualities and by training and experience, many prove unequal to their new job. Some are simply unable to demonstrate the vital yet elusive skills that separate the merely satisfactory from the truly outstanding performers. The reason for much of this failure is that applied skills rely heavily on tacit understanding and capabilities that grow out of the interaction between an individual's embedded personal attitudes and traits and his or her accumulated knowledge and experience.[25]

Whether an individual develops this organizational savvy is extremely difficult to judge in advance. The ultimate problem with behavioural competences is that they attempt to deconstruct what seems to be important about effective managers and leaders and then 'make up' the ideal person for the job, but to use a culinary analogy, how do you un-bake a cake? Even if you could accurately identify the ingredients you would still not have the cake. It is how the ingredients fuse together that is of crucial importance. The sum is not only greater than the parts, but also qualitatively different from any of the basic ingredients. Equally, different environmental conditions will determine the texture and consistency of the finished product.

Again, sports fans know the problems associated with converting promise into star performance. Even footballers at the peak of their game can move clubs and under-perform due to a number of factors including their relationship with the coach and other players, style of play, lack of motivation, or 'culture' of the club. The same is true for club managers. Recruitment based on behavioural competence cannot overcome these problems. Indeed, the focus is on existing competences that are assumed to provide evidence of enduring dispositions such as resilience in difficult circumstances or evidence of 'get up and go'. At best this can offer clues to future performance rather than clear answers.

If the use of Player tactics is on the increase and if these tactics are often difficult for recruiters to identify, it further weakens the validity of the recruitment process and makes it even more difficult to predict future potential, although some of the companies in this study suggested that if people were able to play the selection process in a convincing way they probably had what it takes to survive in the modern business world.

The relationship between recruitment, performance, and productivity is also unclear. Most of the organizations we interviewed believed that many of those on the fast track would include the star performers of the future. They were viewed as a key investment in the future productivity and profitability of the company. However, such views were anecdotal rather than based on systematic evidence. This should not surprise us as human capital theorists simply assume that those who get paid the most must be the most productive because otherwise they would receive lower remuneration. This tautology maybe a comforting explanation for managers of human resources, but it does little to improve the efficiency of companies or a sense of justice.

Very few companies systematically track the performance and careers of their elite recruits, as one recruiter explained 'we seem to be doing a good job as we get very few complaints about the people we select'. But not getting complaints and selecting those that are most likely to add significant value to the company is an altogether different proposition. Again this should not surprise us as Mckinsey's own survey of 400 corporate officers across thirty-nine companies, found that only 26 per cent somewhat or strongly agreed that the board of directors really knows the strengths and weaknesses of their company's top 20–100 executives.[26]

An explanation for this lack of hard evidence is the desire to maintain the mystique of senior management, another is the practical problem of developing adequate measures of the productivity of individuals, especially as the companies depend on the collective efforts of numerous individuals, often working in teams where it is hard to disentangle who contributes what.[27] A further problem is that it is difficult to judge the performance of the fast-trackers relative to other employees, because one is not comparing like-with-like. Even if those on the fast track make rapid advancement within the company it is difficult to ascertain whether this is the result of the personal qualities of the individual or whether it reflects the extra training, mentoring, and advantageous promotion opportunities that they enjoy.

In relation to the productive capacity of the company this is related to an issue that rarely gets a hearing. The fast track may lead to high levels of demotivation among other graduate employees that have been ignored in calculations of 'value added' talent. Mass higher education inevitably means that a growing number of employees will have graduate qualifications, with only a few of these qualifying for the fast track.

Many of those overlooked for preferential treatment may feel that they have not been given a fair chance to prove their worth. That others have been given an unfair advantage because they have the 'gift of the gab' or because they went to the 'right university', rather than because they have superior knowledge or an outstanding record of performance. This will have a significant impact on motivation and retention. Much the same may also apply in the case of non-graduates who may witness younger workers being recruited to more senior positions with no knowledge of the business or proven track record. This issue has become more acute as there are fewer opportunities for career progression within flatter organizational structures. This makes initial recruitment decisions more important as they determine one's position in the organizational pecking order.

This issue was something that concerned Samantha who had recently been appointed to the management fast track of a leading high street retailer:

I've got quite a large team of employees, who I'm in charge of, and I find it quite hard . . . They've really put me in it. And I find there's a bit of an attitude within my store as to I'm a grad . . . Because you know, there's a guy who's in there for example who's an associate manager, and he's worked his way up for a number of years to get where he is, and I've waltzed in there, and I'm where he is after having no experience within the business—I've got no experience within retail really at all. And I'm in exactly the same position and on a better wage than him. And I find there's a bit of animosity. Like just the fact that I go up to head office quite a lot, and he's never been, he sort of gets like 'oh, Samantha's going up there again', you know. And it does put you in a privileged position, but at the same time I feel sometimes like it's a bit unfair, because I don't—I barely know how to use the till, and there're all these people who know their jobs better than I know their jobs, but I'm meant to go in and tell them what to do. And I find that really difficult.

Moreover, while those appointed to fast-track programmes need to demonstrate some managerial competence, it tells us little about the managerial potential of many of those graduates who do not get appointed at this level. During the selection process candidates are told that they are not in competition with others because recruitment decisions are based on benchmark standards so that it is theoretically possible for all those attending a particular assessment centre to be offered a job or alternatively no candidates may be judged to meet the required standard. Therefore if you meet the required standard you get recruited. Conversely, if one does not get appointed one cannot be up to the standard (without this assessment centres lose any claim to scientific rigour). The problem is that these benchmarks are not only set according to the requirements of the job, but also according to the number of applicants. Invariably there are many more candidates than positions to be filled, therefore a key role of the assessment centre is to legitimize the exclusion of candidates who may be perfectly capable of performing managerial functions and of advancement within the organization.

We have also shown that many selection decisions were not 'clear cut'. Who got recruited depended on marginal decisions (this is synonymous with the borderline between a lower and upper-second class mark over which university academics agonize). What determined such decisions was often arbitrary, such as a supporting comment from a senior assessor that took one candidate over the threshold, while another was not so fortunate. At the margins there were also frequent disparities between assessors, despite claims that the criteria for each competence could be clearly applied. In these circumstances small decisions have major consequences for individual life-chances.

The large stakes that companies are betting on a relatively small number of recruits, in terms of training, mentoring, and personal development also made it difficult for those doing the selecting to 'take risks' on people who would probably do a good job, but where doubts remained. When the competition for places is acute there is a tendency to recruit 'safe bets',[28] that is people they can trust. These have the personal and cultural capital consistent with those currently in senior managerial positions.

However, we should not conclude that social considerations must be avoided. We cannot make recruitment objective. Consideration of social fit is inevitable. The key question is not how we rid ourselves of social considerations, but how they can be understood in ways that lead to greater diversity. As De Geus has argued, in companies with a long-term future 'recruits are judged as much on the basis of their fit with the company's values and principles as they are on their ability to fulfil the technical requirements of the job'.[29] So how can we enhance organizational diversity?

Enhancing the Diversity of Talent

Assumption 4:   It is in the enlightened self-interest of companies to diversify their talent pool to ensure that they recruit the best.

In the search for outstanding talent it is assumed that leading organizations embrace individual differences as a source of competitive advantage. 'To maintain competitiveness, organizations must recruit, develop and promote on the basis of competence rather than group membership'.[30] The focus on competence is seen to be a way of advancing diversity, because it is believed to prevent recruitment in one's own image. Most of the organizations interviewed were acutely aware of the political sensitivity of cultural diversity and had explicit statements committing them to its development. Companies clearly wanted to avoid accusations of recruitment based on nepotism, as they sought to neutralize social considerations of all kinds. Recruitment staff ensured that minority groups were represented in the picture galleries of successful appointments that were a key feature of their promotional literature.

The reality was different. At the final stages of recruitment we were struck by the similarities rather than the differences between candidates. There were ethnic minority candidates, but these were often rejected for the reasons discussed in the previous chapter. There was no evidence of positive discrimination. In fact there was little evidence at all because most companies do not collect systematic data on the social backgrounds or the ethnicity of candidates. Even when this evidence was available it was not systematically analysed. The exceptions are usually found in the public sector where recruitment decisions are subjected to political scrutiny.

These issues do not begin or end at the plate glass doors of corporate buildings. They are woven into the fabric of the wider society. The greater diversity within higher education, for instance, is unlikely to lead to diversity in employer recruitment. The pecking order has not changed. We have argued that employers assume that the most talented students are found in the elite universities because they are the most difficult to enter and consequently attract the most talented young people. The top universities actively sponsor such ideas given their reputational concerns to be 'world class'. Such inequalities are now reinforced by differential fees that universities charge their students. This breeds institutional discrimination, as non-traditional students are more likely to find themselves in second chance universities for a host of reasons, including lower examination results, lack of cultural capital, and financial constraints.[31]

In some respects these are the lucky ones. The expansion of higher education has also been associated with a widening gap between the social classes. Those from professional backgrounds are over five times more likely to enter higher education as those from unskilled backgrounds.[32] To its credit the Labour government's report on higher education in England concluded:

This state of affairs cannot be tolerated in a civilised society. It wastes our national talent; and it is inherently socially unjust. We know that the roots of inequality are deep—in the education system, social class differences show themselves from the very earliest years ... We must do everything that can be done to make sure that everyone who has the potential to benefit from a university education has the opportunity to do so.[33]

But as long as leading edge companies target elite universities it will be difficult to extend access to those from less privileged backgrounds, as the middle and upper classes will use all the resources at their disposal to gain access to the top vocational prizes. Widening diversity maybe in the interests of society, but not in the interests of those from privileged families.

We have argued that policies aimed at extending diversity in the workplace have also to contend with the realities of the economy of knowledge. In key areas of the knowledge economy, including consultancy and business services, the value of the company is defined by knowledge claims. Smart buildings, smart cars, smart suits, smart talk, are all part of what is being sold. Such things are not part of the product but the product itself. This imposes limits on diversity when it is seen to conflict with the commercial interests of companies that is captured in an earlier quotation from a senior HR manager in investment banking when he suggested that you can't have diversity and recruit the best, there is inevitably a contradiction. In these circumstances doing a good job depends on looking the part, being at ease with clients, being a suitable ambassador of the company. This social embellishment of knowledge is what adds value to the product. The same basic ingredients can be served up in many different ways, and consultancy companies are the *nouvelle cuisine* of the knowledge economy.

These social and economic limits to diversifying the future upper-echelons of management are difficult to overcome, but this is not to say that things never change. The advances made by middle-class women in access to elite universities along with the managerial and professional fast track reflects an increase in gender diversity. But the fast track is a conservative force that severely limits the scope for further change.

When the number of places is extremely limited there is an inevitable tendency to opt for 'safe bets'. Risky candidates are often those who are socially or culturally distant from those who typically work in senior positions within the organization. An example was a young Asian woman whose parents were from China although she had lived in Britain for most of her life. She was rejected largely because she was diffident about challenging the decisions of senior managers in an interview that was intended to encourage candidates to question business decisions being taken by those in authority. One of the assessors noted 'I've got notes about cultural hang ups here, but I wasn't sure how to express them'. Without sensitivity to such cultural issues, or a legitimate way to discuss them, this candidate was unable to demonstrate her resilience, creativity, and drive in recruitment exercises.

In another example, an Oxford University candidate from a lower socio-economic background was rejected because there was evidence that she had felt socially uncomfortable alongside fellow students and staff in a well-heeled Oxford college, and therefore the assessors felt that she may feel equally uncomfortable with senior colleagues within the organization despite her obvious intellectual abilities. It was felt that she required further development that should be met at her own expense. Therefore, even if non-traditional students get to the final stages of recruitment they are at a disadvantage in socially negotiating their employability.[34]

The issue of diversity is difficult for assessment centres to handle. Recruitment based on competencies is premised on universal standards—matching the right person to the right job. They value uniformity over difference. In such circumstances diversity amounts to little more than offering all an opportunity to prove that they fit the requirements of the organization. Consequently, the privileges of background are beyond comment in the selection process; it is not permissible evidence. Best practice demands that assessors limit their comments to what they see or hear. But what they have seen or heard is the product of social experience packaged in personal capital and on display in interviews and group exercises. This is related to the additional problem that 'we can't conclude that they can't do it, only that they didn't do it', therefore they may have the potential but if it cannot be displayed 'on demand', it is assessed as equivalent to its absence.

In an *aide-memoir* to assessors at one of selection boards, it was noted that:

All descriptions of candidates should be clearly related to the competences sought in the candidates' profile. Reference to background, ethnicity, university, culture or age are best avoided, and should only be included where directly relevant to competences sought.

This is clearly a worthy sentiment as it is likely to rule out explicit discrimination, but it does not resolve the problem of making judgements that are drawn on underlying cultural assumptions. Silence does not make an organization an equal opportunities employer. There were genuine attempts to be fair to all candidates, despite the occasional reference to 'tin pot' universities or 'mumbling due to a Scottish accent'.

The problem is that much of the discrimination is indirect, that is, it is embedded in social institutions, such as material differences in family circumstances, the subject choices of males and females at school that exclude certain career options, or religious and cultural differences that may limit the scope for social experience among Muslim women. Moreover, a level playing field does not make the contestants equal. It does not give them an equal opportunity if they come to the game having followed different training regimes of variable quality.

We were left with the feeling that if organizations were serious about diversity they would not organize assessment centres in the way that they do. A concern to be 'scientific' in their approach was more important than thinking in new and imaginative ways of how to recruit for diversity. Indeed, the longer assessment events went on, the more they 'strained out' individual and social differences between candidates.

Despite all the talk about human resources being the most important thing for competitive advantage, it is typically a low status activity in many organizations. Responsibility for graduate recruitment was often in the hands of young women who had recently graduated from university but companies are unlikely to adopt the same approach in their finance departments. Those in senior managerial positions were felt by these colleagues to have less understanding of the skill requirements of the business. Senior staff tended to talk in generalities about recruiting 'the best' and maintaining or achieving standards of excellence. This often translated into recruiting from Oxbridge and other research universities where the leaders of the future were being groomed for succession. Some recruitment staff felt that these represented outmoded ideas about culture, management, and leadership.

Recruitment staff had a much better understanding of the limitations of such views. These staff had a better understanding of the immediate personnel requirements of the company as they worked closely with divisional managers in identifying graduate numbers for the subsequent year in each part of the business. This gap in understanding between senior management and recruitment staff reflected an age and gender gap, where most of the senior staff were older men. There was also some evidence to suggest that the benchmarking of competences gave recruitment staff a way of constraining senior managers from making arbitrary decisions based on appearance or whether the candidate's father was a member of the same golf club.

Our evidence suggests that conflicting cultural ideas and sentiments exist within the same organization. This does not undermine the value of assessment centres, but it transforms the assumptions on which they are based. They are best organized as a jury system where diversity is the best form of defence. This means that as much evidence is collected as possible that highlights the range of achievements, competences, and capabilities of each individual. These are assessed using a jury panel (assessment team) which recognizes diversity within it, based on age, gender, background, and ethnicity. The 'jurors' should also be involved in every aspect of the recruitment process including the final decision-making meeting.

But little will change until there is a major change in the model of organizational efficiency. This involves rethinking diversity. It is more than a question of ensuring social mix in terms of who gets recruited into tough-entry jobs. The profile of the winner's podium is important because western societies attach considerable importance to achievement based on individual merit rather than social background, gender, or the colour of one's skin. But we also need to rethink how the opportunities within organizations are structured as well as how they are distributed. As Teresa Rees has argued, the mainstreaming of diversity involves more than introducing policies that give people an equal chance to be a 'winner'.[35] It challenges the very nature of the game. Why are many organizations today based on a model of winner-takes-all?[36] How can we move to more inclusive organizational arrangements that recognize the talents and contribution of the majority rather than the few? Without a radical transformation even the most enlightened recruitment staff can do little to overcome the problem of cloning.

The mainstreaming of diversity suggests that the opposition between 'equal opportunities' and 'diversity' is misconceived.[37] The focus on equal opportunities represents the 'bread and butter' of diversity. Companies should collect systematic data about who applies and who gets recruited, alongside evidence about diversity and career progression for all employees and not only the privileged few. Without the focus on equal opportunities, diversity is so watered down to become meaningless. Employees share common social characteristics as well as individual differences. Class, gender, and racial inequalities within the wider society are also found in companies.[38] Therefore, the basic inequalities associated with class, gender, race, ethnicity, disability, and age need to be tackled on a number of fronts including legislation. The enlightened self-interest of employers is a poor substitute, as companies frequently lack the incentive to challenge the problems of recruitment and career development identified in this book.

The focus on diversity is also important because it goes beyond the standard dimensions of inequality, such as gender and race, to consider other differences that deserve consideration such as age, disability, religious affiliation, sexual orientation, and approaches to work. It correctly leads us to consider more than the make-up of the workforce, to examine the nature of worker identities and work activities. It rejects the view of workers as akin to cogs in a machine, in which personality, culture, and individual differences count for nothing.

There is considerable mileage in companies defining their approach in terms of ethical values, making diversity a reality rather than a broken promise. In innovative organizations, operating in multicultural societies, it not only means that the workforce is more likely to reflect their customer base, but that it also gives organizations the capacity to look at the same problems in different ways. Equally, there is little competitive advantage to be gained from being the same as competitors, despite the reputational considerations noted above.

From Sponsored Mobility to Contest Mobility

Given the increasing numbers of highly educated job seekers, inherent problems of identifying the 'star performers' of the future, and issues of diversity and equal opportunities, the management of talent within organizations should be based on a model of 'contest' rather than 'sponsored' mobility.[39] This would allow for a broader range of graduate entry, where progression depends on performance within the organization (this must also recognize the importance of career progression for ambitious employees that have not been to university).[40] Ralph Turner noted that:

> under *sponsored* mobility, elite recruits are chosen by the established elite or their agents, and elite status is *given* on the basis of some criterion of supposed merit and cannot be *taken* by any amount of effort or strategy. Upward mobility is like entry into a private club, where each candidate must be 'sponsored' by one or more of the members. Ultimately, the members grant or deny upward mobility on the basis of whether they judge the candidate to have the qualities that they wish to see in fellow members.[41]

This is similar to the fast track where the careers of successful candidates are 'sponsored' by the organization in ways that are not extended to other managers. Once recruited, members are sponsored within the organization which makes it difficult for others to compete for prized jobs irrespective of effort or performance. Sponsorship also begins on entry to the organization based on the assumption that the assessment process can pick 'winners'. Although sponsorship does not guarantee success, it offers a significant positional advantage, especially in organizations with flat hierarchies, offering relatively few opportunities for senior managerial positions.

In contrast, contest mobility is based on an open contest that reflects individual capabilities, efforts, and performance. It recognizes the limits of early selection and therefore abandons the fast track in favour of a broader recruitment strategy that does not pre-judge senior management potential. The assessment centres will continue to select 'raw' management material with an emphasis on diversity. Once recruited every attempt is made to create a level playing field that gives contestants a wide latitude in the strategies they adopt to achieve high performance. This may involve additional training, support, or mentoring to support employees from diverse backgrounds. However, the prize of a senior and executive managerial position remains in the hands of established elites to give out, but must be based on transparent criteria of performance rather than on elite sponsorship.[42]

A contest model cannot work if companies operate with a revolving door mentality, because it requires investment in a larger proportion of the workforce. It requires a people-centred approach that recognizes the potential of all rather than a few. It requires organizations to focus on the management of talent within their organizations rather than looking to the wider labour market to import talent when it is required. It also requires the reinvention of organizational careers if they are to overcome problems of retention and succession planning. These will not be like the bureaucratic careers of the past because they will be performance driven. Time-serving will offer little advantage unless it is combined with consistent high levels of performance. It may also involve organizations developing alliances for the exchange of staff and secondments to gain experience or where one organization is experiencing a downturn while another business growth.

The reinvention of careers will also require a psychological contract that recognizes the importance of both loyalty and security.[43] This is essential because the knowledge workers of the future must do their best to contribute to the organization while developing their employability and employers must be committed to the career development of all staff. There are good reasons for supposing that many employees would exchange loyalty for security, as it does not rule out the possibility of interesting work.[44]

Woodruffe notes that the rapid turnover of jobs among graduates may not only reflect the idea that 'the culture of moving on is endemic in fresh graduates', but that:

it seems quite possible that the need for graduates to move around is brought about by the way in which they feel underutilized by their first employers, rather than being a matter of immutable fact. An organization might put itself at a great advantage if it recruits high-quality people and ensures that they stay by meeting their needs.[45]

The point about careers is that they are not only of value to individuals in giving a sense of security and direction but they can also be a source of competitive advantage. The management of talent within the organization can be a source of 'flexibility' within rapidly innovative environments. Training involves preparing people to flourish in the social context of work which will vary according to such things as company ethos, culture, organization, size, and industrial sector. As Stasz observed, work context matters in the consideration of skill and performance. While communication, problem-solving, and team-working skills are identifiable in all jobs their nature and importance vary depending on the company.[46] These contextual differences are a vital part of what it means to be productive and can only be learnt 'on-the-job'. Hence, companies play a vital role in developing the individual and collective intelligence on which competitive capacity depends.[47]

The focus on careers would also mitigate Player behaviour to the extent that people would feel that they could advance by showing their 'true' worth. It would allow them to focus on growing within the job, rather than constantly evaluating the value of work activity in terms of its value in the wider job market. But career logjams in lean organizations will make it difficult to find an overall solution to frustration and Player behaviour. This will depend on companies enriching the work experience for the majority rather than the few. It will also require a reduction in status differentials and a narrowing of income inequalities which have now reached obscene proportions.

Conclusion

At the end of Chapter Four we suggested that the knowledge economy points in two directions—the WfT or the liberation of talent. The WfT focuses on the limited pool of outstanding talent that becomes even more important as companies compete on innovation, knowledge, and ideas. Although it is presented as symptomatic of the requirements of the new economy, and is seen to reflect the demands for change and innovation within organizations, it is a response deeply rooted in Western individualism.[48] This model sees employability as a measure of individual contribution and moral worth. It celebrates the Darwinian struggle for success and sees income inequalities as a fair reflection of market contribution. It assumes that organizations are driven by a small elite of leaders that stand head-and-shoulders above the rest of the workforce. It also supports the view that an elite should be identified and developed at an early stage. Once selected their mobility is 'sponsored' within the organization in preparation for the leadership roles they are expected to assume.

The liberation of talent begins with a different view of the knowledge economy. It recognizes that the problems of intelligence and knowledge have changed. There is not a limited pool of innate talent, but rather the major problem today is how to utilize the capabilities of the workforce. This calls for new ways of approaching the management of talent that reflects the fact that in the coming decade around half of all those entering the job market in many developed economies will be university graduates of one form or another. It calls for a 'contest' model of organizational mobility that widens access and broadens progression. This cannot be achieved without imaginative new thinking about the nature of careers.[49] One of the key lessons is that although recruitment issues are important they cannot compensate for the culture of organizations.

But whatever happens organizations will need to deal with the positional issues raised in this book. A contest model does not resolve these conflicts but it could be part of a transformation from the negative-sum game found in many organizations today where the rules of the jungle operate, to a positive-sum game where all derive some benefit even if people inevitably take on different organizational roles.[50]

This analysis leads us to conclude that recruitment for diversity is not an optional extra that can be bolted onto existing organizational structures. It requires a cultural revolution throughout the organization that must be led from the top. It is crucial that senior managers and executives have a better understanding of recruitment issues and challenge the cultural assumptions that may be working against the productivity of their businesses. They are not only being boxed in by outmoded cultural assumptions but they are also missing an opportunity to position themselves in new ways, for instance, being inclusive, open and socially responsible. This may be attractive to large numbers of high calibre graduates that want to work for a diverse, meritocratic, and socially responsible organization.

9

The Great Training Robbery[1]

There is . . . reason for concern about the personal well-being of the growing numbers who do not find that their investments in education are earning them the rewards they were taught to anticipate. The political consequences of latent discontent are not necessarily less threatening to democratic institutions that those of the noisier versions of American disaffection.

Ivar Berg

Peddling Employability

The argument in this book stands in stark contrast to the promise of employability in the knowledge economy—the promise of interesting, well-paid jobs for all those who are suitably qualified. Since the 1960s the proportion of students in higher education in Britain has increased at least fourfold and the proportion in managerial and professional jobs has more than doubled. Higher education has been transformed from the preserve of an elite to a mass pursuit. Many more people are in jobs labelled as managerial or professional. Despite this increase, the proportion of knowledge workers remains much lower than is often assumed and is well below the numbers required to absorb those leaving higher education.

Our analysis of occupational trends in Britain and the United States challenges policy assumptions about the growth in the demand for knowledge workers in the new economy. The problem remains that there are not enough high skilled, high waged jobs to go around. Studies have found up to 40 per cent of graduates in non-graduate work,[2] and this is likely to increase if the government reaches its target participation rate of 50 per cent. Starting incomes for graduates in Britain fell from an average of £13,422 in 2002 to £12,659 a year later.[3] In the United States much of the 'value added' attached to a university education is explained by the falling incomes of those with lower credentials. In other words, the investment in a university degree is a 'defensive' expenditure to reduce the prospect of declining wage levels.[4]

There is growing evidence that university graduates are confronting significant labour market congestion in the competition for fast-track jobs in leading edge organizations, where over twenty well-qualified graduates typically apply for each fast-track appointment. In such circumstances a university degree is rather like a mortgage endowment policy, past returns are no guarantee of future performance. Market conditions change. With many more people qualified for knowledge work the price of that work is likely to fall.

When markets become congested economic orthodoxy tells us that they will clear because supply with generate its own demand. When employers realize that there is a surplus of university graduates they will grow jobs to take advantage of this new pool of talent. But there is little evidence to support this view.[5] A key reason is that many British companies continue to profit from cheap prices rather than the higher skills associated with developing quality goods and services.[6] In a review of trends and future prospects, Ewart Keep reported a large-scale survey of employers that found that 60 per cent of firms had no immediate plans to move into new higher quality product or service areas with higher profit margins.[7] In these circumstances mass higher education is part of the problem rather than the solution, if its *raison d'etre* is to contribute to people's wallets and industrial competitiveness.

It is also difficult to predict the future consequences of economic globalisation. So far is has been low skilled, low waged jobs that have disappeared overseas, but there will be increasing pressures on knowledge workers as more high skilled jobs migrate to low waged countries.[8] This serves as a stark reminder of the duality of employability. The value of one's credentials depends on how one stands relative to others in the job market. Today, that job market is increasingly global.

Therefore, success in the job market not only depends on acquiring the hard and soft currencies of employability, but on the employability of others. The duality of employability highlights the inherent limits to supply-side policies as a way of extending occupational opportunities. Understanding the duality of employability is a necessary corrective to the overoptimism of the pundits of the knowledge economy and its impact on employment. The policy framework for the study of graduate employability needs to be reframed. The evolving system of mass higher education in the United Kingdom has intensified the mismatch between what is required to get a good job and what is required to do a good job. Many graduates may be employable but fail to find employment due to the 'over supply' of suitably qualified candidates.[9]

The focus of policy debates should, therefore, begin with a definition of individual employability that highlights the relative chances of acquiring and maintaining different kinds of employment. This definition focuses attention on the demand as well as the supply for graduate labour. The reality is that one can be employable and unemployed.

The scale of the policy challenge is difficult to exaggerate. If the British workforce is lined up according to how much they are paid, the person in the middle (median) has an annual income of £11,800.[10] If the target of getting half of all young people through university is achieved, there are going to be huge numbers of graduate on low incomes unless there is a massive increase in the number of jobs paying higher wages.

We are not suggesting that supply side issues are unimportant. Some graduates are poorly prepared for the realities of a competitive labour market and contemporary employment. But graduate employability needs to be understood as a public issue concerning the upgrading of the occupational structure and how to organize the competition for a livelihood.[11] This is despite the fact that those we talked to bought into individualistic explanations of success and failure.[12]

The way governments focus on raising universal standards rather than creating a level playing field in the competition for education and jobs, is a public issue of the utmost importance. It enables governments to talk about opportunities for all, and at the same time tolerate the privileges of the middle and upper classes within education, as it is assumed that there are good jobs for all those that reach the required threshold of employability. Again the reality is different, as more contestants enter the competition for tough-entry jobs, issues of equality of opportunity and meritocratic competition become more rather than less important. This has profound implications for the way equality of opportunity has been reduced to little more than equality of access, which ignores the reproduction of unequal life-chances and lifestyles.

Degrees of Worth: Why Some are More Equal Than Others

This book argues that it is misleading to generalize about the economic returns to higher education. More means different, not only in the way people experience university, but also in the value of their credentials in the labour market. Employers evaluate credentials according to the reputational capital they attach to the university or department from which they were issued. Leading employers have always targeted elite universities. Recent political sensitivity concerning issues of diversity led them to emphasize a widening of the talent pool from which to make their selection decisions, but the cost of administering vast numbers of applications has led employers to target their recruitment at those universities where they are most likely to receive applications from 'serious' contenders.[13] This has intensified the entry competition to elite universities.

The hierarchy of universities continues to be used as a key indicator of employability. It is assumed that the best graduates gravitate towards the elite universities. This view is actively promoted by leading universities as higher education has become a global business. The branding of universities and faculty members is integral to the organization of academic enquiry. Claims to world-class standards depend on attracting 'the best' academics and forming alliances with elite universities elsewhere in the world, while recruiting the 'right' kinds of students. Universities play the same reputational games as companies, because it is a logical consequence of market competition.[14]

Here, we find the tautology of privilege: The best students go to the best universities because they are the most difficult to get into. Therefore, no matter how much the university sector expands only a few can be 'the best'. Equally, no matter how much universities lower down the pecking order tailor their provision to develop the employability of their graduates, such activities will typically be seen as 'compensatory': an attempt to make up for the personal and social deficiencies that set them apart from the talent found in top universities. In these circumstances the top vocational prizes go to the graduates from elite universities (although there are exceptions). One leading employer in our research received over 14,000 applications for 400 places. Candidates applying from Oxford University were found to be 29 times more likely to get appointed than someone applying from a new (post-1992) university. This is despite the fact that the academic pecking order does not neatly map onto the hierarchy of managerial competence. First-class minds do not necessarily make first-class managers.

The education system is therefore limited in its capacity to improve the employability of large numbers of students because most universities are limited in their capacity to cultivate the personal and cultural capital required for fast-track appointments. The student profile of the education system tends to reflect the socio-economic make-up of society. The education system tends to reinforce rather than challenge the status quo, despite some evidence of long-range social mobility of those from working-class backgrounds or the challenge to gender or ethnic stereotyping. But less prestigious universities are severely limited in their power to change deep-rooted cultural assumptions that lead employers to stick to the established order of academic (and economic) worth.[15]

There is, however, genuine political concern that young people from disadvantaged backgrounds are failing to get into more prestigious universities at a time when Britain is developing its own 'Ivy League' of universities.[16] This has led to calls to make universities more accountable for their selection decisions. But it was shown that perennial issues of social inequalities in access to education and elite employment were compounded when employers attached greater significance to personal capital. Even gaining qualifications from elite universities is no guarantee of a good job. Credentials are assumed to signify the acquisition of knowledge, skills, and know-how, independent of the social circumstance, gender, or ethnicity of the credential holder.[17] The widening definition of employability to include both soft as well as hard currencies, is assumed at least within the dominant discourse, to signify a broader, work-related curriculum that is open to all through formal education. But we have argued that personal capital reflects the intricate thread of individual identity, human freedom, and social circumstances. Who we are and what we have done in our lives beyond education cannot be separated from employer judgements of our economic worth.

As a result policies aimed at improving the employability of graduates have little impact on the social and educational biographies of those recruited at the elite end of the graduate labour market, although the nature of recruitment has significantly changed. This suggests that a level playing field in the job market cannot be restricted to the competition for credentials, but must be extended to include the most fundamental inequalities in life experience. This has far-reaching consequences for policies of diversity and equal opportunity.

While this may help us to explain why some are more equal that others in the competition for tough-entry jobs, it also points to growing anxiety and insecurity within the middle classes. Those from more privileged backgrounds can no longer capitalize on their cultural backgrounds and 'extracurricular' activities (i.e. university club captain; voluntary work; or extensive travel during a gap year), unless packaged in ways that demonstrate the personal qualities that meet the range of managerial competences organizations have benchmarked as indicative of elite employability. The 'economy of experience' has to be packaged as a *narrative* of employability that must be sold to employers. This suggests a significant extension of economic rationality that extends beyond the credential. The economy of experience is no longer a passive consequence of living a privileged life or coming from a privileged background. It has to be 'worked at' as a reflexive project of the self where the things one does and how they are understood, is captured in terms of individual employability rather than intrinsic human experience.[18]

In sum, this study offered little sign of positive change in the nature of class inequalities. Gaining access to value-added credentials was always a problem for the working classes, but increasingly this is not enough as it has to be complemented by significant investment in personal capital that expose differential access to broader cultural resources (social education). But it does suggest that the elite has been broadened beyond Oxbridge to include other leading universities, but it is still an elite.[19] Equally, the stereotype of Oxbridge Man is no longer the gold standard in a number of organizations. The 'gentlemen' are losing out to female and male 'players' who combine elite credentials with other aspects of personal capital as employers look for 'cosmopolitans' rather than 'locals'.[20] Narrow class experiences, even those of the upper classes, may be discounted as lacking the flexibility to work in different social contexts.

Our focus on labour market entry confirms broader trends towards greater gender equality, although successful women in managerial and professional occupations tend to come from the middle classes. But this does not lead to the conclusion that gender inequalities have been resolved.[21] Much of the research evidence continues to show significant gender inequalities in terms of pay, promotion, and career development.[22] Barriers to senior managerial and professional jobs also hamper their progress, although the 'glass ceiling' is showing some signs of cracking. Cranfield University's annual review of female directors in the FTSE 100 companies, found that eighty-eight women held 101 directorships in 2003 compared to sixty-seven women holding seventy-nine similar positions in 1999. This represents about 12 per cent of the total, but they also found that only seventeen women were executive directors, less that 4 per cent of the total.[23]

People are Our Most Valuable Asset...

Employability policies have been driven by employer concerns that the education system is not delivering the kinds of employees they require. This is assumed to reflect the enlightened realization that business success depends on the knowledge, skills, and commitment of the workforce. Yet, trends in corporate governance, work redesign, and employment policies reveal quite the opposite. In recent decades corporate mission statements emphasize shareholder rather than stakeholder capitalism.[24] The overriding concern is to maximize returns to shareholders, over and above any concern for the interests of the workforce. Much of the restructuring of American and British business has been motivated by cost-cutting, leading to the downsizing of the workforce. Even at the height of the stock market boom at the end of the twentieth century, announcements of record profits were often accompanied by further cuts in the workforce, including managerial and professional workers.

Doing more with less became the order of the day. The need to deliver high rates of return to shareholders imposes a short-termism that encourages companies to use revolving door employment policies. There is little sense of cultivating people over time as they focus on the perennial short-term. In this commercial mood, employers have become impatient with the young and indifferent to the old. A job for life could no longer be tolerated and a commitment to organization careers was abandoned. Beginning workers must be 'oven ready' rather than 'home made'.

It is difficult to avoid the conclusion that employability is about shaping up for a world that is far removed from what most knowledge workers expect. It is also about the offloading of risks and responsibilities onto individuals. But this is not cost-free for employers. Companies may be losing out on huge potential for improved productivity. This is not a question of ignorance, although cultural inertia may play a part, but of priorities and vested interests.

The rise of mass higher education has not led to an abandonment of the fast track in favour of broader schemes of graduate entry. Indeed, our research suggested that many, although not all recruiters felt that the expansion of higher education had not significantly increased the pool of graduate talent. The emphasis on recruiting the best graduates, if anything, intensified the competition for a graduate elite with other leading employers. This finding was consistent with much of the literature on human resource management that highlighted the 'war for talent'.[25] Rather than liberate the talents and skills of all, the war for talent (WfT) asserted that the global knowledge economy increased the importance of exceptional performance by exceptional individuals. Being good is no longer good enough.

In many organizations the knowledge capabilities of employees are well in advance of the capabilities of companies to handle a large pool of higher educated workers. The corporate rhetoric of equal opportunities and diversity policies sits uncomfortably with the underlying cultural assumptions of business organization and efficiency. They remain locked into a set of cultural assumptions that have far-reaching implications for the way work is organized and rewarded. This goes beyond changing attitudes, as there are broader implications for authority, status, power, rewards, and career prospects. Despite much talk about corporate restructuring and transformations in models of organization efficiency, many companies exhibit vestiges of the 'factory' model.[26] Ideas about the limited pool of talent have not been swept away on a tide of educational expansion. On the contrary, the imagery of the WfT has been used to bolster the legitimacy of organizational elites.

Consequently, too much is being invested in too few on inadequate evidence. Although many recruiters expressed genuine concerns about widening diversity, the costs associated with each fast-track appointment encouraged the recruitment of 'safe bets': people like themselves who they could trust. Our analysis challenges this approach on several grounds including the problem of assessing future leadership potential on the basis of existing behavioural competence. We have shown how the assessment centre was given an aura of scientific objectivity through the formal assessment of behavioural competencies, but that this did not relieve recruitment staff from ultimately having to make subjective judgements about who to recruit.

A key role of the assessment centre was to legitimate the decision to reject as well as to hire individual candidates. But while they cannot predict the managerial talent of the future they do give exclusive opportunity rights to a few that have the same knowledge base as other degree holders within the same organization. Our conclusion is that while assessment centres should be maintained the fast track should be scrapped in favour of a 'contest' model of career mobility. This will require employers to take a holistic approach to the management of talent that extends well beyond their hiring decisions. Yet, a new trend has emerged with a growing number of organizations contracting out graduate recruitment at precisely the time that they should be pioneering the management of talent within their organizations. This is intended to cut the costs of recruitment, but it can equally be seen as a way of further distancing employers from selection decisions which are likely to be the subject of increasing public and political scrutiny as occupational opportunities fail to live up to middle-class expectations.

Equally, the analysis of employability, productivity, and social justice must be extended beyond the focus on who gets selected and whether the selection process is fair and efficient. Although this is a vital issue that requires close monitoring and creative approaches from employers to develop selection processes that permit greater diversity. However, the scope for change is limited unless issues of recruitment are located within a wider framework that includes an analysis of work reorganization; how management and leadership roles are defined; and the competences and 'kinds' of people that are perceived to fulfil such roles. It must also highlight how managerial and professional jobs are being redefined not only to meet new technical and personal requirements, but how they serve to produce new distinctions between categories of workers, in circumstances where many more have the knowledge and credentials associated with an elite in the past. At stake is not simply the reproduction of existing divisions, but a power struggle that is reshaping 'productive' inequalities at work.

Little short of a cultural revolution is required in the way organizations utilize the talents and capability of graduates and to meet the expectations of the latter for interesting and meaningful work. But the way companies organize their human resources and especially their approach to graduate recruitment cannot be explained solely as a functional issue of making sure that there are people with the appropriate knowledge and skills to fulfil the strategic mission of the organization. How organizations go about getting done what needs to be done can be achieved in different ways and with different implications in terms of status, authority, and the distribution of rewards. We need to consider the *positional* along with the *technical* division of labour, that is, we need to take full account of the 'social' organization of the workforce. This includes both the allocation of rewards, status, and promotion chances within the organization, as well as reputational issues in terms of the market position of the company within the wider economy.

The democratization of talent through mass higher education, poses a threat to the interests of powerful stakeholders who claim that they are exceptional people deserving exceptional rewards. Indeed, the claims to exceptional rewards seem to have no limits. Many senior managers and executives have justified such rewards as part of a cognitive and business elite distinguished by their extraordinary talent and performance. The WfT fits with their intuitive understanding of the world and their place within it.

The limited numbers gaining university education in the past also confirmed a belief in the limited pool of talent within society as we discussed in the previous chapter. They were by definition a cognitive elite that needed and deserved to be treated differently from the rest of the workforce. 'Sponsorship' seemed both sensible and just. But as far more people are shown to be capable of acquiring advanced knowledge and putting it to productive use, it raises questions about the authority, conditions, and pay of managers and professions.[27] It poses a threat to the legitimate power base of 'management'.

Rather than re-imagine the social organization of work, talent has been redefined. Whereas it relied on expert knowledge and claims to innate superiority to justify privileged positions and rewards, legitimacy now rests on leadership and 'performativity', measured in terms of market value. Knowledge is a part of a broader consideration of personal performance, captured in the idea of charismatic rather than bureaucratic personality. It is based on charisma, energy, and creativity alongside any consideration of knowledge and know-how.[28]

But the democracy of talent also poses problems for those already in post. If market power holds the key to individual employability, then the more difficult it is to enter the company the more it is seen to enhance the labour market power of those already in the company who many be keenly aware of their job prospects beyond their present employer. Such status considerations act as a conservative force in the context of recruitment. Social fit is more than a matter of the appropriate personal chemistry, but also the reaffirmation of elite status that poses a powerful, although largely invisible, barrier to greater diversity.

We have argued that issues of status are not limited to the self-interests of employees but also relate to the branding of organizations. Recruitment is a visible and increasingly important form of corporate branding. Recruitment literature is not only aimed at those organizations ultimately recruit, but also at a larger body of graduates because they are the consumers and clients of the future. Therefore, these companies want to be seen to recruit the best people. Being seen to recruit the best is judged to be a vital source of reputational capital.

This research also highlights the lack of understanding about how companies really work, rather than how they are presented in economic theory or in management textbooks. The view that private companies are the epitome of market rationality, un-swayed by trendy ideas or political correctness is far removed from what goes on in most organizations. The reality is that many companies closely watch their competitors and a herd instinct is *de rigueur*. There is little attempt to challenge existing assumptions about who the best people are, and therefore there is little incentive to break ranks as this may undermine claims to brand leadership.[29]

This not only limits diversity, it also devalues the contribution and development needs of others within the organization, including others with a university education. This makes a nonsense of the idea that companies depend on developing the talents of all. There remains an overriding concern with developing a few rather than nurturing the talents of all. This should not come as a surprise as the research evidence has consistently shown that the more training one has the more training one gets.[30] Moreover, while the rhetoric of employability in the knowledge economy is believed to widen access to high skilled, high waged employment in areas such as management consultancy and investment banking we find an economy of knowledge that depends on the employment of 'expensive' looking, sounding, and acting people. Knowledge work involves selling elite personal capital to clients and customers who expect to deal with the 'right' kind of people: People like them.[31]

But there is no imperative of efficiency that leads companies to utilize the higher educated in the way that they do. There are alternatives. This is why we have emphasized the wealth of talent. Organizations should be encouraged to shift from the fast track, based on a 'sponsorship' model of career promotion, to a 'contest' model where a broader range of graduates are recruited and subsequent progression is based on workplace performance. Recruitment cannot compensate for poor people management. It is not a substitute for investing in training or the management of the broader range of talents found in all organizations, even if much of that talent lies dormant.[32] The emphasis on recruitment rather than training to increase the talent pool negates the importance of institutional processes and structures, along with the responsibility to develop 'their' people.

The Price of Success

Our exploration into graduate employability supports those theories that highlight human agency and social identities, understood within a wider societal context of opportunities and constraints. They are socially constructed out of personal, cultural, and material resources that vary in terms of social circumstances including class, gender, race, and education. In short, people construct their employability but not in circumstances of their own choosing. Moreover, even when people draw on similar resources we have shown that employability is understood and managed in different ways that had consequences for labour market outcomes.

This is far removed from the model of human capital and economic rationality that informs the dominant discourse of employability. Families rarely invest in their children simply to maximize future economic returns. Indeed, decisions about education and employment strategies are often made on very poor, if not incorrect, information. Although young people are encouraged to see higher education as an economic investment, there is little evidence that they have bought into the enterprise culture with an overriding emphasis on making money. Economic rationality is shown to have a limited role in explaining what goes on within higher education and the labour market. It also lacks an appreciation of the unfolding social drama that constitutes the experience of labour market success and failure.

This is not to ignore the importance of income, status, and rewards, especially as the financial cost of credentials continues to mount. The middle and upper classes have a long tradition of using the education system to further their claims to jobs, income, and social superiority, as well as using education to extend these advantages to their children.[33] But a characteristic of post-industrial societies is the importance attached to personal achievement and self-actualization. The issue is not only one of how to make a living, even a good one, but finding work that is a source of personal interest, satisfaction, learning, and growth.[34]

They understand that if one wants an interesting job with a good salary there is little choice other than to go to university. Indeed, the more people that enter university the more important this becomes as non-graduates are pushed further and further down the pecking order of employability towards low waged service sector employment. This questions the assumption that if people had better careers information and accurate knowledge of their chances of getting particular kinds of jobs, they would choose differently. It fails to understand that if people want managerial or professional employment there is little choice other than to enter the competition for tough-entry universities and jobs.

The problem confronting individuals and families is not only the intensity of this competition, but also that the rules of the game have changed. Credentials are not a form of exchange like money; they represent the hard end of the soft business of recruitment. Credentials 'signal' less about the things that prospective employers want to know.[35] In the bureaucracies of the past the qualities of disciplined and consistent performance based on clearly defined rules and authority relations were not that different from that required for success in the education system. After a period of adjustment it could reasonably be assumed that the same consistency of performance would lead into middle or senior management. But as the competition has been extended beyond the paper chase to include the less tangible criteria of behavioural competences, this leaves individuals with the problem of how to demonstrate their employability.[36]

Employability demands that individuals give more of themselves. Here, the work–life balance has become a public issue not only because of longer working hours or concerns about gender equality at work, but also because private identities are in danger of being squeezed out under the growing pressure towards the commodification of the self.[37] As Robert Jackall has observed, 'The real task for the ambitious manager . . . becomes how to shape and keep shaping others' perceptions of oneself . . . so that one becomes seen as "promotable".'[38] Therefore the price of success maybe the experience of self-denial, the suppression of feeling, interests, and activities that do not conform to the perceived requirement of an occupational career.

The middle classes are increasingly caught in an 'opportunity trap'.[39] What looks like an extension to personal freedom, limits freedom. The price of success is increasing due to the competitive demands of getting ahead in knowledge-driven economies. We have to run faster, for longer, just to stand still.[40] This reveals the unintended consequences of individual actions and government policies. When the routes to success are limited, individuals and families have little alternative other than to do similar things to get ahead. But if everyone adopts the same tactics the costs in terms of time, effort, and money may not reap the expected benefits.[41] This has led middle-class families to adopt ever more desperate measures to win a positional advantage.

Frank and Cook note that the widening inequalities in occupational rewards has:

> lured some of our most talented citizens into socially unproductive, some-times even destructive, tasks. In an economy that already invests too little for the future, they have fostered wasteful patterns of investment and consumption. They have led indirectly to greater concentration of our most talented college students in a small set of elite institutions. They have made it more difficult for 'late bloomers' to find a productive niche in life.[42]

The distinction between the Players and Purists represent different responses to the opportunity trap. It also strikes at the very heart of middle-class sensibilities and the meritocratic creed that it has enunciated over several decades. They may share similar cultural experiences and aspirations but their approaches to employability reveal conflicting views of achievement and the rules of the game. It challenges the claims to middle-class superiority based on equality of opportunity rather than market power.[43] This is an internal class struggle that is not limited to political ideology, but is reflected in the way graduates are coming to understand who they are, where they are heading, and what are legitimate ways of achieving their ambitions.

Our analysis suggests that increasing congestion in the elite labour market will lead more graduates to adopt Player tactics. Indeed, we can anticipate the rise of the 'player' society. But when confronted with the prospects of downward social mobility, many middle-class families are likely to conclude that market realities cannot be ignored. A sense of fair play becomes secondary to winning.[44] This is reinforced by the dull compulsion of student debt that increases the stakes attached to finding a well-paid job after graduation.

It seems inevitable that with so many qualified candidates applying for limited places that individuals will seek to differentiate themselves in any way they know how. Yet, many in this study were culturally confused, as some believed that the Players were cheats, while others took a more pragmatic view—'if you can't beat them, join them'. This carries the danger that future generations of high achievers will be schooled and hired in a culture of cynicism, as Oscar Wilde observed people know the price of everything and the value of nothing, which Ralph Fevre has called the demoralization of economic behaviour.[45]

Player behaviour is, therefore, not only a consequence of market congestion but reflects the demise of business ethics. Many British and American companies exist just-for-profit. They exist to make more and more money for their shareholders. What is missing, and this is also true for notions of employability, behavioural competence, and the WfT, is any consideration of individual or corporate ethics, morals, and integrity. If companies have little integrity then people will behave with little integrity. The dominant message to young knowledge workers is that this is a 'dog eats dog' world, so look after number one because no one else will. Employment is a fling rather than a commitment of marriage, in which the short-term needs of each partner dominate.[46]

Richard Sennett suggests that under modern capitalism we have witnessed a 'corrosion of character', that is, a decline in the ethical value we place on our own aspirations and on our relations with others.[47] This corrosion of character reflects an economic climate that radiates indifference:

It does so in terms of the outcomes of human striving, as in winner-takes-all markets, where there is little connection between risk and reward. It radiates indifference in the organization of absence of trust, where there is no reason to be needed. And it does so through reengineering of institutions in which people are treated as disposable. Such practices obviously and brutally diminish the sense of mattering as a person, of being necessary to others.[48]

In these circumstances people will seek those jobs that appear to offer personal fulfilment in their own right, as this is the only source to true meaning left. But this corrosive process is far from complete, as people search to give meaning and purpose to their lives, without the benefit of occupational careers. There is considerable scope for companies to highlight ethical purpose, both in terms of a commitment to their employees and broader social purpose.[49] Companies that have a clear sense of ethical purpose are likely to attract and recruit people who want to make a difference beyond the bottom line. But this will require an altogether different evaluation of the purpose of business, work, and careers.

There seems little doubt that the management of graduate expectations will become an increasingly important issue, as young adults are encouraged to see the costs of university education as a worthwhile investment in their occupational futures. The expansion of occupational careers in the 1950s and 1960s were not only a source of personal continuity and direction, but a source of social stability. As Harold Wilensky observed at the time, they gave, 'continuity to the personal experience of the most able and skilled segments of the population—men [or women] who otherwise would produce a level of rebellion or withdrawal which would threaten the maintenance of the system'.[50] Today, not only has individual employability become a risky business, but also a much larger proportion of people are being encouraged to aim higher, whereas the overriding role of the educational system in the past was to 'cool out' the masses.

This is likely to extend the simmering frustration of the poor to sections of the middle classes when labour market realities fail to fulfil social expectations. In a related study to this one, Smetherham records a conversation with a male graduate five years after university that captures this sense of frustration:

I'm mortified...I think school and university life completely sets you up with the wrong expectations of what the rest of your life's going to be. Because the impression that I got from school and university, was that...if you've got the self-discipline to work hard and apply yourself and you do well at it, then you will be rewarded...And all I've been is held back, harassed, ignored—I've enjoyed working with the people that I've worked with...but I've never, never ever been given the opportunities that I thought I would be given.[51]

There is also the prospect that more young people will decide that the price of success is too great. Some graduates will shun this twenty-first-century rat race, in search of areas of study and employment that continue to offer scope for individual authenticity and self-discovery. We may not return to the days of student revolts as young adults came to reject the suburban routines of the good life, but we can anticipate a reappraisal of the nature of success and greater emphasis on quality of life issues, as the struggle for competitive advantage in education and the job market takes an increasing toll on individual well-being.

Conclusion

In the 1960s Ivar Berg argued that the relationship between education and jobs in America amounted to a great training robbery because there was little evidence that better-qualified employees were the most productive and that the use of credentials to screen people for decent jobs excluded the socially disadvantaged who found it impossible to match the credential performance of more affluent students. He also pointed to the under-utilization of talent and suggested that rather than concentrate on upgrading the supply of labour we should focus on the overall demand for employment.

Despite major changes over the last forty years or more, this mismanagement of talent continues today. This book challenges the dominant discourse of employability that harbours a number of unsubstantiated claims for a burgeoning knowledge economy. It challenges the assumption that there are graduate jobs for all those who develop the appropriate employability skills, and if they fail to find suitable employment, that they are incompetent in some crucial respect. It challenges the burden of responsibility that has shifted to the individual who now has a moral obligation to be employable. Our analysis found a serious mismatch between what it takes to get a good job and what it takes to do a good job. It questions the idea that there is the best person for the job and that the role of the assessment centre is to identify that person. Moreover, while there have been changes in the nature of managerial work the assessment of the intangible qualities of individuals has become an important source of legitimation as more graduates meet the knowledge requirements of managerial and professional employment.

Yet, our conclusion is not altogether negative. It encourages us to rethink the purpose of education and how we organize the competition for credentials. It raises fundamental questions about what it means to be employable and the role of higher education in contributing to the economic livelihoods of students as well as the requirements of a vibrant democracy. It also raises key questions for companies about the way they recruit, tackle issues of diversity, and manage their human resources in a context of mass higher education. Additional questions are raised in relation to the purpose and goals of organizations and the kinds of people they wish to recruit to key positions.

This book also has ramifications for individuals and families in how they understand the 'price' of success and failure in the twenty-first century. And for governments it raises issues of efficiency and justice in that the knowledge economy does not solve but brings into sharp relief. Most importantly, it calls for a national debate as the knowledge 'dividend' associated with a university education may be declining at precisely the time that students and their parents are being encouraged to see education as a private investment rather than a public good.

Notes

Chapter 1

1. This quotation is taken from Tony Blair's Labour Party Conference Speech in Bournemouth, 1999.
2. For example, see Bell, D. (1973), *The Coming of Post-Industrial Society* (New York: Basic Books); Neef, D. (ed.) (1998), *The Knowledge Economy* (Boston: Butterworth-Heinemann).
3. Brown, P. and Lauder, H. (2001) *Capitalism and Social Progress* (London: Palgrave).
4. We will resist the use of quotation marks around 'knowledge' work throughout the book while acknowledging that there is little agreement over its definition. While some adopt a broad definition to include virtually anyone who deals in 'information', others such as Brint (2001) and Thompson et al. (2001) work with more restricted definitions. We will deal with this issue in greater detail in Chapter Three. However, in this book the idea of a knowledge-based economy is restricted to the labour market for those with university credentials who represent an increasingly large proportion of labour market entrants. These are purported to be the 'knowledge' workers of the future and are expected to command high levels of general and specialist knowledge. But it is important not to conflate the acquisition of expert knowledge within higher education with actual employment opportunities for using advance knowledge in the conduct of one's employment. This book will argue that there is serious market congestion that may lead many university graduates to end up in jobs offering considerably less than they bargained for. Brint, S. (2001), 'Professionals and the "Knowledge Economy": Rethinking the Theory of Postindustrial Society', *Current Sociology*, 49/4, 101–32; Thompon, P., Warhurst, C., and Callaghan, G. (2001), 'Ignorant Theory and Knowledge Workers: Interrogating the Connection Between Knowledge, Skills and Services', *Journal of Management Studies*, 38/7, 923–42.
5. Michaels, E., Handfield-Jones, H., and Axelrod, B. (2001), *The War for Talent* (Boston: Harvard Business School Press).
6. The role of the assessment centres will be discussed in detail in Chapter Six. Also see Searle, R.H. (2003), *Selection and Recruitment: A Critical Text* (Basingstoke: Palgrave).

7. Marglin, S.A. (1982), 'What Do the Bosses Do? The Origins and Functions of Hierarchy in Capitalist Production', in A. Giddens, and D. Held (eds.), *Classes, Power and Conflict: Classical and Contemporary Debates* (Basingstoke: Macmillan).

8. Rose, N. (1999) *Governing the Soul: The Shaping of the Private Self* (London: Free Association Press); Thompson, P. and Warhurst, C. (eds.) (1998), *Workplaces of the Future* (Basingstoke: Macmillan).

9. Giddens, A. (1991) *Modernity and Self Identity: Self and Society in the Late Modern Age* (Oxford: Polity), p. 6.

10. Frank, R.H. and Cook, P.J. (1996), *The Winner-Takes-All Society* (New York: Penguin).

11. Fevre, R. (2003), *The New Sociology of Economic Behaviour* (London: Sage).

12. This study also stands at the crossroads between sociology, management, education, economics, social psychology, and social policy. This presents formidable demands in terms of the sheer volume of literature and the challenge of developing an interdisciplinary approach.

13. Mills, C.W. (1970), *The Sociological Imagination* (Harmondsworth: Penguin).

14. This highlights the inevitable tension, if not contradiction, between the approach national governments follow to narrow inequalities in the competition for a livelihood and to promote social diversity and the interests of individuals and families to maintain or enhance their social privileges through education and the labour market. Social justice and efficiency may depend on people acquiring the knowledge, skills, and capabilities that extend occupational opportunities to all with the ability and commitment to succeed, but from the perspective of individuals and their families the overriding concern is to secure a positional advantage in order to secure elite employment. See Brown, P. (2003), 'The Opportunity Trap: Education and Employment in a Global Economy', *European Education Research Journal*, 2/1, 142–80.

15. Hirsch, F. (1977), *The Social Limits to Growth* (London: Routledge and Kegan Paul).

16. Ashton and Green (1996), *Education, Training and the Global Economy* (Aldershot: Edward Elgar); Brown, P., Green, A., and Lauder, H. (2001), *High Skills: Globalization, Competitiveness and Skill Formation* (Oxford: Oxford University Press).

17. For a related discussion see Brown, P. (2000), 'The Globalization of Positional Competition?', *Sociology*, 34/4, 633–53.

18. Reich, R. (1991), *The Work of Nations* (New York: Simon & Schuster).

19. Frank and Cook (1996), op. cit.

20. Pfeffer, J. (1994), *Competitive Advantage Through People* (Boston MA: Harvard Business School Press.

21. Brown, P. and Scase, R. (1997), 'Universities and Employers: Rhetoric and Realities', in A. Smith and F. Webster (eds.), *The Post-Modern University?* (Milton Keynes: Open University Press).

22. Alvesson, M. (2001), 'Knowledge Work: Ambiguity, Image and Identity', *Human Relations*, 54/7, 863–86; Scarbrough, H. (1999), 'Knowledge as Work: Conflicts in the Management of Knowledge Workers', *Technology, Analysis and Strategic Management*, 11/1, 5–16.

Chapter 2

1. Hirsch, F. (1977), *The Social Limits to Growth* (London: Routledge).
2. Drucker, P. (1993), *Post-Capitalist Society* (Oxford: Butterworth-Heinemann); Thurow, L. (1999), *Building Wealth: The New Rules for Individuals, Companies, and Nations in a Knowledge-Based Economy* (New York: Harper & Collins).
3. Smith, A. (1976 [1776]), in. R.H. Campbell and W.B. Todd (ed.), *An Inquiry into the Nature and Causes of the Wealth of Nations* (Oxford: Clarendon Press), p. 782.
4. Marshall, G. and Swift, A. (1993), 'Social class and social justice', *British Journal of Sociology*, 44/2, 187–211.
5. This was not shared by all as neo-Marxists continued to emphasis the exploitation and alienation of labour in the interests of the capitalist class.
6. Durkheim, E. (1933 [1893]), *The Division of Labour in Society*, transl. G. Simpson (New York: Macmillan), p. 377.
7. Young, M. (1961), *The Rise of the Meritocracy* (Harmondsworth: Penguin).
8. Bell, D. (1973), *The Coming of Post-Industrial Society* (New York: Penguin).
9. Bell, D. (1977), 'On Meritocracy and Equality', in J. Karabel and A.H. Halsey (eds.), *Power and Ideology in Education* (New York: Oxford), p. 607.
10. Stewart, T.A. (2001), *The Wealth of Knowledge* (London: Nicholas Brealey).
11. Ghoshal, S. and Bartlett, C. (2000), *The Individualized Corporation: A Fundamentally New Approach to Management* (London: Random House), p. 8.
12. Michaels, E., Handfield-Jones, H., and Axelrod, B. (2001), *The War for Talent* (Boston, MA: Harvard Business School Press).
13. Ibid., pp. 4–5.
14. Jamieson, D. and O'Mara, J. (1991), *Managing Workforce 2000: Gaining the Diversity Advantage* (San Francisco: Jossey-Bass).
15. Mills, C.W. (1959), *The Power Elite* (Oxford: Oxford University Press).
16. Of course, some organizations have a long tradition of using assessment centre techniques, most notably the British Civil Service.
17. Kanter, R. (1989), *When Giants Learn to Dance* (London: Simon & Schuster).
18. Holbeche, L. (1998), *Motivating People in Lean Organizations* (Oxford: Butterworth-Heinemann).
19. Cappelli, P. (1999), *The New Deal of Work: Managing the Market-Driven Workforce* (Boston: Harvard Business School Books).
20. Arthur and Rousseau (eds.) (1996), *The Boundaryless Career: A New Employment Principle for a New Organizational Era* (New York: Oxford University Press); Peiperl, M., Arthur, M., Goffee, R. and Morris, T. (eds.) (2000),

Career Frontiers: New Conceptions of Working Lives (Oxford: Oxford University Press).

21. Arthur and Rousseau (1996), op. cit., p. 4.
22. Ibid. (1996), p. 6.
23. Ibid. (1996), p. 373.
24. See Keep, E. (1999), 'UK's VET Policy and the "Third Way": Following a High Skills Trajectory or Running up a Dead End Street?', *Journal of Education and Work*, 12/3, 323–46; Ashton and Green (1996), *Education, Training and the Global Economy* (Aldershot: Edward Elgar); Brown, P., Green, A. and Lauder, H. (2001), *High Skills: Globalization, Competitiveness and Skill Formation* (Oxford: Oxford University Press); Lloyd, C. and Payne, J. (2002), 'Developing a Political Economy of Skill', *Journal of Education and Work*, 15/4, 365–90.
25. Hillage, J. and Pollard, E. (1998) *Employability: Developing a Framework for Policy Analysis*, EfEE Research Briefing No. 85. p. 1.
26. Drucker (1993), op. cit.; Kanter, R. (1989), op. cit.
27. Leadbeater, C. (1999), *Living on Thin Air: The New Economy* (London: Viking), pp. 228–9.
28. Bogdanowicz, M.S. and Bailey, E.K. (2002), 'The Value of Knowledge and the Values of the New Worker: Generation X in the New Economy', *Journal of European Industrial Training*, 26/2/3/4: 125–9, p. 127.
29. Cappelli (1999), op. cit., quoted in Michaels, Handfield-Jones, and Axelrod (2001), op. cit., p. 6.
30. Brown, P. (2003) 'The Opportunity Trap: Education and Employment in a Global Economy', *European Educational Research Journal*, 2/1, 142–180.
31. Beck, U. (1992), *Risk Society: Towards a New Modernity* (London: Sage).
32. Fukuyama, F. (1999), *The Great Disruption: Human Nature and the Reconstitution of Social Order* (New York: Free Press).
33. Brown, P. and Lauder, H. (2001), *Capitalism and Social Progress: The Future of Society in a Global Economy* (Basingstoke: Palgrave).
34. Hesketh, A.J. (2003) 'Employability in the Knowledge Economy: Living the Fulfilled Life or Policy Chimera?' Paper awarded the Carolyn Dexter Best Paper Award, *Democracy in a Knowledge Economy*, Academy of Management Annual Conference, Seattle, USA, 1–6 August; Ohmae, K. (1996), *The End of the Nation State* (London: Harper & Collins); Rosecrance, R. (1999), *The Rise of the Virtual State: Wealth and Power in the Coming Century* (New York: Basic Books).
35. Reich, R. (1991), *The Work of Nations* (New York: Simon and Schuster).
36. *The Economist*, (2003) 'A Survey of Capitalism and Democracy', June 28, p. 8. See also Larry Elliott 'Pigs will not clean their own sties', *Guardian*, 22 November, 2002. He reports figures presented by Paul Krugman that show that between 1970 and 1999 the average adjusted salary rose by around 10% from $32,522 to $35,864. By comparison the top 100 CEOs saw their remuneration increase from $1.3 m to $37.5 m, more than a 1,000 times the pay of ordinary workers.

37. Hesketh, A. (1999), 'Towards an Economic Sociology of the Student Financial Experience of Higher Education', *Journal of Education Policy*, 14/4, 385–410.
38. Labour Party (1997), *Election Manifesto* (London: The Labour Party).
39. Brown and Lauder (2001), op. cit.
40. For an interesting discussion of the sociology of economic behaviour, see Fevre, R. (2003), *The New Sociology of Economic Behaviour* (London: Sage).
41. The global labour market does not operate as a 'free' market (Castells 1996, n. 42; Held et al. 1999). Nationality continues to operate as a vital tool for restricting the competition for jobs by excluding millions of well-qualified workers from other parts of the world such as skilled software engineers from India competing for IT jobs within the European Community or North America (Kobrin 2000).
42. Castells, M. (1996), *The Rise of the Network Society* (Oxford: Blackwell).
43. Kobrin, S. (2000), 'Development after Industrialisation: Poor Countries in an Electronically Integrated Global Economy', in N. Hood and S. Young (eds.), *The Globalization of Multinational Enterprise Activity and Economic Development* (Basingstoke: Macmillan).
44. Brown (2003), op. cit.
45. One company in a sector characterized by labour shortages, received approximately 6,000 applications for 300 jobs, an odds ratio of 20–1. A year later, about the same number of applicants were competing for only 100 positions on their graduate programme. Hence, their relative chances declined from 20–1 to 60–1, despite a consistent quality of candidates.
46. Hirsch (1977), op. cit.
47. Braverman, H. (1974), *Labor and Monopoly Capital: The Degradation of Work in the Twentieth Century* (New York: Monthly Review Press).
48. Holmes, L. (1995), 'Skills: A Social Perspective', in A. Assiter (ed.), *Transferable Skills in Higher Education* (London: Kogan Page). Bloomer, M. and Hodkinson, P. (2000), 'Learning Careers: Continuity and Change in Young People's Disposition to Learning', *British Education Research Journal*, 26/5, 583–97.
49. Arnot, M., Weiner, G., and David, M. (1999), *Closing the Gender Gap: The Post War Era and Social Change* (Cambridge: Polity Press); Crompton, R. (ed.) (1999), *Restructuring Gender Relations and Employment: The Decline of the Male Breadwinner* (Oxford: Oxford University Press); Halford, S., Savage, M., and Witz, A. (1997), *Gender, Careers and Organisations* (Basingstoke: Macmillan).
50. Fromm, E. (1949), *Man for Himself: An Enquiry into the Psychology of Ethics* (London: Routledge).
51. Modood, T. and Acland, T. (1998), *Race and Higher Education* (London: Policy Studies Institute, PSI); Carnoy, M. (1996), *Faded Dreams: The Politics and Economics of Race in America* (New York: Cambridge University Press).
52. Frank, R.H. and Cook, P.J. (1996), *The Winner-Takes-All Society* (New York: Penguin), p. 3.

53. The same trend has not been found to the same extent in continental Europe, where neo-liberalism is less evident.
54. Simmel, G. (1990 [1907]), in D. Frisby (ed.), *The Philosophy of Money* (London: Routledge).
55. Ehrenreich, B. (1989), *Fear of Falling: The Inner Life of the Middle Class* (New York: Pantheon).
56. Brynin, M. (2002), 'Over qualification in Employment', *Work, Employment and Society*, 16/4, 637–54.
57. Boudon, R. (1973), *Education, Opportunity and Social Inequality: Changing Prospects in Western Society* (New York: John Wiley), p. 4.
58. Ibid., p. 6; Brown (2003), op. cit.
59. Tawney, R.H. (1982 [1921]), *The Acquisitive Society* (Brighton: Wheatsheaf).
60. Brown, P., Hesketh, A., and Williams, S. (2003), 'Employability in a Knowledge Economy', *Journal of Education and Work*, Spring, 16/1, 107–26.
61. Bourdieu, P. and Boltanski, L. (1978), 'Changes in Social Structure and Changes in the Demand for Education', in S. Giner and M. Archer (eds.), *Contemporary Europe: Social Structure and Cultural Change* (London: Routledge and Kegan Paul).
62. The extent of this varied between countries where higher education was severely restricted in countries such as Britain and Germany, but this was far less the case in the United States.
63. The picture in Europe is uneven in terms of graduation rates. There are significant differences between the Netherlands and the United Kingdom as opposed to Germany. This highlights the importance of a comparative perspective as the social construction of positional competition is subject to importance variations. The dual system in Germany has channelled large numbers of young adults into training programmes that offer access to decent job opportunities without the requirement of higher education. Whether the dual system will continue to perform this role in the future is a moot point (Lauder, (2001), '*Innovation, Skill Difusion and Social Exclusion*', in P. Brown, A. Green, and H. Lauder. High Skills: Globalization, Competitiveness and Skill Formation (Oxford: Oxford University Press).
64. Purcell, K. (2002) *Qualifications and Careers: Equal Opportunities and Earnings Among Graduates*, Equal Opportunities Commission. www.eoc.org.uk/research.
65. Arnot, Weiner, and David (1999), op. cit.; Osborne, M., Rees, T. et al. (2000) *Science Policy in the European Union* (Brussels: European Commission).
66. Smetheram, C. (2004), *The Employability of First Class Graduates*, School of Social Sciences, Cardiff University, PhD (unpublished).
67. Frank and Cook (1996), op. cit.
68. Hirsch (1977), op. cit., p. 5.
69. Collins, R. (1994), *Four Sociological Traditions* (Oxford: Oxford University Press), p. 146.

70. Ibid., p. 146.

71. Hirsch (1977), op. cit.

72. Unlike money, credentials are not a currency of exchange but one of entitlement. If you have the appropriate qualifications you are entitled to enter the competition for specific kinds of employment. It confers an entitlement to barter.

73. Bendix, R. (1956), *Work and Authority in Industry* (New York: Wiley)

74. Merton, R. (1949), *Social Theory and Social Structure* (New York: Free Press).

75. Ibid., p. 196. However, in Whyte's account of the 'organization man', it is suggested that the organization not only consumed much of the time and energy of the official, but also placed considerable demands upon his (sic) family. See Whyte, W. (1965), *The Organization Man* (Harmondsworth: Penguin).

76. Is has been the latter which has been the main focus of human capital theory. Equally, the importance attached to technical knowledge will vary considerably depend upon the nature of the employment. See Rose, N. (1999), *Governing the Soul: The Shaping of the Private Self*, 2nd edn (London: Free Association Books); Du Gay, P. and Salaman, G. (1992) 'The Cult(ure) of the Customer', *Journal of Management Studies*, 29, 615–33; Casey, C. (1995), *Work, Self and Society: After Industrialism* (London: Routledge); Thompon, P., Warhurst, C., and Callaghan, G. (2001), 'Ignorant Theory and Knowledge Workers: Interrogating the Connection Between Knowledge, Skills and Services', *Journal of Management Studies*, 38, 923–42.

77. Scarbrough, H. (1999), 'Knowledge as work: conflict in the management of knowledge workers', *Technology Analysis and Strategic Management*, 11/1, 5–16, p. 7.

78. Drucker, P. (1999), *Management Challenges for the 21st Century* (Oxford: Butterworth-Heinemann), p. 21.

79. Mason, G. (2002), High Skills Utilisation Under Mass Higher Education: Graduate Employment in Service Industries in Britain', *Journal of Education and Work*, 15/4, 427–56.

80. Gerth, H. and Mills, C.W. (eds.) (1967), *From Max Weber* (London: Routledge), p. 246.

81. Shils, E. (1968), 'Charisma' *International Encyclopedia of the Social Sciences*, 2, 286–90.

82. Gerth and Mills (1967), op. cit., p. 54.

83. Brown, P. and Scase, R. (1994), *Higher Education and Corporate Realities: Class, Careers and the Decline of Graduate Careers* (London: UCL Press).

84. Brown, P. (1995) 'Cultural capital and social exclusion: some observations on recent trends in education, employment and the labour market', *Work, Employment and Society*, 9, 29–51.

85. Alvesson, M. (2001), 'Knowledge Work: Ambiguity, Image and Identity', *Human Relations*, 54/7, 863–86, p. 863.

86. This is not to suggest that *social* qualifications were eliminated in recruitment to bureaucratic organizations. The selection of elites has traditionally been associated with a 'cultural code' consistent with images of masculine managerial authority; expert knowledge; and the right school tie Scott, J. (1996), *Stratification and Power: Structures of Class, Status and Command* (Cambridge: Polity Press); Goffee, R. and Scase, R. (1995), *Corporate Realities* (London: Routledge). Rather, if employers are rewarding the certified display of middle class self-discipline as Collins, R. (1979), The Credential Society: A Historical Sociology of Education and Stratification (New York: Academic Press) assumes, there has not only been a change in its form, but it has become an explicit element of employer recruitment practices (see Brown, 1995 op. cit.: 41).

87. Rose (1999), op. cit.

88. For a discussion of such techniques as sources of surveillance see Foucault 1977; Cohen 1985; McKinlay and Starkey, K. (eds.) (1998), Foucault, Management and Organization Theory: From Panoptican to Technologies of the self (London: Sage).

89. Thomson, K. (1998), *Emotional Capital: Capturing Hearts and Minds to Create Lasting Business Success* (Oxford: Capstone); Goleman, D., Boyatzis, R., and McKee, A. (2002), *The New Leaders* (London: Little, Brown).

90. Holbeche, L. (1998), *Motivating People in Lean Organizations* (Oxford: Butterworth-Heinemann).

91. Two excellent studies of education, cultural capital and the middle classes are Ball, S. (2003) *Class Strategies and the Education Market: The Middle Classes and Social Advantage* (London: Routledge Falmer); and Power, S., Edwards, T., Whitty, G., and Wigfall, V. (2003) *Education and the Middle Class* (Buckingham: Open University Press).

92. Brown and Scase (1994), op. cit.

93. It is also more than 'habitus' with a voice!

94. There are a growing numbers of self-help books that encourage us to 'reinvent the self' for personal and business success. But rarely is any consideration given to the 'self' as a social construct. These books present the self as ahistorical, 'you can be whatever you want to be': empty vessels to be filled with the latest techniques to succeed in the market for elite jobs. See Bourdieu, P. and Passeron, J. (1977), *Reproduction in Education, Society and Culture* (London: Sage); Bourdieu, P. (1998), *Practical Reason: On the Theory of Action* (Cambridge: Polity).

95. Bourdieu, P. (2000), 'Making the Economic Habitus: Algerian Workers Revisited', *Ethnography*, 1, 17–41.

96. In the study of employability it is important to understand the nature of cultural capital in different 'fields' such as education as opposed to the labour market. It may be deployed in the education system to facilitate academic success, but at the same time contradict changing models of

organizational efficiency and leadership that place a high premium on 'personal qualities' rather than 'academic abilities'.

97. Bourdieu, P. (1977), *Outline of a Theory of Practice* (Cambridge: Cambridge University Press), p. 95.

98. The strengths and limitations of the concept of habitus have been widely debated. See, for instance, Jenkins, R. (1992), *Pierre Bourdieu* (London: Routledge).

99. Bourdieu (1977), op. cit., p. 32.

100. Savage, M., Barlow, J., Dickens, P., and Fielding, T. (1992), *Property, Bureaucracy and Culture: Middle Class Formation in Contemporary Britain* (London: Routledge).

101. Rees, G., Fevre, R., Furlong, J., and Gorrard, S. (1997), 'History, Place and the Learning Society: Towards a Sociology of Lifetime Learning', *Journal of Education Policy*, 12/6: 485–97.

102. Fromm (1949), op. cit.

103. Fischer, I. (1927), *The Nature of Capital and Income* (London: Macmillan).

Chapter 3

1. These data are extrapolated from those kindly provided by the US Bureau of Labor Statistics (BLS) and our extrapolations of Wilson's (2001) summary of the current size of UK occupations. Further elaboration of these sources follows below.

2. Leadbeater, C. (1999), *Living on Thin Air: The New Economy* (London: Viking).

3. Chao, E.L. (2001), 'Message from the Secretary of Labor', *Report on the American Workforce*, US Department of Labor (Washington: DOL), p. 2.

4. Carnevale, A.P. and Desrochers, D.M. (2002), *The Missing Middle: Aligning Education and the Knowledge Economy* (Washington: US Department of Education).

5. Blair, T. (2002), 'My Vision for Britain', *The Observer*, 10th November, p. 26.

6. Thrift (2001), ' "It's the romance, not the finance, that makes the business worth pursuing": disclosing a new market culture', *Economy & Society*, 30/4, 412–23, p. 415.

7. Kling, J. (1995), 'High performance work systems and firm performance', *Monthly Labor Review*, May, 29–36, p. 29.

8. Reich, R. (1991), *The Wealth of Nations* (London: Simon and Schuster).

9. Drucker, P. (1993), *Post-Capitalist Society* (Oxford: Butterworth and Heinmann), p. 30.

10. Alvesson, M. (2001), 'Knowledge work: Ambiguity, image and identity', *Organization*, 54/7, 863–86.

11. Landes, D (1999), *The Wealth and Poverty of Nations* (London: Abacus), p. 276.

12. OECD (1999), 'Measuring Knowledge in Learning Economies and Societies', Draft Report on Washington Forum, National Science Foundation

and the Centre for Educational Research and Innovation, Paris: OECD, p. 1. www.oced.org/els/papers/papers.htm.

13. Cortada, J.W. (1998), 'Introducing the knowledge worker', in James W. Cortada (ed.), *The Rise of the Knowledge Worker* (London: Butterworth Heinmann), p. xiii.

14. Ibid., p. xiv.

15. Blair, T. (1998), 'Foreword by the Prime Minister' to *Our Competitive Future: Building the Knowledge Driven Economy, the government's competitiveness white paper* Cm 4176 (London, DTI), p. 5.

16. Cortada, J.W. (2001), *21st Century Business: Managing and Working in the New Digital Economy* (London: Prentice Hall), p. 6.

17. There are obvious problems with this claim. The link between the economic well-being of a nation state and the skills of its indigenous workforce are coloured by the presence of multinational organizations whose capital base may lie outside the borders of where even the majority of its workforce is located. Different economic sectors are in different modes of economic development and cycles (e.g. the recession of the manufacturing sector in the United Kingdom during the dot.com boom in the late 1990s).

18. Leadbeater (1999) op. cit., p. 18.

19. Hamel, G. and Prahalad, C.K. (1994), *Competing for the Future* (Boston: Harvard Business School Press), p. 35.

20. Holman, D. (2000), 'A dialogical approach to skill and skilled activity' *Human Relations*, 53/7, 957–80, p. 964.

21. For example see Fitz-enz, J. and Davidson, B. (1984) *How to Measure Human Resources Management* (New York: McGraw-Hill); Fitz-enz, J. (2000), *The ROI of Human Capital: Measuring the economic value of employee performance* (New York: Amacom); Mayo, A. (2001), *The Human Value of the Enterprise: Valuing PEOPLE as Assets—Monitoring, Measuring, Managing* (London: Nicholas Brearly Publishing).

22. Gini, A. (2001), *My Job, My Self: Work and the Creation of the Modern Individual* (New York: Routledge), p. ix.

23. Ulrich Beck, cited in Giddens, A. (1998), *The Third Way: The Renewal of Social Democracy* (Cambridge: Polity), p. 36.

24. US Department of Commerce (DOC), US Department of Education (DOE) & US Department of Labor (DOL) (1999), *21st Century Skills for 21st Century Jobs* (Washington: DOC/DOE/DOL), p. 1, original emphases.

25. US Department of Labor (DOL) (2001), *Office of the 21st Century Workforce* (Washington: US Department of Labor), p. 7, our emphasis.

26. Reich, R. (1991), *The Work of Nations*, p. 77.

27. Ibid., p. 83.

28. Ibid., pp. 84–5.

29. Ibid., p. 174.

30. Ibid., p. 174.

31. Ibid., pp. 174–5.
32. Ibid., p. 176.
33. It is interesting to note here that Reich does not suggest that routine production services can be exported globally. In many ways it is this phenomenon that has contributed to the economic debate over globalisation (e.g. Omhae, 1995).
34. Reich (1991), op. cit., p. 208.
35. See footnote 2, p. 174.
36. Not including the government workers and those involved in work using a combination of these three skills which Reich decided not to categorize, the shares of the US labour force represented by each of the typologies become symbolic analysts (27%), in-person workers (40%) and routine production (33%).
37. Ibid., pp. 179–80.
38. Cortada (2001), op. cit.
39. Drucker (1993), op. cit., p. 75. Although it is worth noting here that Cortada, unlike Reich, estimated the proportion of those doing knowledge work in 1960 to be as high as 42% rising to 52% by 1980 (Cortada (2001), op. cit., pp. 5–6.
40. Reich (pp. 181–4) does offer a framework for categorizing workers into symbolic analysts:

> That a job category is officially classified "professional" or "managerial" likewise has little bearing upon the function its occupant actually performs in the world economy. *Not all professionals, that is, are symbolic analysts.* Some lawyers spend their entire working lives doing things that normal people would find unbearably monotonous—cranking out the same old wills, contracts, and divorces, over and over, with only the names changed. Some accountants do routine audits without the active involvement of their cerebral cortices. Some managers take no more responsibility than noting who shows up for work in the morning, making sure they stay put, and locking the place up at night. (I have even heard tell of university professors who deliver the same lectures for thirty years, long after their brains have atrophied, but I do not believe such stories.) None of these professionals is a symbolic analyst. (Reich, 1991: 181, our emphasis)

41. These data are derived from Silvistri (1995, n. 42 table 1) and Hecker (2001, n. 54 tables 1 & 2).
42. Silvestri, G.T. (1995), 'Occupational Employment to 2005', *Monthly Labor Review*, November 1995, pp. 60–87.
43. Although we stress again that these proportions are based on aggregations of data utilizing the BLS's's own classifications at a lower level. As we discuss below, our own classifications of these data reveals a different picture.

44. With projections estimating the number of additional jobs to be around 15%, or 22 million jobs, this total would seem on the surface to be easily attainable.

45. Esping-Andersen, G. (1999), *Social Foundations of Post-Industrial Economies* (Oxford: Oxford University Press).

46. Just thirteen out of the thirty fastest growing occupations in the United States during the next decade will require an education beyond compulsory schooling age and some on-the-job training (see Hecker, 2001, n. 54 table 3: 79). And just nine out the thirty occupations accounting for the largest job growth will require a minimum qualification of a first degree (see Hecker, 2001, n. 54 table 4: 80).

47. These reworked data are reported in table 3.4: The Re-Classification of In-Person Service and Routine Production Occupations.

48. Berg, I. (1970), *Education and Jobs: The Great Training Robbery* (New York: Praeger). Dore, R. (1976), The Diplomatic Disease: Education, Qualification, and Development (London: George Allen and Unwin).

49. Reich (1991), op. cit.

50. We would like to thank Daniel Hecker of the US Department of Labor for providing access to this data. The use of this data obviously reflects our interpretation of the evidence!

51. We acknowledge here a personal conversation with Professor John Burgoyne of Lancaster University Management School during which the distinction between knowledge *worked* and knowledge *worker* was made.

52. Braverman, H. (1974), *Labor and Monopoly Capital: The Degradation of Work in the Twentieth Century* (New York: Monthly Review Press), p. 423, original emphases.

53. Langdon, D.S., McMenamin, T.M., and Krolik, T.J. (2002), 'US labor market in 2001: economy enters a recession', *Monthly Labor Review*, February 2002, 3–33. Although it is interesting to note that constant referral is being made to the jobless growth that has accompanied the recent economic upturn. For example, in December 2003 just 1,000 new jobs were created in the entire US economy against a projection of 150,000 for the same month.

54. Hecker, D. (2001), 'Occupational employment projections 2000–2010', *Monthly Labor Review*, November 2001, pp. 57–84, table 6: 83.

55. Following further political devolution in Britain, this document only deals with higher education in England.

56. Clarke, C. (2003), 'Foreword by the Secretary of State for Education and Skills' in *The Future of Higher Education* Cm 5735 (London: TSO), p. 2.

57. DFES, 2003, *The Future of Higher Education*, 1.22, p. 16.

58. Wilson, et al. (2001, n. 60, table 5: 63). Our re-categorization of the 1990 edition of the Standard Occupation Codes (SOC) into the three types of work is as follows knowledge workers (kw): Corporate managers and administrators, Managers/proprietors in agriculture and services, Science and engineering professionals, Teaching professionals, Health professionals,

Other professional occupations, Science and engineering associate professionals, Health associate professionals and Other associate professional
occupations; as *in-person services*—Secretarial occupations, Personal service
occupations, Buyers, brokers and sales representatives, Other sales occupations; and as *routine production*—Clerical occupations, Skilled construction
trades, Skilled engineering trades, Protective service occupations,
Industrial plant and machine operators, assemblers, Drivers and mobile
machine operators, Other occupations in agriculture, forestry and fishing
and Other elementary occupations. We attach the caveat here that we are
reliant upon the aggregations utilized by the UK's DfES. More detailed
analysis of UK occupational data at lower levels is currently being undertaken by the authors.

59. The direct comparison is with table 1 above that is based on BLS data
rather than our re-coding which significantly reduces the proportion of
symbolic analysts to 20% in 2000. We were able to repeat the same recoding for the UK data as this was unavailable at the time of writing.

60. Wilson, R.A., Green, A., Homenidou, K., & Cambridge Econometrics (2001),
Projections of Occupations and Qualifications 2000/2001 (London: DfES).

61. Ibid., p. 41.

62. Ibid., p. 41.

63. DFES (2003), op. cit. 1.3, p. 10.

64. Ibid., 7.21, p. 83.

65. Pryor, F.L. and Schaffer, D.L. (2000), *Who's Not Working and Why?
Employment, cognitive skills, wages, and the changing U.S. Labor Market*
(Cambridge: Cambridge University Press).

66. Ibid., p. 68, our emphasis.

67. Brynin, M. (2002), Overqualification in Employment', *Work, Employment
& Society*, 16/4, 637–54. Battu, H. and Sloane, P. (2000), 'Over education
and crowding out in Britain' in L. Borghans and A. de Grip (Eds.) The
Over educated Worker? (Cheltenham: Edward Elgar); Aston, L. and
Bekhradnia, B. (2003), Demand for Graduates: A Review of the Economic
Evidence, Higher Education Policy Institute. www.hepi.ac.uk/articles/
docs/graduatesmain.pdf; Keep, E. and Mayhew, K. (2004 forthcoming),
'The Economic and Distributional Implications of Current Policies on
Higher Education', *Oxford Review of Economic Policy*. Smetherham, C.
(2004), 'First Class Women in the World of Work: Employability and
Labour Market Orientations', Working Paper No. 45, Cardiff School of
Social Sciences, www.cardiff.ac.uk/social/publications/workingpapers/
workingpapers.html

68. Keep, E. and Mayhew, K. (1999), 'The Assessment: Knowledge, Skills and
Competitiveness', *Oxford Review of Economic Policy*, 15/1, 1–15; Mason, G.
(1999) 'Product strategies, workforce skills and 'high-involvement' work
practices', in P. Capelli (ed.), *Employment Practices and Business Strategy*
(New York: Oxford University Press).

69. See Chapter 3, Note 67.
70. Brynin (2002), op. cit., p. 650.
71. Wilson, Green, Homenidou, & Cambridge Econometrics (2001), op. cit.
72. Alongside the *trend* estimate is the *balance* demand scenario, this assumes that the demand for high skills labour (using the proxy of a bachelor's degree) will broadly follow the supply of such personnel.

> By 2010 in the balance demand scenario, over 20 per cent of those employed are projected to have a degree. However, these remain heavily concentrated in SOCs 1–3 (and to a lesser extent in 7.1, Buyers, Brokers and Sales representatives). There are also significant increases in many lower level occupations, although the overall level remains low. (Wilson et al., 2001: 67)

> At one in every five new jobs, the balanced demand scenario is significantly less than the 80% of future jobs requiring a degree cited in *The Future of Higher Education*. More likely, perhaps is the third and final assumption used by Wilson to predict future occupational growth; namely *fixed penetration rates*, which simply estimate future demand for graduates will remain at 1999 levels. This inevitably begs the question of whether organizational demand for graduates is as robust as policymakers would like to suggest.

73. Keep, E. (2004), After Access: Researching Labour Market Issues, in J. Gallacher (ed.), *Researching Access to Higher Education* (London: Routledge). Equally, other official statistics in the United Kingdom, puts the current demand for first degree level qualifications or equivalent at 29% of the workforce. A figure substantially less than the proportion of the future labour force expected to be equipped with similar high skills in the projections discussed above. Also see Wolf, A. (2002), *Does Education Matter?* (London: Penguin).
74. Although these organizations account for a relatively small proportion of the 400,000 graduates entering the UK job market each year.
75. The AGR's annual survey does not obtain a response rate of more than 70%. The major graduate recruiters, however, do file their returns. For this reason, we feel confident that our estimations of the numbers of graduates recruited by those organizations who do not respond to the survey are more likely to be over-estimations as opposed to under-estimations. There is an alternative view offered by the AGR itself, which estimates that there are approximately 1,000 companies with dedicated graduate recruitment programmes. These figures are based on personal correspondence with Carl Gilleard, Chief Executive of the AGR.
76. Higher Education Statistics Agency, (HESA) (2003), *Students in Higher Education Institutions* 2001/02, table 0A.
77. Even taking the AGR's estimate of 1,000 dedicated graduate recruitment programmes in the UK, and adopting the median number of graduates per programme (thirty-one vacancies, see AGR (2003), *The AGR Graduate*

Recruitment Survey 2003, Winter Review, Chart 2.2, p. 11.), we still estimate a ratio of thirteen graduates per vacancy. A more generous interpretation of this data, utilising the *mean* number of vacancies (sixty-two vacancies per company) as opposed to the median, raises the number of graduate vacancies to 62,000: a ratio of nearly seven graduates per vacancy.

78. AGR (2001) *Graduate Recruitment Report* (Warwick: AGR), p. 21.
79. Purcell, K. and Pitcher, J. (1996), *Great Expectations: The New Diversity of Graduate Skills and Aspirations* (Manchester: Higher Education Careers Services Unit).
80. Purcell, K. (2000), *Changing Boundaries in Employment* (Bristol: Bristol Academic Press); Purcell, K., Hogarth, T., and Simm, C. (1999), *Whose Flexibility? The Costs and Benefits of Different Contractual and Working Arrangements for Employers and Employees* (York: Rowntree Foundation).
81. *Source*: Purcell, K. (2002), *Qualifications and Careers: Equal opportunities and earnings among graduates*, Working Paper Series No. 1 (Manchester: Equal Opportunities Commission), table 1, p. 6.
82. Ibid., table 1, p. 30.
83. Derived from Wilson, Green, Homenidou, & Cambridge Econometrics (2001), op. cit., table 4.5, p. 39.
84. See Chapter 3, Note 67.

Chapter 4

1. Michaels, E., Handfield-Jones, H., and Axelrod, B. (2001), *The War for Talent* (Boston: Harvard Business School Press), p. xiv.
2. Ibid.
3. This includes brochures and material from corporate websites.
4. Michaels, Handfield-Jones, and Axelrod (2001), op. cit.
5. Ibid., p. 3.
6. In the interests of anonymity, we do not identify any of the participating companies in this research.
7. Michaels, Handfield-Jones, and Axelrod (2001), op. cit., p. 3.
8. Cohen, D.S. (2001), *The Talent Edge* (Toronto: John Wiley), p. xvi.
9. Michaels, Handfield-Jones, and Axelrod (2001), op. cit., p. 126.
10. Holbeche, L. (1998), *Motivating People in Lean Organizations* (Oxford: Butterworth-Heinemann).
11. Michaels, Handfield-Jones, and Axelrod (2001), op. cit., p. 5.
12. Woodruffe, C. (1999), *Winning the Talent War* (Chichester: John Wiley), p. 11.
13. Michaels, Handfield-Jones, and Axelrod (2001), op. cit., p. 6.
14. Cappelli, P. (1999), *The New Deal at Work* (Boston: Harvard Business School Press).
15. Tulgan, B. (2001), *Winning the Talent Wars* (London: Nicholas Brealey), p. 24.
16. Frank, R.H. and Cook, P.J. (1996), *The Winner-Takes-All Society* (New York: Penguin).

17. Tulgan, for example, suggests that this 'is great for the economy. Free markets are very efficient (though not without casualties), and efficient systems reproduce effective behavior. Whereas the feudal employment system caused employers to bear much of the risk (and the costs) of fluctuations in the market value of individuals' skills and abilities, the market-driven model diversifies this risk (and the costs) among individuals themselves' (Tulgan, 2001: 26).

18. Michaels, Handfield-Jones, and Axelrod (2001), op. cit., p. 7.

19. Ibid., p. 7.

20. Ibid., p. 6.

21. Leadbeater, C. (1999), *Living on Thin Air: The New Economy* (London: Viking).

22. This suggests that graduates need to pay more attention to the philosophy and values of the company rather than the initial starting package.

23. Woodruffe, C. (1999), op. cit. Typically, there is little or no reference to the expansion of higher education or the large numbers of candidates applying for the extremely limited opportunities for fast-track positions. This is handsome compensation for the decline in the numbers of 25–44-year-olds that will decline by 6% between 1998–2008 in the United States, and the fact that in the United Kingdom the number of under-25-year-olds dropped around 14% in the last three decades of the twentieth century (Woodruffe, 1999: 101).

24. Michaels, Handfield-Jones, and Axelrod (2001), op. cit., p. xii.

25. Ibid., p. xii.

26. Ibid., pp. xii–xiii.

27. Ibid., p. xiii.

28. Tulgan (2001), op. cit., p. 32.

29. Brown, P. and Lauder, H. (2001), *Capitalism and Social Progress* (Basingstoke: Palgrave).

30. Zuboff, S. (1984), *In the Age of the Smart Machine: The Future of Work and Power* (New York: Basic Books).

31. Bourdieu, P. and Passeron, J.C. (1964), *The Inheritors: French Students and their Relationship to Culture* (London: University of Chicago Press); Brown, P. (1995), 'Cultural Capital and Social Exclusion: Some Observations on Recent Trends in Education, Employment and the Labour Market', *Work, Employment and Society*, 9/1, 29–51.

32. Sumner, G.W. (1952), *What Social Classes Owe to Each Other* (Caldwell, Ohio: Caxton).

33. Kandola, R. and Fullerton, J. (1998), *Diversity in Action: Managing the Mosaic*, 2nd edn (London: Chartered Institute of Personnel and Development), p. 37.

34. Greenslade, M. (1991), 'Managing Diversity: Lessons from the United States', *Personnel Management*, December, pp. 28–32.

35. Johnson, R. and Redmond, D. (2000), *Diversity Incorporated: Managing People for Success in a Diverse World* (London: Financial Times/Prentice Hall), pp. 2–3.

36. Woodruffe (1999), op. cit., p. 102.
37. Ibid., p. 103.
38. O'Reilly, C.A. and Pfeffer, J. (2000), *Hidden Value: How Great Companies Achieve Extraordinary Results with Ordinary People* (Boston: Harvard Business School Press).
39. Bendix, R. (1956), *Work and Authority in Industry: Ideologies of Management in the Course of Industrialization* (New York: John Wiley).
40. Ibid., p. 440.
41. Gramsci, A. (1971), *Selection from the Prison Notebooks of Antonio Gramsci* (London: Lawrence and Wishart).
42. Whyte, W. (1965), *The Organization Man* (Harmondsworth: Penguin).
43. Bendix (1956), op. cit., p. 441.
44. Tulgan (2001), op. cit., p. 25.
45. Companies could increase the level of knowledge required say to Masters level or even to Research Degree level, but much business knowledge is generic and not highly specialist, although there are obvious exceptions.
46. Weber, M. (1948), H.H. Gerth and C.W. Mills (ed.), *From Max Weber: Essays in Sociology* (London: Routledge and Kegan Paul).

Chapter 5

1. Kakabadse, A.P., Nortier, F., and Abramovici, N.-B. (eds.) (1998), *Success in Sight: Visioning* (London: International Thompson).
2. Hacking, I. (1986), 'Making up people', in Thomas C. Heller, Mortan Sosna, and David Wellbery (eds.), *Reconstructing Individualism: Autonomy, Individuality and the Self in Western Thought* (Stanford: Stanford University Press).
3. For example, see Peck, J. (2000), 'Structuring the labour market: a segmentation approach', in Stephen Ackroyd and Steve Fleetwood (eds.), *Realist Perspectives on Management and Organisations* (London: Routledge).
4. Bethell-Fox, C.E. (1989), 'Psychological Testing', in Peter Herriot (ed.), *Handbook of Assessment in Organizations* (Chichester: Wiley), p. 308.
5. Handyside, J.D. (1989), On Ratings and Rating Scales', in Peter Herriot (ed.), *Handbook of Assessment in Organizations* (Chichester: Wiley), p. 672, our emphasis.
6. Thomas International (Undated), *The People Partnership* (Bucks: Thomas International).
7. DfEE (1999), *Policy Action Team on Skills: Final Report* (London, DfEE), p. 30.
8. Labour Party (2001), *Ambitions for Britain: Labour's manifesto 2001* (London: Labour Party), p. 13.
9. Association of Graduate Recruiters (AGR) (2003), *Graduate Recruitment Survey, Winter* (Warwick: AGR).
10. For example AGR, 1995; NCIHE, 1997; CVCP/DfEE/HEQE, 1998; DfEE, 2000.

11. See Jessop, B. (2003), *The Future of the Capitalist State* (Oxford: Polity); Jessop, B. (2000), 'The state and the contradictions of the knowledge-driven economy', in John Bryson, Peter Daniels, Nick Henry and Jane Pollard (eds.), *Knowledge, Space, Economy* (London, Routledge); Peck, J. and Theodore, N. (2000), 'Beyond Employability', *Cambridge Journal of Economics*, 24, 729–749.
12. Warhurst, C. and Nickson, D. (2001), *Looking Good and Sounding Right: style counselling in the new economy* (London: Demos), p. 10.
13. See Feltham, R.T. (1989), 'Assessment centres', in Peter Herriot (ed.), *Handbook of Assessment in Organizations* (Chichester: Wiley).
14. Jenner, S. and Taylor, S. (2000), *Recruiting, Developing and Retaining Graduate Talent* (London: Financial Times/Prentice Hall), p. 77.
15. Cohen, D.S. (2001), *The Talent Edge: A Behavioral Approach to Hiring, Developing, and Keeping Top Performers* (Toronto: John Wiley and Sons), p. 75.
16. AGR (1998), *The Newcomer's Guide to Graduate Recruitment* (Cambridge: AGR), p. 98, original emphasis.
17. Boudreau, J.W. (1989), 'Selection utility analysis: a review and agenda for future research', in M. Smith and I.T. Robertson (eds.), *Advances in Selection and Assessment* (New York: John Wiley); Buckley, M.R. and Russell, C.J. (1999), 'Validity Evidence', in Robert E. Eder and Michael M. Harris (eds.), *The Employment Interview Handbook* (London: Sage).
18. AGR (1998), op. cit., p. 40.
19. Ibid., p. 40.
20. Handyside, J.D. (1989), 'On Ratings and Rating Scales', in Peter Herriot (ed.), *Handbook of Assessment in Organizations*, p. 671.
21. Ibid., p. 672.
22. Ibid., p. 675.
23. Bhaskar, R. (1998), 'Philosophy and scientific realism', in Margaret Archer, Roy Bhaskar, Andrew Collier, Tony Lawson, and Alan Norrie (eds.), *Critical Realism: Essential Readings* (London: Routledge), p. 27.
24. Holmes, L. (1995), 'Skills: a social perspective', in A. Assiter (ed.), *Transferable Skills in Higher Education* (London, Kogan Page), p. 22.
25. AGR (1998), op. cit.; IRS (1998), *Graduate Recruitment and Sponsorship: The 1998 IRS Survey of Employer Practice, Employee Development*, Bulletin No. 107. November.
26. Jenner, S. and Taylor, S. (2000), op. cit.
27. Public Sector Case Study Company Graduate Management Training Scheme Brochure, 2001.
28. Copi, I.M. and Cohen, C. (1998), *Introduction to Logic*, 10th edn (New Jersey: Prentice Hall), p. 217.
29. Ibid., p. 471.
30. Ibid., p. 482.
31. Rorty, R. (1980), *Philosophy and the Mirror of Nature* (Oxford: Basil Blackwell).

32. Boje, D.M., Alvarez, R.C., and Schooling, B. (2001), 'Reclaiming story in organization: Narratologies and action sciences', in Robert Westwood and Stephen Linstead (eds.), *The Language of Organization* (London, Sage).

33. C.f. Hacking (1986), op. cit., p. 228.

34. Ibid., p. 223.

35. Ibid., p. 229.

36. Rosalind H. Searle (2003), *Selection and Recruitment: A Critical Text* (Basingstoke: Palgrave), p. 260.

Chapter 6

1. Bridges, W. (1995), *Job Shift: How to Prosper in the Workplace Without Jobs* (London: Nicholas Brealey).

2. Our study was not intended to be representative of all graduates entering the UK labour market. Most of those we interviewed had reached the final stage of the selection process with at least one leading private or public sector organization. Most of the thousands who apply to these companies have already been eliminated on the grounds of relatively weak applications or initial interview. There are some graduates who have no interest in a fast-track management job or in making a professional career a central life interest. Michael Tomlinson's PhD research in the School of Social Sciences at Cardiff University clearly shows that some graduates 'retreat' from or 'reject' the competition for tough-entry graduate jobs. Of the sixty graduates interviewed for this book there was a fairly even gender balance, although as already noted very few were from working-class backgrounds or from the ethnic minorities. Most were from more prestigious universities but only a minority studied at Oxford or Cambridge University.

3. Brown, P. and Scase, R. (1994), *Higher Education and Corporate Realities* (London: UCL Press).

4. See, Wajcman, J. and Martin, B. (2002), 'Narratives of Identity in Modern Management: The Corrosion of Gender Differences?' *Sociology*, 36/4, 985–1002; Bradley, H. (1999), *Gender and Power in the Workplace* (Basingstoke: Macmillan).

5. See Reay, D., Ball, S., David, M., and Davies, J. (2001), 'Choice of Degree or Degree of Choice?: Social Class, Race and the Higher Education Choice Process', *Sociology*, 35/4, 855–74. This research shows that students from ethnic minorities are also less likely to apply for fast-track jobs because they do not think they stand a chance of getting appointed and because they may feel that these jobs are not appropriate for 'them'.

6. These are intended as descriptive terms that leave aside issues of political correctness or moral preference. It should be remembered that the Purists

are also playing to win, but according to meritocratic rather than market rules of the game. The political legitimacy attached to meritocratic competition during the second half of the twentieth century enables the Purists to claim historical precedent, much like a sports federation confronted with demands to make significant changes to the rules of the game. The Purists are the defenders of the standards of fair play. Occupational selection should be based on merit demonstrated by individual effort and ability in an open and fair competition. In other words, occupational selection for the best jobs must reflect their innate and moral superiority that should not be 'faked' by tailoring oneself to the recruitment criteria of employers. The idea of the Purist also relates to Gidden's notion of the 'pure relationship'. Here, the Purists view the use of assessment centres as an attempt to match the right person to the right job, that requires a high level of personal disclosure to ensure that the recruiting organization has the necessary data to make an accurate judgement.

7. Gerth, H. and Mills, C.W. (eds.) (1967), *From Max Weber* (London: Routledge).
8. This includes those that have very little idea, interest or simply rejected the whole notion of managing one's employability. These are very few in number in this study because they had all applied for fast-track jobs.
9. Goffman, E. (1959), *The Presentation of Self in Everyday Life* (New York: Doubleday Anchor); Atkinson, P. and Housley, W. (2003), *Interactionism* (London: Sage).
10. Lots of work on transition from education to employment has highlighted the significance of social identity.

Chapter 7

1. Goffman, E. (1959), *The Presentation of Self in Everyday Life* (New York: Doubleday Anchor).
2. Harvey, L. and Green, D. (1994), *Employer Satisfaction* (Birmingham: QHE/Esso), table 3, p. 21.
3. National Committee of Inquiry into Higher Education (NCIHE, 1997), *Main Report* (London: HMSO).
4. NCIHE Appendix 4 (1997), *National Committee of Inquiry into Higher Education Appendix 4: Consultation with employers* (London, HMSO).
5. Brown, P. and Scase, R. (1994), *Higher Education and Corporate Realities* (London: UCL Press), p. 144.
6. Mason, G. (1996), 'Graduate Utilisation in British Industry: The Initial Impact of Mass Higher Education', *National Institute Economic Review*, 156, 93–103.
7. Brown and Scase (1994), op. cit., p. 119.
8. Witz A., Warhurst C., and Nickson D. (2003), 'The Labour of Aesthetics and the Aesthetics of Organization', *Organization*, 10/1, 33–54.

9. Alvesson, M. (2001), 'Knowledge work: Ambiguity, image and identity' *Organization*, 54/7, 863–886, 877.

10. Ibid.

11. Deetz, S. (1997), 'Discursive Formations, Strategized Subordination and Self-surveillance', in Alan McKinlay and Ken Starkey (eds.), *Foucault, Management and Organization Theory* (London: Sage).

12. Foucault, M. (1988), 'Technologies of the Self', in L. Martin, H. Gutman, and P. Hutton (eds.), *Technologies of the Self* (Amherst, MA: University of Massachusetts Press), pp. 16–49, p. 18.

13. Witz, Warhurst, and Nickson (2003), op. cit.

14. Bourdieu, P. (1990), *The Logic of Practice* (Cambridge: Polity).

15. Research in organizational settings has suggested such values come from daily discursive practices, for example, Knights, D. and Willmott, H. (1985), 'Power and Theory in Social Practice', *The Sociological Review*, 33, 22–46.; Knights, D. and Willmott, H. (1989), 'Power and subjectivity at work: from degradation to subjugation in social relations', *Sociology*, 23, 535–58; Knights, D. and Collinson, D. (1987), 'Disciplining the shop floor: a comparison of the disciplinary effects of managerial psychology and financial accounting', *Accounting, Organizations and Society*, 12, 457–77.

16. Alvesson (2001), op. cit., p. 865.

17. See Brown, P. and Hesketh A.J. (2004), 'I Say Tomato, You Say Tamayto: Critical Realism and the Labour Market Process', in S. Ackroyd and S. Fleetwood (eds.), *Realism in Action in Organisation and Management Studies* (London: Routledge).

18. We should, therefore, stress that employers would not recognize the above mental constructs of employability as something that they *formally* use during an assessment centre. Nevertheless, our presentation of these findings to over fifty graduate recruiters at the Association of Graduate Recruiters' Annual Conference in 2002 was met with strong recognition and approval.

Chapter 8

1. Mills, C.W. (1956), *The Power Elite* (New York: Oxford University Press), p. 141.

2. O'Reilly, C.A. and Pfeffer, J. (2000), *Hidden Value: How Great Companies Achieve Extraordinary Results with Ordinary People* (Boston, MA: Harvard University Press), p. 2.

3. See Marglin, S.A. (1982), 'What Do the Bosses Do? The Origins and Functions of Hierarchy in Capitalist Production', in Giddens, A. and Held, D. (eds.), *Classes, Power and Conflict* (London: Macmillan); Gorz, A. (1989), *Critique of Economic Reason* (London: Verso); Shenhav, Y. (1999), *Manufacturing Rationality* (Oxford: Oxford University Press); Fevre, R. (2003), *The New Sociology of Economic Behaviour* (London: Sage).

4. Creating a sense of crisis is, of course, not always a bad thing if the proposed changes redirect the energies of employees in the appropriate direction.

5. Michaels, E., Handfield-Jones, H., and Axelrod, B. (2001), *The War for Talent* (Boston: Harvard Business School Press), p. 126.

6. See Ralph Fevre (2003), op. cit.

7. Fox, A. (1974), *Beyond Contract: Work, Power and Trust Relations* (London: Faber and Faber).

8. Brown, P. and Lauder, H. (2001), *Capitalism and Social Progress: The Future of Society in a Global Economy* (Basingstoke: Palgrave).

9. Goleman, D. (1996), *Emotional Intelligence* (London: Bloomsbury), p. 160.

10. Pfeffer, J. (2001), 'Fighting the War for Talent is Hazardous to Your organizations Health', Research Paper No. 1687, Graduate School of Business, Stanford University.

11. Cohen argues that 'Organizations no longer have the time, resources, and flexibility to coax nascent talent while shedding the employees who fail to make a strong positive impact. The financial and competitive hit is too hard, and the opportunity costs too high … a company that can identify and recruit more top performers from the outset has a tremendous advantage over any competitor' (Cohen, 2001: 19).

12. See Halsey A.H., Heath, A.F., and Ridge, J.M. (1980), *Origins and Destinations* (Oxford: Clarendon); Brown and Lauder (2001), op. cit.

13. Companies could increase the level of knowledge required say to Masters level or even to Research Degree level, but much business knowledge is generic and not highly specialist, although there are obvious exceptions.

14. Some employers are suspicious of those with top grades, not only because of concerns about grade inflation, but also because the personal attributes required for academic success are different from those required to make a successful manager. Academic success is privatized. In the humanities and social sciences, lectures are accompanied by library study (where talking is not permitted!), and the submission of individual assignments. In this environment teamwork is cheating. The opportunity for discussion is often limited to seminars, but growing student numbers has led all universities to increase the size of seminar classes which reduce the chance to debate issues in a small group. Equally, because seminar participation is rarely assessed student attendance cannot be taken for granted. Much of relevance to the experience of work is extra-curricular. Education rewards the highest grades based on academic performance alone, whereas the workplace operates with a broader range of personal qualities.

15. Zuboff, S. (1988), *In the Age of the Smart Machine: The Future of Work and Power* (New York: Basic Books).

16. Brown and Lauder (2001), op. cit.

17. Talent is ultimately a social construction. The historical transformation of work over the last century suggests that 'it is often social hierarchy and the world views associated with it that restrict the unfolding of human

capacity, and not the limitations of natural endowment' (Sabel, 1982: 224). What is equally evident is that much of what constitutes personal capital is the result of social learning. However, we have shown that assumptions about 'nature' will continue to influence recruitment decisions and about talent, but these have been extended beyond cognitive ability, to incorporate drive, tenacity, self-reliance. But this form of Social Darwinism is 'socially' corrupted etc.

18. Fevre (2003), op. cit.
19. Lasch, C. (1995), *The Revolt of the Elite and the Betrayal of Democracy* (New York: W.W. Norton), p. 39.
20. This is taken from the executive summary of the Universities UK report Enhancing Employability, Recognising Diversity, see www.Universities UK.ac.uk/employability.
21. Ghoshal, S. and Bartlett, C. (1997), *The Individualized Corporation* (London: Random House), p. 220.
22. Ibid., p. 223. Moreover, Woodruffe notes that even within a sector there are differences in organizational values and culture. 'Anyone who has derived a tailor-made list for an organization will know how organizations have their own language which subtly conveys their priorities in their own code. All this would be lost with a generic list.' (Woodruffe, C. Winning the Talent War (Chichester: John Wiley), 1999: 121). We are back to the importance of cultural codes and the chemistry between the individual and the company. Competences don't tell us much about 'social fit.'
23. Kelly, R. (1998), *Star Performer* (London: Orion Business Books).
24. The idea of generic talent must also be challenged as the 'social fit' between the individual and the organization holds the key to performance. Cohen notes that 'an employee who is a top performer in one organization cannot be transferred readily into another, because the behaviors required are different' (2001: 57).
25. Ghoshal and Bartlett (1997), op. cit., p. 233
26. Michaels, E., Handfield-Jones, H., and Axelrod, B. (2001), *The War for Talent*, p. 172.
27. Pfeffer, J. and Sutton, R.I. (2000), *The Knowing Doing Gap: How Smart Companies Turn Knowledge into Action* (Boston, MA: Harvard Business School Press).
28. Brown, P. and Scase, R. (1994), *Higher Education and Corporate Realities* (London: University College London Press).
29. De Geus, A. (1997) 'The Living Company', *Harvard Business Review*, March–April, 51–59, p. 9; O'Reilly and Pfeffer (2000), op. cit., pp. 69–74.
30. Kandola, R. and Fullerton, J. (1998), *Diversity in Action: Managing the Mosaic*, 2nd edn (London: CIPD), p. 11.
31. See Reay, D., Ball, S., David, M. and Davies, J. (2001), 'Choice of Degree or Degrees of Choice? Social Class, Race and the Higher Education Choice Process', *Sociology*, 35/4, 855–74.

32. See *The Future of Higher Education*, figure 2, p. 17 (DfES, 2003).
33. Ibid. The problem is that many of the education and labour market policies that the British government has pursued will reinforce rather than ameliorate existing inequalities. See Lauder, H., Brown, P., and Halsey, A.H. (2004), 'Sociology and Political Arithmetic: Some Principles of a New Policy Science', *British Journal of Sociology*, 55, 3–22.
34. The overriding problem is one of class, cross-cut by issues of gender, ethnicity, race, and age.
35. Rees, T. (1998), *Mainstreaming Equality in the European Union: Education, Training and Labour Market Policies* (London: Routledge). Rees' main concern has been gender equality but she also argues that a mainstreaming agenda must be 'concerned about the inter-relationship among different equality dimensions', p. 193. For anyone who believes that issues of gender equality have been resolved, even from the middle classes, should read Rees' more recent work with colleagues on women in science. See, Rubsamen-Waigmann et al. (2003) *Women in Industrial Research: A Wake Up Call for European Industry* (Luxemburg: European Commission), and Osborn, M., Rees, T. et al. (2000) *Science Policies in the European Union: Promoting Excellence Through Mainstreaming Gender Equality* (Luxemburg: European Commission).
36. Frank and Cook (1996), *The Winner-Takes-All Society* (New York: Penguin).
37. Cornelius, N. (ed.) (2002), *Building Workplace Equality: Ethics, Diversity and Inclusion* (London: Thomson).
38. Tackney, N.D., Tamkin, P., and Sheppard, E. (2001), *The Problem of Minority Performance in Organisations* (Eastbourne: Institute of Employment Studies).
39. Turner, R. (1960), 'Sponsored and Contest Mobility and the School System', *American Sociological Review*, 25, 855–67.
40. The idea of 'sponsored' and 'contest' mobility was popularized by Ralph Turner in the 1960s to highlight different models of credential competition. Here, the terms have been modified to make them relevant to a work rather than educational context. It is worth quoting Turner's original use of the term 'contest' as well as 'sponsorship'.

   Turner wrote, '*Contest* mobility is a system in which elite status is the prize in an open contest and is taken by the aspirants' own efforts. While the "contest" is governed by some rules of fair play, the contestants have wide latitude in the strategies they may employ. Since the "prize" of successful upward mobility is not in the hands of the established elite to give out, the latter are not in a position to determine who shall attain it and who shall not' (1960: 856).

   Our use of the term contest is different because in an organizational context the contest is still judged by senior staff rather than by an objective criterion such as a formal academic examination. Many aspects of job performance involve a subjective interpretation of contribution and future potential. Under a 'sponsorship' model privileged status is given by recruitment staff on behalf of the organization on the basis of leadership potential. Membership is granted or denied on the basis of whether candidates are judged to have the personal qualities that they require for a future in senior positions. Once recruited, members are sponsored within the organization in ways that make it difficult for others to compete for prized jobs irrespective of effort or performance.

41. Ibid., p. 856.
42. The flatter the organization the more this is the case because there is more competition for senior positions. Those with a competitive advantage at the outset are most likely to command such posts.
43. Reichheld, F.F. (1996), *The Loyalty Effect* (Boston, MA: Harvard Business School Press).
44. Roller coasters can be exciting but can get a bit exhausting and tiresome after a while. It is okay when you are young, in demand, and there is a buoyant labour market.
45. Woodruffe, C. (1999), op. cit., pp. 108–9.
46. Stasz, C. (1997), 'Do Employers Need the Skills They Want? Evidence from Technical Work', *Journal of Education and Work*, 10/3: 205–24.
47. Brown and Lauder (2001), op. cit.
48. Bendix, R. (1956), *Work and Authority in Industry: Ideologies of Management in the Course of Industrialization* (New York: John Wiley).
49. See Peiperl, M., Arthur, M., Goffee, R., and Morris, T. (eds.) (2000), *Career Frontiers: New Concepts of Working Live* (Oxford: Oxford University Press); Peiperl, M., Arthur, M. and Anand, N. (eds.) (2002), *Career Creativity: Explorations in the Remaking of Work* (Oxford: Oxford University Press); Collin, A. and Young, R.A. (eds.) (2000), *The Future of Career* (Cambridge: Cambridge University Press).
50. For a discussion of positive and negative sum games see Thurow, L.C. (1981), *The Zero-Sum Society: Distribution and the Possibilities for Economic Change* (New York: Penguin); Hirsch, F. (1977), *Social Limits to Growth* (London: Routledge).

Chapter 9

1. This title is taken from Ivar Berg's classic study of *Education and Jobs: The Great Training Robbery* (New York: Praeger), 1970.
2. See Chapter 3 What Knowledge Economy.
3. See Bygrave, M. (2003), 'Degrees of Difference', *The Observer,* 21 September.
4. Thurow, L. (1977), 'Education and Economic Equality', in J. Karabel and A.H. Halsey (eds.), *Power and Ideology in Education* (New York: Oxford University Press). From the mid-1990s graduate incomes began to rise in absolute terms but these have already tailed off as the euphoria of the

Internet revolution evaporated (see Brown and Lauder, 2003). Mishel, L., Bernstein, J. and Boushey, H. (2003), 'The State of Working America, 2002/2003', (Ithica, NY: Cornell University press).

5. Mason, G. (2002), 'High Skills Utilization Under Mass Higher Education: Graduate Employment in Service Industries', *Journal of Education and Work*, 154/4, 427–56; Battu, H. and Sloane, P. (2000), 'Overeducation and Crowding Out in Britain', in L. Borghans and A. De Grip (eds.), *The Overeducated Worker? The Economics of Skill Utilization* (Cheltenham: Edward Elgar).

6. Porter, M. and Ketels, C. (2003), UK Competitiveness: Moving to the Next Stage, Department of Trade and Industry (DTI) Economics Paper No. 3, London: DTI/Economic and Social Research Council (ESRC).

7. Keep, E. (2004), 'After Access: Researching Labour Market Issues', in J. Gallacher (ed.), *Researching Access to Higher Education* (London: Routledge); National Skills Task Force (2000) *Skills for All: Research Report of the National Skills Task Force* (Sudbury: DfEE), p. 117.

8. Deloitte Research (2003), www.deloitte.com/dtt/cda/doc/content/Offshoring.pdf.

9. Aston, L. and Bekhradnia, B. (2003), 'Demand for Graduates: A Review of the Economic Evidence', Higher Education Policy Institute, www.hepi.ac.uk/articles/docs/graduatesES.pdf; Felstead, A., Gallie, D., and Green, F. (2002), *Work Skills in Britain 2001* (London: DfES); Brown, P. and Lauder, H. (forthcoming), 'Globalisation and the Knowledge Economy: Some Observations on Recent Trends in Employment, Education and the Labour Market', School of Social Sciences, Working Paper No. 43. http://www.cardiff.ac.uk/socsi/publications/working Papers/; Wolf, A. (2002), *Does Education Matter?* (London: Penguin).

10. Chote, R. and Wakefield, M. (2003), 'You Might be Richer than You Think', *The Guardian*, 29 September.

11. Brown, P., Green, A. and Lauder, H. (2001), *High Skills: Globalization, Competitiveness and Skill Formation* (Oxford: Oxford University Press); Ashton, D.N. and Sung, J. (2002), *Supporting Workplace Learning for High Performance Working* (Geneva: International Labour Office).

12. As McDonald states,

No longer will public policy aim at ensuring that there are a sufficient number of jobs for everyone who wants to work. Instead the unemployed are to be managed in such a way that they will mobilize their personality as resource—they are to be the principal architects of their self-creation, entrepreneurs of the self (McDonald 1997: 71–2).

Kevin McDonald (1997), 'Social transformation: new problems, new possibilities', in P. James, W. Veit, and S. Wright, *Work of the Future: Global Perspectives* (St Leonards, NSW: Allen and Unwin), p. 71–2.

13. The problem with the wealth of talent is that organizations are swamped with potential applicants that give them little incentive to diversify their

recruitment beyond a small number of leading universities. Paradoxically, employers argue that widening diversity is required to enrich their pool of managerial talent, yet fear that any broadening of their publicity would lead to a flood of applications that are virtually impossible to administer. Therefore, there is a tendency to maintain a narrow recruitment strategy.

14. Currie, J. and Newson, J. (eds.) (1998), *Universities and Globalization: Critical Perspectives* (London: Sage); Brown, P. (2000), 'The Globalisation of Positional Competition?' *Sociology*, 34/4, 633–53; Naidoo, R. (2003), Review Essay: Repositioning Higher Education as a Global Commodity: Opportunities and Challenges for Future Sociology of Education Work', *British Journal of Sociology of Education*, 24/2, 249–59.

15. Brown, P. and Scase, R. (1994), *Higher Education and Corporate Realities* (London: UCL Press); Ainley, P. (1994), *Degrees of Difference: Higher Education in the 1990s* (London: Lawrence and Wishart).

16. Department for Education and Skills (DfES) (2003), *The Future of Higher Education* (London: DfES).

17. Of course, some such as Collins and Bourdieu have argued that the credential is a 'badge' of class membership. It certifies class status.

18. Obviously, these can and often do overlap.

19. The Russell Group of British universities are the University of Birmingham; Bristol; Cambridge; Cardiff; Edinburgh; Glasgow; Imperial College, London; King's College, London; Leeds; Liverpool; London School of Economics; Manchester; Newcastle upon Tyne; Nottingham; Oxford; Sheffield; Southampton; University College, London and Warwick.

20. Gouldner, A.W. (1957), 'Cosmopolitans and Locals: Toward an Analysis of Latent Social Roles', *Administration Science Quarterly*, 2: 281–306.

21. Equal Opporunties Commission (EOC) (2003), 'Facts about Women and Men in Great Britain, 2003', www.eoc.org.uk/cseng/research/factsgreat-britain2003.pdf.

22. Purcell, K. (2002), *Qualifications and Careers: Equal Opportunities and Earnings Among Graduates*, Working Paper Series No. 1, Equal Opportunities Commission.

23. Connon, H. (2003), 'Top Jobs for the Girls? Far Too Few in Our Lifetime', *The Observer*, 16 November.

24. Lazonick, W. and O'Sullivan, M. (2000), 'Maximizing Shareholder Value: A New Ideology for Corporate Governance', *Economy and Society*, 29/1, 13–35.

25. Michaels, E., Handfield-Jones, H., and Axelrod, B. (2001), *The War for Talent* (Boston: Harvard Business School Press).

26. Brown and Lauder (2001), op. cit.

27. This is a lesson companies have learnt. They are not limited as in the past to having to cultivate their own talent through long-term career structures, or fear that if some of their managers/professional left new

staff would be difficult to find. Declining working conditions for many managers/professional reflects this as companies have also learnt, especially from the Japanese, that workers lower down the hierarchy are not thick and stupid and can be trusted to take responsibility for many aspects of their own work without close supervision from management.

28. Also, how the market is used to lever up salaries and remuneration packages. Rather than pointing to their contribution within the company they make market demand, no matter how artificial a key bargaining chip.

29. Alvesson, M., Robertson, M., and Swan, J. (2001), 'The Best and the Brightest: The Role of Elite Identity in Knowledge-Intensive Companies', CMS Conference, July, Manchester, UK.

30. Felstead, A., Gallie, D., and Green, F. (2002), *Work Skills in Britain 2001*, (London: DfES); Keep, E. (2003), 'Too True to be Good—Some Thoughts on the "High Skills Vision" and on Where Policy is Really Taking Us', Paper presented at the SCOPE conference on the High Skills Vision, Warwick University, September.

31. What this also reveals is that the problem of diversity is a broader social issue that cannot be resolved without a societal transformation in our understanding of 'talent', this must include the attitudes of customers, clients, and employers.

32. Pfeffer, J. (1998), *The Human Equation: Building Profits by Putting People First* (Boston, MA: Harvard Business School).

33. Halsey, A.H., Heath, A., and Ridge, J. (1980), *Origins and Destinations: Family, Class and Education in Modern Britain* (Oxford: Clarendon).

34. This is reflected in the range of subject choices at degree level, where what is fashionable may not coincide with economic utility. Many who enter university remain vague about what they want to do with the rest of their lives, so they opt for something that interests them. What interests them is inevitably shaped by social messages delivered on a daily basis, especially through the media, leading to the popularity of subjects such as cultural studies, media studies, forensic science, and criminology, that attract far more people than can realistically expect to find related employment. Indeed universities have become sensitized to consumer tastes. When they consider new programmes of study or expanding the intake into particular fields of study, market testing pays no attention to the chances of their students finding jobs relating to their area of study or any consideration of labour market conditions. They focus exclusively on student demand. If there are people willing to take a particular degree, then provision will be made in a desperate bid to increase university income. Many others study established degree subjects such as English Literature, History, or Sociology because it interests them and they know that many employers use the university degree as a generic benchmark, without specifying a preference for a particular field of study.

However, it is wrong to assume that the problem is that young people are now pursuing their childhood fantasies of being a pop star or astronaut. These young knowledge workers are not simply chasing glamour and the big money, they want the opportunity to grow as people and to make a difference.

35. Students with the highest exam scores, such as those in mathematics, tell employers little about the potential of these students to become leading mathematicians, as those with the best examination results may be better at remembering formulae, rather than having the creative imagination required to advance or apply knowledge in new ways. This is precisely why employers use the discourse of employability to move beyond the credential, to define the range of personal, people, and problem-solving skills that constitutes an effective manager.

36. Self-employment remains a high risk strategy, most people will remain employees.

37. Rose, N. (1999), *Governing the Soul: The Shaping of the Private Self*, 2nd edn (London: Free Association Books).

38. Jackall, R. (1988), *Moral Mazes: The World of Corporate Managers* (New York: Oxford University Press), p. 64. See also www.sunyit.edu/~harrell/billyjack/book_reviews.htm.

39. Brown, P. (2003), The Opportunity Trap: Education and Employment in a Global Economy, *European Education Research Journal*, 2/1, 142–80.

40. Boudon, R. (1973), *Education, Opportunity and Social Inequality* (New York: John Wiley).

41. Of course, the social elites will try to adopt tactics that make use of their exclusive resources, especially the ability to pay for expensive private education and tutoring that is beyond the means of the many middle class families.

42. Frank, R. and Cook, P. (1995), *The Winner-Takes-All Society* (New York: Penguin), pp. 4–5.

43. For a discussion of meritocratic and market rules relate to conflicting middle class ideologies, see Brown (1995, 2000).

44. Bell, D. (2002), *Ethical Ambition* (London: Bloomsbury), *The Observer*, 10/11/02.

45. Fevre argues that remoralization must begin with a debate 'about what values matter to us from the start, 'what sort of lives we want to lead, what sort of society we want to have — and then we judge the sort of economic behaviour that goes on all around us against these values'. Fevre, R. (2003), *The New Sociology of Economic Behaviour* (London: Sage), p. 244

46. Of course, it is usually the employer who is in the ascendancy as employees depend on employment for their economic livelihoods.

47. Sennett, R. (1998), *The Corrosion of Character: The Personal Consequences of Work in the New Capitalism* (New York: W.W. Norton), p. 10; Jackall, R.

(1988), *Moral Mazes: The World of Corporate Managers* (New York: Oxford University Press).

48. Sennett (1998), op. cit., p. 146.
49. Reichheld, F. (1996), *The Loyalty Effect: The Hidden Force Behind Growth, Profits and Lasting Value* (Boston, MA: Harvard Business School).
50. Wilensky, H.L. (1960), 'Work, Careers and Social Integration', *International Social Science Journal*, 12, 543–60, p. 555.
51. Smetherham (2004), 'First Class Women in the World of Work: Employability and Labour Market Orientations', Working Paper No. 45, Cardiff school of Social Sciences, www.cardiff.ac.uk/socsi/publications/workingpapers/workingpapers.html.

Index